WHAT WERE THEY xxx! LIKE TO FLY?

Gene Smith

Motorbooks International
Publishers & Wholesalers ®

First published in 1990 by Motorbooks International
Publishers & Wholesalers, P O Box 2, 729 Prospect
Avenue, Osceola, WI 54020 USA

Motorbooks International books are also available at
discounts in bulk quantity for industrial or sales-
promotional use. For details write to Special Sales
Manager at the Publisher's address

Library of Congress Cataloging-in-Publication Data
Smith, Murlin Gene.
    What were they like to fly? / Murlin Gene Smith.
        p.   cm.
    ISBN 0-87938-440-9 (soft)
    1. Airplanes—Miscellanea.   I. Title.
TL671.S566 1990   90-6381
    629.133—dc20   CIP

On the Front cover: This view shows how heavily armed
an F-4 Phantom can be. *Jim Benson*

On the back cover: Dressed for action, author Gene Smith
prepares to board one of the Coon-Ass Militia's (122nd
TFS 159th TFG Louisiana Air Guard) F-15s

Printed and bound in the United States of America

Contents

Foreword

Confessions of a type hog

I remember exactly when it started. I was just three and had gone into the front yard to play.

A trumpet vine twined around the trellis on the front porch, and a hummingbird was busy drinking nectar from the flowers. He was a beautiful little thing, all iridescent feathers and shiny obsidian eyes and whirring sounds.

But his beauty was incidental.

The hummingbird had a means of locomotion much superior to mine. In the twinkling of an eye, he could dart from place to place on his pointy little wings—up, down, in, out, sideways, even backward with exquisite control. He could hover in midair for minutes at a time, if he chose.

I, on the other hand, was restricted to waddling along on the ground, laboriously climbing over obstacles, and, often as not, snagging my clothing in the effort.

I envied that hummingbird. I still do.

I had other problems, too. I grew severely myopic shortly afterward. At a single stroke, those pointy eyeballs took me forever out of reach of the military fighter pilot's career I wanted. I test about 20/200 without glasses, but—very fortunately—correct to 20/20. No matter.

When I was 5½, the world went up in flames as Hitler invaded Poland, and Britain and France declared war. Night after night I lay on the living room rug and listened spellbound to the sonorous tones of Edward R. Murrow reporting the Blitz direct from London. Occasionally in the background I could hear the bark of an anti-aircraft gun, the dull distant crump of bombs and the far-off drone of engines.

Other boys studied baseball, memorized batting and pitching statistics. I studied airplanes and their armament, memorized performance figures. My dreams were filled with the graceful shapes of winged things, and at night in my bed I would drift off to sleep vowing firmly that my eyes would get better. They did not, of course.

Years later, I finally remarked to a friend of mine, a major general and the adjutant general of my state, that men like him still irritate me. Astonished, he asked why. Because, I explained, the taxpayers trained him and ten thousand more like him to fly some of the finest airplanes ever built; *paid* him to do it, and all they could do was complain about their low pay rates.

I would have paid the government!

Personally, I said, I identified more with another friend, a colonel with eleven air-to-air victories in P–38s and P–51s over Europe. A short, pudgy little man with wavy black hair, he looked at me one day with his merry brown eyes and said abruptly, "You know, I never had so much fun as when I was runnin' around over Europe, shootin' at people."

Indeed.

As for me, I was denied even a high-paying airline career. Another friend, a veteran captain with a major carrier, once hurried to tell me they'd just relaxed the acceptance standards; they were now taking people with 20/70 eyesight.

I laughed—and thanked him.

Resigned finally, I joke today that I am the only blind commercial pilot most folks are likely to meet; a Mister Magoo of the airways. Then I hasten to add that according to the FAA it's alright if I'm blind. Since I haven't hit anything yet, I carry a waiver attesting to the fact that I'm not likely to.

But wishes really do come true, if you truly want them badly enough, and the day came when I learned to fly—out of a little 2,000 ft. runway with wires at both ends.

I was married by then, and thrice a father. Both wife and children resented the time daddy spent with airplanes instead of with them. They still do, I suppose.

But I pointed out to my wife that she wouldn't let me chase other women, and she wisely kept silent after that. The children promptly grew up, as children will, and were mostly glad that dad wasn't forever poking his nose into their affairs, anyway.

So it came to pass that I began plotting reasons we needed an airplane in the family.

The first bargain I found was a lovely plum-colored Stinson Voyager, which my wife rejected on the ground that she didn't like the color. The next was a sleek and classic Bellanca Cruisair. Like the Stinson, it had a 165 hp Franklin. She turned that one down because she didn't like low-wing airplanes; the wing blocked the view of the ground. My third choice was a 135 hp Piper Pacer, freshly restored and immaculate, for sale quite reasonably on our own home field.

At that point my bride looked at me very seriously and declared there was no way our family needed a four-place airplane.

I learned, finally.

I came home one evening not long afterward and announced, "Guess what, baby?" And when she asked what, I replied, "We own a Luscombe!"

It was a 1946 8E Silvaire with an 85 hp Continental, full electric and starter, running lights and metalized wings. I flew that airplane for eight years and probably 600 hours, and I'm sure I'll never again have so much flying for so little money. It cruised at 112 mph on 4.9 gallons of gasoline, and I covered much of the United States in it, much of the time without a radio.

It was a pretty little airplane, too, with its polished aluminum and green trim. Lord, I got tired of polishing on that thing! So did the rest of the family.

So one day I came home, and to my wife I said, "Guess what, baby?" And when she asked what, I replied, "We own two airplanes." I had just bought a 1948 Monocoupe 90AL, one of eleven built with hydraulic toe brakes and the 115 hp Lycoming O-235C-1. Regrettably, I had to sell the Luscombe soon afterward, but the two were from the same stable, and the Monocoupe was much the rarer bird. More fun, too, in truth.

We've been going together nearly twenty years now, the Monocoupe and I. And though I grow exasperated with her at times, I suspect we'll be together some time longer. I once joked to a friend that when I die, I want them to strap me into the Monocoupe, set fire to it and launch me, like a Viking chieftain in his flaming dragon boat. He looked at me in horror and exclaimed, "Oh, you wouldn't do *that* to that pretty little airplane, would you?"

These days, of course, the Monocoupe is no longer alone, and now I tell people, You know how airplanes are: Turn your back on them and they'll get together in a corner of the hangar and breed, and first thing you know, you have a whole little flock.

I still need a couple more, though. A fighter would be nice. And a nice vintage twin—maybe a Beech 18 or a Cessna Bobcat or perhaps a Grumman Goose. Then I love the Helio Courier, too. It would sure be nice to have one of those on amphibious floats. . . .

Boys never quit dreaming.

But writers are lucky. Sometimes they get a chance to fly some of the machines all of us would like to own. If I can't own all those lovely flying machines, at least I can flirt with them now and again. And I do. At this point I'm probably closing in on 170 different types of airplanes flown.

One memorable weekend this summer, I flew these six airplanes in this order in a little over two days: A Yugoslavian Soko Galeb jet; a Stinson L-5G; a Beech C-45 (civil D-18); acro-great Bevo Howard's old 1941 factory clipwing Cub, now with a 180 hp engine; a Lockheed C-60 Lodestar; and a Supermarine Spitfire Mk. IX.

As they say, it's hard work and the pay is low, but someone has to do it.

Meanwhile, my wife long ago resigned herself to the fact that my head can be turned by nearly any pretty set of wings that comes along. To paraphrase Will Rogers: I never met an airplane I didn't like. Of course, I like some better than others. . . .

This book is a selection of stories about a few of the memorable airplanes I've been lucky enough to meet so far.

I hope you enjoy it.

Chapter 1

Curtiss JN–4D Jenny

Grand Old Girl

When this report was written, N2404 was the world's only OX-powered Jenny flying. At publication of this book there are half a dozen, plus another four with other engines (like the air-cooled Tank conversion), and who knows how many there will be by the turn of the century?

Who would have guessed that the Jenny would be flying into the twenty-first century? Even in such severely reduced numbers?

Flying a Jenny is a trip backward in time, of course, because unless you're a masochist you don't fly a Jenny just for fun. The whole exercise is much like riding a horse. It's a major operation just to get the thing out of the hangar, prepare it for flight, get it back to the hangar and put it away.

In short, you really have to want to fly, to fly a JN4D!

On the other hand, this is the airplane that taught the nation to fly; that nurtured the barn-stormers; that made a generation aware of airplanes and aviators. Its historical significance is pivotal. And it is fun!

It's been my great good fortune to fly the stock Jenny, the Tank conversion and the four-aileron Canuck. The last is best.

I pulled a big 8½ ft. prop through twelve times and paused, panting. "Okay," I called. "Let's try it." I grabbed the bottom of the blade and took a running step to my right, turning to yell "Clear" over my left shoulder.

Dan Neuman spun the magneto booster handle furiously. I could see his shadowed arm moving on the side of the fuselage. Nothing happened. We tried it again. Then we tried it twice more. Nothing.

"Maybe it's not primed yet," said Neuman. "Can you see gas dripping out of the vent tube yet?"

I couldn't. I went back to priming. I pulled the prop through another dozen times, and finally a single droplet of gas peeped shyly out of the tube, hesitated, and fell silently into the lush grass of Anoka, Minnesota's Anoka County Airport. Two more raced after it.

"All right," I gasped. "I've got gas." Neuman nodded. I gave the bottom blade a mighty yank, and jumped aside.

"I didn't hear you yell 'Clear,'" said Neuman, motionless in the cockpit. Very cautious man, that Neuman. Fine, safety-conscious veteran airline pilot.

Grimly, I staggered back over to the prop.

Neuman is proud of his compression. Most OX-5s only go about 30 or 40 lbs., even when they're tight. But Neuman replaced the old dual, wide compression bands with two narrow bands at the top and then put two thin oil rings in the bottom cut-out on each of the eight big cylinders. Then he hand-lapped them all individually, taking the procedure right out of the Pratt & Whitney R-2800 manual. *His* OX-5 goes 85 lbs. of compression, and I was feeling every pound.

I fiddled at positioning the prop, stalling while I psyched myself into one more good try. Then I gave it a Samson heave and sprang far out to the side, bellowing "Clear!" like a Marine drill instructor.

The prop, of course, had stopped the instant I let go of it. But Neuman cranked the booster as if he didn't even notice.

Hallelujah!

The damn thing started. Just like that. One moment the prop was motionless, the next it was a shining blur, and thin traces of blue smoke puffed briefly out of the short stacks. Those silly little rocker arms began to jiggle nervously like a cricket about to jump, and suddenly the Jenny was a live thing.

I ran around the wing and scrambled hastily into the front cockpit—but not so hastily that I didn't watch where I put my feet. I had the feeling if I didn't, Neuman might reach up and clout me with an end wrench.

It was my own fault. He'd offered me choice of seats, and like a fool I took the front one, where he could watch what I was doing. But all the instruments were in the back, and I figured it was better to have him back there where he could more easily minister to this beast's unknown whims.

The leather padded seat was comfortable, and my feet fell naturally on the smallish rudder bar. The control stick looked like a ball bat stuck in the floor. In front of me was a fold-down observer's writing desk and a pair of chrome-hooded cockpit lights. On my left was a familiar throttle lever capped with a black knob. That was all.

Out on the cowling ahead of the windshield was a single teardrop gauge. It said "empty" on the left and "full" on the right and it was a lot nearer to the left than to the right. Way out in front was a radiator cap, just like on Granddad's Hupmobile. It had a round dingus sticking up with a white circle in the middle and a thermometer that went right through it.

About the time I got the cloth flying helmet on and the heavy military-style safety belt buckled, the throttle knob went all the way forward. At idle, the noise filtering through the helmet flaps had been merely noticeable. Now it was remarkable. I realized why most OX-5 Club members are a little deaf. The OX-5 at full throttle sounds like an outsize Singer run by gasoline.

The rocker arms waved frantically in the sudden breeze and the Jenny began to roll. It trundled ahead

The Curtiss JN series of military airplanes really brought aviation to North America. Early models helped Pershing chase bandits in Mexico in 1911–12. The later JN–4D trained the Army Air Service pilots for World War I. Sold as surplus after the war, they served barnstormers well, bringing flight to little towns all over America. More than 2,600 were built, but in 1969 this was the only totally original flying Jenny. St. Paul, Minnesota, airline pilot Dan Neuman restored N2404 and his wife Vona hand-sewed the clear doped Irish linen cover. By 1989, nine Jennies were flyable.

heavily for about a plane length and a half, then Neuman shoved the stick to the stop and the steerable tailskid lifted out of the grass.

The Jenny gathered herself with a rush, was suddenly light on the wheels, and we were airborne within about 200 ft., as if she were an old hand at this.

She is, in a way.

She had logged only twenty-seven hours since remanufacture—a term used advisedly—but the manufacturer's plate in the cockpit said N2404 was one of a series of 400 built under contract by the Springfield Aircraft Corporation between October 1917 and October 1918 to government order. That's half a century in anyone's logbook.

Of more than 2,600 built, N2404 is the world's only OX-powered Curtiss-Wright JN-4D still flying, and she is beautiful. She is covered in clear-doped Irish linen with hand-sewn seams, and has 1 in. rib-stitching on the four mainplanes and rib tape with hand-frayed edges, all courtesy of Dan's wife, Vona Neuman, a craftswoman of the old school. She learned her trade by recovering a Beech 17.

"I quit keeping house and everything," she said. "I just had to sew on it. Some winter nights, this house smelled so bad we could hardly stand it." The eleven coats of dope, of course, are nitrate. Vona Neuman, so careful of her precise 1 in. spacing, was shocked later when she examined a factory Jenny fabric job in the Smithsonian and learned that original ribstitch spacing was haphazard.

N2404 is built of the best quality aircraft spruce and ash; thirty percent of the fuselage wood and seventy percent of the wings is well aged. Nearly all the copper-plated fittings and flying wires and the piano wire bracing in the front of the cockpit are original.

Steel tube landing gear, a two-place front cockpit and a steel tail—all fitted for barnstorming back in the 1920s by the brothers DeMass of Chesterton, Indiana, first civilian owners—have been replaced with original parts.

Five engines were cannibalized to produce the bellowing OX-5 in the nose.

It is shrouded in cowlings handmade by Dan Neuman using a wooden form to pound the side cooling gills to shape. Although Neuman makes his living as a senior 707 captain for Northwest Airlines, he is also an A&P. The metalwork is as precise as Vona Neuman's ribstitching.

The hodgepodge cockpit instrument panel was junked and original instruments substituted, though the airspeed indicator is from a JN-4H, and the only thing known about the compass is that it's a "vintage" unit of the proper era, supplied by the University of Minnesota. The front pit has new wood, but is otherwise original.

The booster mag was optional on OXs, and is used in N2404 because the Scintilla mags don't provide the low rpm hot spark of original types. Like cars of forty years ago, the Jenny has a lever to advance or retard the spark.

The airplane is a bit overpowering shoehorned into Neuman's spacious hangar, dwarfing a Monocoupe 90A and a half-restored Siemens-powered Waco. It is, after all, a large machine. It is 27 ft. 4 in. long and stands 9 ft. 10⅝ in. The wingspan is 43 ft. 7⅛ in.

It is such a tight fit that it will go in only at an angle, and clearance is less than 3 in. per side. Neuman handles all moving personally. Because of the skid and because the aft fuselage is quite heavy, he uses a special tail dolly that he built from heavy steel tubing and a pair of Buhl Pup wheels.

Stuffed in odd corners around the airplanes are enough spare parts to build another Jenny, including an OX-5 that Neuman calls "better than this one." There is also a Hall-Scott, a *six*-cylinder Liberty, a Curtiss Conqueror D-12, a German rocket motor, an

Crafted of wood, wire, fabric and dreams, the Jenny seems frighteningly fragile—but she taught a generation to fly, survived a decade and a half of casual misuse and now seems likely to fly on into the twenty-first century. In service, ultraviolet rays from the sun quickly destroyed the strength of the fabric, and airplanes had to be re-covered every couple of years, until airmen learned to paint their airplanes with silver dope: aluminum powder in a clear base. Spidery construction is evident in this exacting restoration to original condition.

80 hp LeRhone rotary and another converted to a radial, miscellaneous other radials and God knows what else. He's been collecting stuff for twenty-one years.

The sheer number of wires needed to hold a Jenny together is amazing. An incautious pilot could hang himself preflighting this bird. In flight, some vibrate madly while others are taut, in varying degrees depending on the attitude at the moment—an indication the whole contraption is working as it should.

The maze of wires and the slow speed, of course, made the Jenny so popular for wing-walking, plane-changing and other larger-than-life stunts now frowned upon by the federal bureaucracy.

Because the fuselage is a simple rectangular structure without internal bulkheads, it's easy to glance behind the pilot's seat and check clear back to the rudder post for wasps' nests and other impedimenta. In fact, the whole airplane is so open to inspection it's almost embarrassing, like finding someone's grandmother naked at a garden party.

The "baggage compartment" behind the rear seat is just big enough for maps, an extra helmet and goggles, gloves and maybe a hankie. It's so small it isn't even placarded with a weight restriction.

Factory specifications list an initial climb rate of 200 fpm but N2404 will better that handily. She will reach 2,500 ft. in seven minutes. The book says power loading on a JN-4D is 21.3 lbs. per hp, but the factory rated an OX-5 at 1425 rpm static and 1550 to 1600 airborne, full throttle. Neuman's engine will turn up

100 rpm more on the ground and at least 50 in the air, swinging a stock 59 in. pitch Sensenich. A 60 in. pitch is full cruise. The engine idles contentedly at 500 rpm.

Climb and glide speed is 50 to 55 mph, mostly the latter. The airplane cruises at 63 mph and stalls without warning at about 40. Cruise rpm is 1450, causing Neuman to remark, "There isn't much difference between full throttle and cruise in that engine." He says 1450 gives him 63 to 65 mph on 7 to 7½ gph which means the book figure of 2¼ hours full-throttle endurance is pretty accurate for the twenty-one-gallon tank.

The OX-5 is indifferent to diet, running happily on eighty-octane avgas, standard auto regular or ethyl in any proportion. It burns no oil. Neuman uses a forty-weight non-detergent, and in twenty-seven hours had changed oil three times, including a change after five hours' initial ground running.

Pilot and passengers are quite conscious of wind noise through the Jenny's maze of wires, and an airspeed indicator is a luxury that could be handily discarded. After a few minutes in the JN-4D, a pilot automatically keeps an ear tuned to the wind's wild song.

The rocker arms and valve guides—which must be individually lubricated after each flight—send a fine spattering of oil across the windshields in the first few minutes, but it soon subsides. The OX is basically a clean engine.

Both ailerons and elevator are surprisingly light, particularly the ailerons. Both compare favorably

The JN-4D is not heavy, but it's a big airplane, and its tail skid and many wires make it awkward to move around. It takes two men and a boy to get one in and out of the hangar, and preparing for flight consumes the better part of an *hour. Post-flight chores take nearly as long; all this no matter how long you fly. You've really got to want to fly to fly a Jenny!*

with current production general aviation types despite their unbalanced surfaces. The rudder is heavier, due largely to the short moment arm of the weeny rudder bar.

It's easy to see why this bird was much loved by wing-walkers and such. It's predictable and stable and, despite the low 5.5 lbs. per sq. ft. wing loading, it's not much affected by thermals. There's so much stuff hanging out in the breeze that it takes a good jolt to affect its stability.

Secrets of handling the Jenny are power, airspeed and attitude, just like every other airplane built. Neuman says, "It's an attitude airplane more than anything else," and he's right, but a little judiciously applied power can do a lot to straighten out handling errors.

We tried no real maneuvers, since Neuman was obviously ready to deck me from behind at the least sign of aerial madness, but the Jenny leaves the feeling it'll do about anything you want to do if it's done with finesse. The airplane is unlikely to do it for you. It gives the definite impression that if you fly yourself into some embarrassment, you're going to have to fly yourself out—the hallmark of a good trainer.

Despite the Jenny's history of long and yeoman service in the hands of reckless barnstormers and feckless fledglings, Neuman handles it with a lover's tenderness, and I did, too. I almost think he'd rather bend his 707.

With two aboard, the Jenny is definitely tail heavy. Since there is no trim, constant slight forward stick pressure is needed to maintain level flight.

Neuman even nixed stalls, reporting that, with the lifting tail and the aft-loaded condition, the airplane has a tendency to flat spin. But he says the controls just go suddenly loose and things get very quiet. The stall is straight ahead, and he reports a maximum 150 ft. altitude loss.

Forward visibility is surprisingly good off the ground, out over the long cowl and between the cylinder banks, but nose-high approaches demand angle vision.

Controls are easy to coordinate, and while it will maneuver satisfactorily feet-on-the-floor, it pays to use rudder in bank recovery. If you don't, there's a sudden breeze against your cheek.

The first fifteen degrees of bank take a definite effort in a Jenny, but then the airplane wants to tighten the turn—a result of the lack of wing dihedral. Steeper banks take some throttle to maintain altitude and airspeed.

Throttled back, the Jenny has a relatively high sink rate: on the order of 500 fpm with power, with the nose well down. The OX-5 is very smooth at cruise power, with a distinctive rippling bang-bang-bang from the slow-turning V-8. But the engine loads up in fifteen or twenty seconds even at low positive settings, and begins to complain.

Two hundred feet is plenty of ground roll for a Jenny takeoff, but climb-out is something else again. You have plenty of time to admire the frantic wiggling of the valve rocker arms on the 90 hp OX–5 V–8, also built by Curtiss. A

JN–4D is quite roll-resistant. It loops okay, but the figure won't be round. Gear is soft, virtually guaranteeing good landings.

This is what it's all about! Jenny cruises at 62–63 mph, and the near-total lack of instrumentation gives new meaning to the old phrase, "flying by the seat of your pants." It's a real experience. . . .

Both Neuman and I have heard that an OX with short stacks will quickly develop warped valves if the airplane is slipped in cool temperatures. He avoids slips.

The airplane takes a little power in the round-out to stop the sink and allow at least minimal flare. There is zero float, as in most biplanes.

Landings are soft. With an empty weight of 1,430 lbs. and a gross of 1,920, this is not a particularly small airplane, and you think of those big 26x4 in. clincher high-pressure tires beneath and expect a roll-out like a farm wagon.

Then the wheels rumble across the rough turf and there is only minimal fuselage vibration. The roll-out is about seventy yards, since Neuman prefers wheel landings for better visibility and to spare the tailskid. It pivots thirty degrees either side of center and doubles as the Jenny's only braking system, but it's a tad on the fragile side. S-turns and a head over the side are of course *de rigeur* for taxiing.

Neuman tries to avoid crosswind landings, but he says the Jenny takes them well despite the narrow gear and the 18 in. clearance between the turf and the bamboo wingtip skids.

There's some post-flight work involved in flying N2404. The first item, of course, is to carefully wipe down the whole airplane to remove any oil stains, grass or other smudges from the spotless finish. The entire airplane sparkles, and the fussiest diner could eat off the cockpit floor without a murmur. Hell, he could eat off the inside of the bottom engine cowling!

Then there's the matter of squeezing it back into the hangar, lubricating all those exposed working parts on the OX and, perhaps, checking the Prestone/water mix in the radiator.

Maybe it's fortunate that present JN-4D production is limited. It took Neuman eighteen years to collect the pieces for N2404, and 3½ years to build her after that. At that rate, he'll have traded in his 707 on a 747 before he turns out another. Besides, he's having trouble with labor relations.

Vona says, "No more!"

First printed in *Air Progress*, February 1970.

Chapter 2

Curtiss Robin

Topeka Robin

The Robin is another one of those historically significant airplanes.

It really was the first successful air charter airplane; the businessliner of its day, and a machine a fixed-base operator could make money with. Its utter reliabilty, relative cruise efficiency and long range endeared it to aviation entrepreneurs from coast to coast.

It also set more records than any of us can remember, including some truly amazing time-aloft marks, although the records, of course, were made with those models sporting the Wright radials. OX–5 engines in the 1920s and early 1930s were not noted for reliability. The record-setting continued for years. In fact, war clouds were gathering over Europe when Douglas "Wrong Way" Corrigan made his famous flight to Ireland in a Robin.

Robins are not really fun to fly, but there is a period charm to their wicker seats, high control inputs and total lack of visibility directly ahead. Modern pilots find looking out the sides takes a little getting used to. Fortunately, they are extremely docile.

Dr. Leland M. Weber is a short, silver-haired dentist who seems vaguely familiar to most people.

Among non-fliers, it may be because he resembles at least five of the Seven Dwarfs. But among antique airplane buffs, he really is familiar. His usual post on summer weekends has been in a lawn chair at a fly-in, beneath the broad wing of N9223, one of the slickest Curtiss Robins still flying.

"I bought it to use as a tow plane for gliders," Weber said four years ago when a well-known Florida aircraft dealer unloaded it at Ottumwa, Iowa. It had been in regular use as a Seattle-based photo plane until shortly before, but at the time, it was distinguished chiefly by a gold-plated doorknob, threadbare tires and a long list of minor ailments.

The ferry pilot who delivered it a month later declined to land on the runway. He didn't think the tires would stand it. He was right. A week later, one suddenly blew out while the airplane sat peacefully in the hangar.

But N9223 has since received well over a thousand man-hours of tender loving care, an unspecified but large amount of A&P labor, myriad small repairs and a new paint job.

The plane has flown maybe seventy hours in that time. No one seems any more interested today in keeping an accurate log than at any other time in her long and checkered career. Weber estimates she's flown perhaps 15,000 hours or more in her forty-one year history. No one really knows. Certainly not Weber, the plane's twenty-seventh owner.

N9223 has flown in Mexican heat and Northern cold. She's hopped passengers at county fairs, looped and slow-rolled at forgotten air shows, trained pilots and been used for some things still-living former owners just won't discuss.

"The reason there aren't many Robins left is because all the rum-runners used them to haul liquor from Cuba or Mexico," says Weber earnestly. "But every time the Feds caught one, they'd confiscate it and burn it."

When Topeka, Kansas, dentist Leland Weber (right) donated his 1929 Curtiss C–1 Robin to the Experimental Aircraft Association (EAA) in the fall of 1969, Paul Poberezny himself came down to collect it and ferry it back. The

EAA resold the airplane in the late 1980s, after Weber's death. Airplane originally had a six-cylinder, 170 hp Curtiss Challenger engine with double-throw crankshaft, but has carried a 225 hp Lycoming for years.

There's no question but that, in 1930, the Robin would have made an excellent booze bus. If you can get something into the narrow fuselage, you can fly off with it. On the other hand, there aren't many other forty-one-year-old airplanes around, either.

Old N9223 has towed no gliders—nor is she likely to. Before moving to the Experimental Aircraft Association's museum in Hales Corners, Wisconsin, she was Topeka Municipal Airport's unofficial mascot and a showpiece regular at antique fly-ins throughout the Midwest.

Seven of the thirteen Robins still active now sport 220 to 225 hp Continental or Lycoming radials. Old N9223 is one of them. She was a C–1 model, 296th of her kind, when she rolled off the Curtiss-Robertson Airplane Manufacturing Company production line at Anglum, Missouri. Her power then was a six-cylinder, 170 hp Curtiss Challenger with a double-throw crankshaft. Now it's the big Lycoming.

This is a far cry from the 90 hp OX-5 used in the first Robins, and the abundant power, the thick Curtiss C-72 airfoil and a truly astonishing sink rate combine to make today's Robin a very respectable short-field airplane. It takes an awful load, a young jungle or a full-fledged swamp to keep those high-pressure 30x5 in. tires on the ground for more than 100 yards.

Like most old airplanes, N9223 is more at home on a pasture than an asphalt runway, a new steerable tailwheel notwithstanding. And she can get downright willful in a gusty Kansas crosswind.

The split-axle outrigger-type landing gear is anchored to the forward wing struts and has a 96 in. tread. Stout and equipped with air-oil oleos, it soaks up stresses and strains that would wreck a lesser airplane. That's fortunate, because the mechanical brakes are no better than they have to be.

"Doc groundloops her nearly every time he lands, but she's never lifted a wheel yet," says Ray Rundell, a Topeka police officer and old soaring buddy who's put most of the time on N9223 in the past few years.

"The first time I flew it, I was scared. I hadn't flown anything for two years. But he couldn't find anybody else to fly it, so I got in and took off. I made my first turn and I thought, 'What're you doin' here?' But I shot a couple of landings and—I've been flying it ever since. It's the heaviest, most powerful thing I ever flew," Rundell said.

Actually, the Robin is not difficult to fly. It's just hard work. The work starts with pulling the 98 in. Hamilton Standard ground adjustable propeller through half a dozen turns to swage accumulated oil out of the bottom cylinders. But, since the original inertia-type hand-cranked starter has been replaced with an electrical one, no one has to stand outside and wind.

Starting procedure calls for ten slow shots of prime, magneto switches on both, throttle full forward and then back to cracked, master and generator switches on, and punch the button. A placard on the panel says, "Start on Right Mag," but Rundell recommends both. It seems to make no difference.

The Lycoming grinds, the big prop makes a slow circle and the engine fires, a cloud of blue smoke swirling back from the rusty-red exhaust stack along the right side of the fuselage. The cowling and the custom panel vibrate gently, instruments dancing in their shock mounts.

The engine ticks over at 550 rpm, but will idle well at 450 after warming. Once rolling, the plane will taxi smartly at 600 rpm. Ground check is at 900 to 1000 rpm—"as high as you can hold it with the brakes"—with 75 rpm drop on either mag and little effect from the carburetor heat.

Ground handling is positive, but rather like steering a DC–3 without jockeying the throttles.

The tower clears Robin N9223 for Runway 35, and we make an intersection takeoff, for we have no need for the other half mile of paving. The power comes in gently and there is no real need for right rudder.

The rpm winds around to 1850, and the Robin gets light on the wheels almost immediately. With the tail in the air, she's inclined to wander, and the heavy rudder usually is well behind in correcting.

At 100 yards and 50 mph, she flies off, showing an initial climb rate of 1,600 fpm—the only real advantage of the big engine. The original Challenger had an advertised 102 mph cruise, and this airplane certainly will do no better than that, even allowing for instrument error.

But grossed out, this bird will climb 1,000 fpm, and Weber was told that as a photo plane it flew regularly at 20,000 ft. With only a pilot aboard and the prop set now for cruise, she'll touch 2,000 fpm briefly at Topeka's 1,000 ft. elevation.

The plane climbs happily at 60 mph, and at 80 still will indicate 600 fpm with temperatures far at the low end of the dial.

The first turn, at 500 ft., is a real indication of how the Robin flies—like a Mississippi flatboat or Disney's Dumbo in advanced age. The rudder is guaranteed to develop a good set of leg muscles on any pilot within a few days' flying. Once the pilot rudders into the turn, it's not enough just to ease the foot pressure when the bank is established. It takes definite opposite rudder to stop the tail's swing and straighten out the unbalanced control surface.

There's plenty of noise in the Robin's cabin, despite extra-thick insulation, but it doesn't have the fury of an opposed engine sound. It's a soothing bang-bang-bang from the seven big cylinders up front. The

The first successful air taxi, the three-place Robin was utterly reliable, setting numerous endurance records. Because it would fly with anything you could stuff into it, the type also was popular with rumrunners during Prohibition. Big, unbalanced controls made the airplane tiring to fly, but it's as safe as a government bond.

cabin gets its share of exhaust fumes, and it's a good idea to leave the side window well cracked.

Power off, the airplane stalls at an indicated 38 mph (the book says 45 mph actual) with a gentle, barely discernible break, and mushes downward, the rate of descent oscillating from 450 to 1,000 fpm. A slight aileron correction is enough to keep it straight ahead.

Power on (1200 rpm), the break comes at the same speed, but she's a far fiercer bird. There's a sharp pitch-down and the airplane falls off on the right wing, demanding a heavy rudder foot for recovery.

Normal cruise is at 1650 rpm, and gets 75 mph indicated air speed for 11 gph fuel consumption. Maximum cruise is 1750 rpm, 85 mph IAS and 14 gallons.

If the air is smooth, the airplane flies very comfortably hands-off, providing the pilot keeps his feet on the rudder pedals. If the air is rough, the Robin will make a pilot earn his time.

Forward visibility is a phrase invented well after the Robin's heyday. It was designed when the world was agog about Lindbergh's solo trans-Atlantic flight—and if Lindbergh didn't need to see where he was going, why should anyone else?

Speed is not the Robin's long suit. None of them will do more than 105, and most top out at closer to 100. Nevertheless, this type of airplane, too, flew the Atlantic, in 1939—in the hands of Douglas "Wrong Way" Corrigan, who ended up in Ireland.

Like many older airplanes, there's a definite delay between control application and response. Again like many, it takes definite effort to stop the control movement, except for the elevator. This, due to the long stick and excellent leverage, is quick and positive. Aileron and rudder are quite stiff.

There's a fair amount of adverse yaw in a bank, but the Robin doesn't quarrel about holding bank angles up to sixty degrees or more. She's stable and uncomplaining in slow flight at 45 mph, but it takes judicious throttle juggling, averaging about 1500 rpm, to hold her there without sinking. Surprisingly, there's almost no apparent difference between high- and low-speed control pressures, though greater stick travel is noticeable below 60.

In-flight visibility is good if not panoramic. It's fair along either wing, poor level to either front quarter and superlative down and to either side through the deep knee-level windows. Like the windshield, these are the original safety glass and as distortion-free as a shop window. The roll-up glass cabin windows have been replaced by plexiglass, 50 lbs. lighter.

The pilot sits centered in the lonely front seat, head poking into a narrow, recessed well between the wings and capped by an almost useless overhead window. Brace wires run diagonally across the well and can leave him with crisscross cranium bumps in rough weather.

The two passengers share a bench seat in the rear. Narrow-shouldered, skinny passengers are preferred.

Despite the low stall speed, approaches are best made somewhere between 65 and 80 mph IAS. Below 65, the sink rate is something fierce. In fact, at 65 it's 1,800 fpm. At 80 it's 1,000 fpm and pilot's choice between a tight pattern and a power approach. Controlling the sink with throttle is easy, and it's natural to set up a 600 to 700 fpm descent with about 1200 rpm.

Trying to flare at speeds below 60 is not advised, because the airflow over the elevator isn't enough to raise the heavy nose. My first Robin landing was on turf at 50 mph with a 160 lb. man in the back seat. The flare started fine, but with full back stick I got a beautiful wheel landing instead of the three-pointer I'd been reaching for. The long-stroke oleos travel 4½ in., and make wheelers a joltless experience.

An 80 mph approach gives a nice flare and soft landings on hard-surface runways, and with the stick back firmly, the airplane is not hard to handle. The wide gear makes her want to roll straight ahead, but sometimes a little help doesn't hurt. With only the pilot aboard, she's a little squirrely on the roll-out down around 40 mph.

Trim is a ratcheted Johnson bar on the left side, just beneath the throttle. It looks like something stolen off a corn planter, and is of limited help in lightening control pressures on landing.

On the ground, there is no such thing as forward visibility. Thus, with the nose high for landing, the pilot is technically blind ahead. The deep side windows provide a very satisfactory substitute, however, and keeping an equal amount of runway showing on both sides quickly becomes natural. S-turns are mandatory for taxi, especially if there might be something up ahead somewhere.

N9223 had an empty weight of 1,576 lbs. when she left the factory in April 1929, a gross of 2,440, an 864 lb. useful load and 394 lbs. of payload with fifty gallons of fuel in the two wing tanks and five gallons of oil aboard. Now, at forty years old, she's put on a little weight.

The engine is 75 lbs. heavier than the Challenger, and there's 25 lbs. of lead in the tail to balance it. A little equipment has been added, a little removed. What with one thing and another, present dry weight—measured—is 1,825 lbs., and gross weight is considered to be about 2,755, of which 500 lbs. is payload. The 12.5 cu. ft. luggage compartment is limited to 50 lbs.

Original range was given as 510 miles. Now it might be 420, leaned out at about 7,500 ft. and cranked back to 1600 rpm. Climb was listed at 650 fpm and now is vastly improved. Ceiling was 12,700 ft. Now it is unknown, but far higher than anyone wants to take it without oxygen.

The steel tube fuselage measures 25½ ft.; the mixed-construction wings span 41 ft. and the airplane stands 8 ft. high. The constant-chord wing measures 6 ft. from nose to trailing edge and the wing area totals 224 sq. ft. The wings feature routed spruce spars and stamped duralumin ribs—a new process for the time.

Curtiss sold something over 750 Robins in several different models at prices ranging from about $8,000 down to $5,995 and followed them with the similar six-place Thrush.

The first really successful US monoplane design, the boxy Robin introduced more people to flying than any single plane until the J-3 Cub, and Robins set a long string of records.

The few remaining Robins are conversation pieces; they're interesting to fly, and they're great attention-getters. They are forgiving and far from hard to master, but they do demand muscle and they're just not "fun" airplanes.

First printed in *Air Progress*, March 1970.

Chapter 3

Howard DGA–6

Mister Mulligan

Benny Howard's famous DGA–6 was always a star-crossed airplane. The design posted some remarkable feats, but it had an unhappy history, too.

Flying at 20,000 ft. to avoid weather, Harold Neumann succumbed to hypoxia and crashlanded in the Rocky Mountains on the way to California to position the airplane for the 1934 transcontinental dash.

He explained that Howard had ordered him to fly at that altitude and, when he asked about oxygen, pooh-poohed the need for it. Neumann passed out at the controls and only came to in a mountain valley. Fortunately, there was an airstrip nearby. Less fortunately, there was a 20 kt. direct crosswind blowing and Neumann was still woozy. Howard was so mad he fired Neumann by telegram, but Neumann's wife, Inez, promptly jumped down Benny's throat and made him hire Neumann back.

The second time, Benny and his wife, "Mike," were roaring east in the 1936 Bendix when Mulligan *shed a prop blade and the plane crashed in the desert. Both were injured, and Benny lost a leg. The wrecked* Mulligan *was abandoned where it fell.*

Years later, Bob Reichert salvaged the usable pieces, "rebuilt" the airplane—and promptly killed himself and his wife trying to set a new pylon speed record. He struck the desert floor at nearly 300 mph, cartwheeled and exploded.

Jim Younkin, owner of this beautiful Mister Mulligan *replica, has reason to be cautious.*

It makes no difference. I'm like Neumann. If I had that airplane, I'd fly the wing struts off it, and enjoy every minute.

"I really hate to fly this airplane," said Jim Younkin as we pushed the big, white, radial-engined brute backward across the taxiway and into the grass in front of Younkin's shop hangar.

Sweat popped out on my temples as I pushed on the wing strut and tried to concentrate more on what Younkin was saying and less on my incipient slipped disk.

I asked him why he felt that way. Was *Mister Mulligan* disappointing to fly? Looking at it, I couldn't see how it possibly could be.

Younkin shook his head. "It's sure a nice flyin' airplane," he said, confirming once again the old pilot's claim that if it looks good, it'll fly good. Then he added, "Boy, if you ever lost your engine, it'd be too bad."

Why, I asked? Didn't it glide well? Younkin shook his head again. "It glides fine," he said. "It glides fast!" He paused and added sadly, "It's too bad it scares me like it does."

So what's the problem, I asked? Younkin shrugged. "I just don't feel comfortable flyin' that big, heavy, high-powered airplane around at my age. I don't feel as comfortable with it as I would like to feel."

His Travel Air 4000 or his 1931 Stinson Junior S are more his speed these days, Younkin implied. Or even his Travel Air Mystery Ship, currently on loan to the EAA Museum in Oshkosh, Wisconsin. "The Travel Air is more relaxing to fly than this airplane," he explained of the Mystery Ship. "It's more docile. It's like a sport airplane. This is heavy. You make power approaches, and it's so awkward to handle on the ground that you don't just go out and play with it like you should. That Mystery Ship, compared to this, it's like flyin' a Cub."

This from a man who not only built and test flew painstaking replicas of two of the most famous and successful (and beautiful) racing planes of the 1930s, but totally restored—and tested—four antique airplanes as well. And who has flown all of them to a variety of aviation events the length and breadth of this country!

This from a man who has flown *Mulligan* repeatedly into the organized madness of Oshkosh, who has crossed the Rockies to take it to the Reno Air Races, who has dodged southern thunderbumpers to attend the Tullahoma bash. . . . Perhaps most impressively, this is a man who has many times flown his big white charger in and out of Blakesburg, Iowa's rough, bumpy, sloping Antique Airfield turf strip. This is a 5,000 hour pilot who has—by his own estimate—logged 125 hours at *Mulligan*'s controls, making him the most experienced DGA–6 pilot in history, by far.

You just don't know whether to believe him or not, when he talks like that!

After all, Jim Younkin is only fifty-seven. He's been flying for more than thirty years; has shaped his life around aviation and its needs—and still does, though

he officially "retired" long ago. Both his older brothers are pilots (Navy veterans of World War II). His son Bobby earns his own living flying. Jim Younkin personally designed all the Mitchell autopilots through the Century IV, once owned part of the company and still holds "between 15 and 20" patents in the field.

See what I mean?

On the other hand, watch him around his airplane and you have to take Younkin's statements seriously, for he is clearly a worrier at the controls. And when he backs off for a few minutes to let someone else have a crack at *Mulligan*, he's nervous as a man who's just learned his house is on fire and nobody has either a bucket or a hose.

You have to wonder. . . .

One thing's for certain: *Mulligan* is one fantastic flying machine!

It has fingertip-light, trigger-quick ailerons, highly responsive tailfeathers and a performance envelope broad enough to turn most homebuilders pea green with envy.

The original airplane carried a Pratt & Whitney R-1340S1D, sporting a 14:1 supercharger and a Smith electric variable-pitch propeller which enabled it to pump out 830 hp on 100 octane fuel for racing. The

A scaled-up Monocoupe, Benny Howard's DGA–6 racer was unique in several respects. It was the only airplane to win both the Bendix transcontinental dash and the Thompson trophy around the pylons at Cleveland—and to post both *wins in the same year: 1935. It also was the only civilian airplane in history capable of carrying passengers and luggage while still outrunning the Army's first-line fighters.*

S1D is no longer available. Neither is the big blower or the Smith propeller. Younkin's exacting replica must make do with the heavier R-1340AN-1, a military engine developing a maximum 600 hp for takeoff and 550 METO (maximum, except take-off). The AN-1 carries a 10:1 blower and a Hamilton-Standard constant-speed, but the combination still is potent enough to allow it to loaf along at a 230 mph cruise at 10,500 ft. and, probably, hit a top of 250 mph.

The Hamilton-Standard lacks the blade pitch range it needs to fully exploit the airplane's incredible performance envelope, says the builder. It jumped off fine on the first test flight, but quickly ran out of fine pitch. Younkin came back and adjusted the stops, so now it doesn't get off nearly so well—but the prop won't hit the forward stop until 10,500 ft. Now, he says, "What I've got is a constant speed prop up to 10,500 and then it's a fixed pitch."

The original airplane claimed an initial sea level climb rate of 2,800 fpm, pulling 550 hp, and 4,450 fpm pulling 830 hp. "Normal" top speed (sea level, 550 hp) was listed at 251 mph; 550 hp cruise 231 at sea level; 262 at 1,000 ft. and 292 at 17,000—the optimum altitude for the 14:1 blower and the Smith prop. Claimed sea level Vmax, on 830 hp, was 287 on 100 octane—the configuration used in the Thompson Trophy Race of 1935.

That's based on a 2,600 lb. empty weight and a normal category gross of 4,100 lbs., providing a useful load of 1,500 lbs. At those weights, the airplane's 150.7 sq. ft. of wing yielded a wing loading of 30.7 lbs. per sq. ft. and a power loading of 7.65 lbs. per hp. In its Bendix cross-country configuration, gross weight shot up to 5,300 lbs., useful load to 2,700 and wing loading to 39 lbs. per sq. ft. Yet, despite the fact that the airplane had a wing loading roughly comparable to a Spitfire fighter, landing speed with the little drag flaps extended to their full thirty degrees was listed at a comfortable 64 mph.

Mulligan had a 66 in. chord, an NACA 2412 airfoil and a span of 31 ft. 8 in., a length of 25 ft. 1 in. and was 11 ft. 9 in. high in flight position. Younkin's replica, of course, has the same dimensions and weights as the original—and the same wing loadings.

It weighed around 4,000 lbs. the way we were flying it on a muggy, 85 degree June day in northern Arkansas, and when the lever-action throttle went forward and the big Pratt & Whitney began to roar, there was no question we were going flying, performance-limited Hamilton-Standard or not!

Heading into a 5 knot wind, the tail came up in probably 150 yards and we were off the asphalt at around 900 or 1,000 ft. Pulling 30 in. and 2000 rpm, the airplane quickly assumed a ten-degree nose-up attitude and the rate of climb needle flickered briefly at 2,000 fpm before falling back to fluctuate between 1,500 and 1,800.

"It'll get to altitude in a hurry," said Younkin, adding that he got 2,800 fpm at full throttle while flying at Tullahoma, Tennessee, with two passengers aboard.

Furthermore, it comes down the same way! "If you want to descend 3,000 fpm, why, you just stick the nose down," said Younkin. Definitely my kind of airplane!

And, if the truth were known, probably Jim Younkin's, too. The thing is, as my wife remarked, "He's so laid back he's almost prone."

I first met Jim Younkin when he started showing up at Midwest fly-ins in his beautifully restored Travel Air 4000, ten years ago, but it was a good deal later before I got to know him. It was probably three years before I heard him say more than ten words all in a bunch.

He is a saturnine, taciturn man who dips a little snuff, walks around in worn-out jeans and an old shirt and generally looks like he's straight off a hillside hardscrabble farm.

You'd never dream he's a former college engineering teacher and creative genius whose design talents embrace not only his autopilots but even the house he lives in. Certainly no one would suspect he plays saxophone in a local bar every Saturday night!

The fact is, Jim Younkin's a fake. He's not even an Arkansawyer! The family moved to the state from Iowa when he was a high school freshman.

All the Younkin boys were bitten by the aviation bug back in Iowa—hard. As kids, they built and flew rubber- and gas-powered models and were "just caught up in aviation," as he explains it.

When World War II came along, both Bob and Bill became Navy pilots, and Jim was on his way to following in their footsteps when the war ended and he traded in his extended six-year Navy obligation for a fast eighteen months in the Army.

After the war, Jim studied electrical engineering at the University of Arkansas, Bob became a crop duster and FBO and Bill drifted off into running an automotive maintenance facility.

Jim Younkin taught at the University of Arkansas. Then, seeking to combine his EE background and his interest in aviation, he went to work at Collins Radio. There, a mechanical engineer told him what general aviation needed was a low-cost slaved gyro. The upshot of that was that both of them left Collins, and Younkin developed the slaving system in his home shop.

He sold it to Aviation Instruments in Houston—and himself along with it. There, he got into design work on AIM gyros, trying to make them producible. While he was so engaged, AIM got a request to manufacture a steering system for a Beech drone using a fluxgate compass and a rate gyro. Again, Younkin developed a working system. That in turn caught the attention of Don Mitchell, who'd been trying to do the same thing, and soon Mitchell pirated Younkin away to his little plant in Mineral Wells, Texas.

That was in 1962. For Mitchell, Younkin designed the first heading bug built into a 3 in. vertical-card

The original Mulligan carried an 830 hp version (though this power level was not sustainable on the 87 octane fuel of the era) of the Pratt & Whitney R-1340 with a 13.85:1 blower and could hit 292 mph at 17,000 ft. It also climbed 4,450 fpm at full power. Jim Younkin's exacting replica makes do with 600 hp and a 10:1 supercharger, but still cruises at better than 250 mph and climbs 2,800 fpm. Note that this early 1930s design still provides better performance than any other single-piston-engine general aviation airplane around.

gyro and a whole series of successful autopilots. When the firm was sold in 1967, Younkin stayed on, but two years later he moved part of his engineering operation back to Arkansas and did preliminary design work from there for another ten years before officially retiring.

But of course he didn't, really.

Bob had traded for the remains of the Travel Air, a former crop duster, and got Jim interested in restoring it even while he was still doing engineering consulting. Telling of it, Younkin laughed, explaining: "It was kind of a case of trading two $500 cats for a thousand-dollar dog. You couldn't even tell it was a Travel Air!

"It had a metal fuselage, Cessna 195 gear, Frise ailerons, square tipped wings. . . . By the time we got through restoring it, it was 85 percent homebuilt."

The Travel Air was finished and flying in 1976, and soon was winning awards at aviation events throughout the Midwest. Also finished shortly afterward was a Stearman which he restored in his spare time, so to speak.

Because of his problems with the Travel Air restoration, Younkin decided his next project was going to be either pure homebuilt—or a restoration where all the pieces were already there.

That's when he determined to replicate the famous Travel Air Mystery S racer of 1929. He'd already started on it when "the Stinson just kinda turned up." He restored the fuselage on the latter, then set it aside until the racer was finished.

The *Mystery Ship* was flying in 1979, the Stinson in 1980. Both, of course, exhibited the flawless workmanship and attention to detail that has characterized all Younkin's work.

He took the *Mystery Ship* to Oshkosh in 1979, and it was on that trip that he decided to build the DGA-6. "I had just built probably the best one you could pick, but I had gotten into a pattern, it seemed, and the obvious choice for another would be *Mister Mulligan*. So, after a few beers, I decided that would make a good project."

Younkin explains his all-time favorite airplane is the Grumman F3F, but he figures no one ever will be able to replicate that because of the number of sophisticated parts found in it which can't be easily duplicated.

Mulligan, on the other hand, "was built in a shop with no more facilities than I had. There's nothing on this airplane that you could not duplicate."

The original *Mulligan* was built in the old American Eagle factory at Kansas City Municipal Airport by young Eddie Fisher and a couple of helpers to a concept laid down by Ben O. Howard and detailed by Gordon Israel. It was essentially an overgrown Monocoupe 110 Special with, as Howard had promised, "the biggest engine I can find."

The result is history.

Mulligan was the only airplane ever to win both the Bendix transcontinental dash from Burbank to Cleveland and the Thompson Trophy pylon race in the same year. It also was the only passenger-carrying enclosed cabin airplane ever to make a name for itself in the Unlimited classes. It was like no other airplane before or since.

When *Mulligan* turned up on the qualifying line of the Thompson Trophy race on Labor Day morning, 1935, its engine had never been opened up at low altitude. Pilot Harold Neumann flew it just fast enough to qualify. Then he opened the throttle to see what he could get. What he got was several scorched cylinders, which were barely replaced in time for the race that afternoon. The time margin was so thin there was no time even for any kind of run-up test.

It was a hot day; probably around 100 degrees Fahrenheit or hotter, and the start time had been moved up because of a threatening thunderstorm. Rolling into place for the race horse start, Neumann found Roscoe Turner on the pole in his big golden Wedell-Williams, its thousand-horse P&W rumbling. Next to him was Sylvester J. "Steve" Wittman in his wicked little red and silver homebuilt, *Bonzo*, half of it taken up by the mighty Curtiss Conqueror V-12. Outboard of *Mulligan* were Roger Don Rae in the Keith-Rider *Firecracker*, Art Chester in *Jeep*, Marion McKeen in *Miss Los Angeles* and Joe Jacobson in *Mike*. Finally, there was a big Seversky amphibian piloted by Lee Miles. All had their engines idling.

Originally, Neumann had intended to use *Mulligan*'s controllable-pitch prop and fast takeoff to get the jump on the pack and lead from the first. But race officials, with a revised (and better) weather forecast in hand, stalled more than half an hour to launch on the original schedule, thereby leaving the whole field idling at the starting line—heating up.

When the flag finally dropped, Neumann gunned his engine—and to his horror it nearly quit, victim of fouled plugs. The rest of the racers took off without him as he coaxed *Mulligan* off the field under part throttle, using every foot of sod and arriving at the scattering pylon teetering on the thin edge of a stall.

He was two laps into the race before the fouling burned off the plugs and Neumann was able to set the power and prop pitch he intended to use for the rest of the race. His revised strategy was simply to finish the race—in the money, if possible.

He began passing the slower entrants about midway through the race and, toward the end, when he overtook Wittman's ailing *Bonzo*, he figured he had second place cinched. He saw Turner, the leader, landing, went ahead and flew two more laps to finish his own distance and add a little insurance, and landed.

When he reduced the power, the engine packed up on him again, leaving him idling in the middle of the air field, unable to move. Disgusted, he climbed out just as a race official drove up, hugged him, and announced, "You won! You won!"

The long idling period had taken its toll on Roscoe Turner's engine, too, and he had been forced to drop out a lap short, streaming smoke and flames! And that's how *Mulligan* won the Thompson.

It may be stories like that that bother Jim Younkin and lead to his conservatism at the controls. "Race pilots had a strange way of lookin' at things," he said, talking of Neumann. "If he had this *Mulligan*, he'd fly it every damn minute, 'til the wings fell off. But I think of too many things that can go wrong. . . ."

And he's had problems getting this engine to run just right, too. Something about too much fuel pressure. He says he intends to change the carburetor, but just hasn't gotten to it yet. "The worst problem I had with it was comin' back from Reno, takin' off from Cheyenne," Younkin related. "At that altitude, there was just a narrow range where it'd work for takeoff power." He was carrying two passengers, "a lot of baggage and a lot of fuel, and the tail was so heavy you couldn't hardly taxi."

But it is a measure of his painstaking research, his exacting ways and his craftsmanship that the replica racer flew hands off on its first test flight. Except for the prop adjustment, the only needed modifications were to cure some in-flight fuel venting and to add a stiffener to the trailing edge of the engine cowling.

Younkin's departure point in the project was the detailed three-views and cutaways done by Paul R. Matt for the Historical Aviation Album back in 1975, supplemented by all the data he could mine from the late Eddie Fisher's memory and all the photos he could find. "I spent hours and hours researching all

Younkin's replica DGA-6 incorporates some control system improvements that remove the heavy feel of the original and leave it a positive delight to fly. The DGA-6 sired an airplane manufacturing company and a whole series of similar airplanes, the most common of them the wartime DGA-15P, built for the Navy. The Younkin Mulligan *is much more fun to fly!*

the pictures," he said, fishing out an example. "You can still see the pencil marks I drew on there."

He located a junk Howard DGA-15 and, where possible, used original Howard parts: many fittings, the stabilizer jack screw and cabin pitch trim assembly, the flap motor and assembly, the pedals, the firewall. The wing hardware is modified Howard. The engine mount is a custom unit exactly like a commercial Howard but one inch shorter. The tail tubes are as per Howard and so on.

He spent days just calculating the precise curvature of the metal fairing that provides a fillet between the wing and fuselage juncture.

On the other hand, he made some deliberate—but unobtrusive—changes in the original design, too, deciding "there was no reason to copy their mistakes."

For example, when the Howard team built *Mulligan*, they simply copied most of the Monocoupe's design features, including its horribly heavy ailerons.

Building his replica, Younkin saw no reason to put up with that. He modified the aileron nose configuration and added internal counterbalances for flutter protection. The original aileron actuators were simple bent tubes attached to the bellcranks, which Younkin didn't like. And although he left them in place for looks, he substituted internal idler arms moving straight fore and aft.

On the original, simple round tubes projecting between lower cylinders provided induction air for the carburetor and oil cooler. Younkin's are bigger, and rectangular, for better volume. Additionally, he paid a great deal of attention to providing a good heating and ventilating system. Flaps were hinged at the bottom, instead of copying the original's top-mounted piano hinges, but with a totally closed top line in the retracted position. He also deleted the Monocoupe-style external gap seals on the elevator and rudder, substituting a system of internal seals.

Howard's racer had a one-piece bump cowling, for some reason—meaning the prop had to be removed anytime a mechanic wanted to work on the engine. Younkin's is split into three pieces, for convenient access. But, like the original, it's made of metal. Nine pieces, in fact, all cut and welded together right there in Younkin's shop, with bumps welded over the cylinder cut-outs and finally heat-treated. "Stupidity, brute force and determination" produced that cowling, says Younkin. "That's probably what built this whole airplane."

The thirty-gallon oil tank sported by the original ship has been replaced with a nine-gallon tank in the replica, but it's mounted in the same place. Wing and fuselage tanks hold a total of 125 gallons of fuel and, as in the original, the rear seat passengers sit directly on the gas tank. Since the Pratt & Whitney burns thirty gallons an hour, *Mulligan* has a four-hour endurance—but that represents a still-air range of 920 miles!

Younkin mounted the pitot tube out beyond the strut, in the hope it would read more accurately than in the original location. And, of course, the panel has modern circuit breakers, modern instruments and radio—and a loran! But the rest of the airplane is pure quill *Mulligan*.

The tailwheel, for example, is rigidly mounted and partially enclosed in a streamlined fairing, which means whenever *Mulligan* turns, the tailwheel tire must skid sideways, scrubbing off rubber. Younkin has worked out the design for a fifteen-degree swiveling, locking tailwheel that would make taxiing considerably easier, "but I just don't want to give up that fairing." He glanced at the 10 in. tire and added: "I think this is the fourth tailwheel tire, and it's gone, just about. I figure $6 or $7 an hour for tailwheel tires. The things cost about $120 plus labor—and that's without too much local flying."

The advantage to the present system, of course, is that any tendency to swing on takeoff or landing is automatically dampened as long as the tailwheel is on the ground—a plus that Harold Neumann, at any rate, feels is worth the aggravation.

Younkin isn't sure just how many hours went into the *Mulligan* project, but it has to be well over 10,000—the equivalent of five man-years! "I worked on it about three years an average of 40 hours a week," he said, and began ticking off the contributions of other men, coming up with another 5,000. "There's no telling what it's got in it," he summed up. "It's got too much, I can tell you that!"

The fuselage is a 4130 welded steel tube structure with wood formers and stringers and partial mahogany cover. The all-wood two-spar wing likewise is covered with mahogany plywood, in turn covered with fabric and hand-rubbed dope.

The result is a slick, very fast airplane. I leveled out at 7,500 ft. MSL, and set up cruise power of 28 in. at 2050 rpm. The airspeed indicator walked rapidly up the dial and stabilized at 220 IAS—252 true at our 9,000 ft. density altitude. Not bad for a sticky, hazy, bumpy summer day!

There was a slight lateral instability at cruise; the faintest hint of a tendency to hunt left and right, like a Bonanza, prompting Younkin to remark on the need for a rudder lock for comfortable cross-country flying.

Dutch rolling the airplane rapidly from wingtip to wingtip while holding the nose on a point, I quickly discovered the ailerons were as nice as anything I'd ever flown. The rudder also was quite light and very powerful ("Too powerful!" growled Younkin), with a slight hesitation before it became effective. The elevator, though not really heavy, was surprisingly much heavier than the other controls.

The overhead elevator trim (there is no rudder trim) was powerful and precise in effect, and the overall impression of the airplane was of a comfortable, powerful four-place Monocoupe with about a twenty percent added margin of stability. "It's sure a nice instrument airplane," and is certified as such, reported Younkin. And, though the cockpit noise level is uncomfortably high for unprotected ears, "that's no problem if you've got a (good modern) headset."

Clearing the area with fast 180 degree turns left and right, using about sixty degrees of bank, I rolled back to level flight, eased the throttle back to idle, slipped the prop lever to full forward and began sneaking the stick back into my lap as Younkin hunched forward, his hands tensed.

The power off straight-ahead stall came at 70 IAS, with a rapid but gentle bob of the nose. The airplane fell straight ahead, but there was a noticeable decrease in roll stability at the break. I caught it quickly by releasing the back pressure and adding a shot of power, but not before I lost 100 ft. of altitude—certainly more than acceptable in a two-ton airplane of this class.

I did another, with the same result, then set up 18½ in. MP and tried a mild power stall. This time, *Mulligan* hung on down to 65 IAS and broke much the same way as before. The stall was gentler—but the altitude loss was still 100 ft.

I sneaked a look at Younkin out of the corner of my eye. He seemed on the verge of a nervous breakdown. So, regretfully, I abandoned my stall work and just played with the airplane for a few minutes, doing some mild climbs and descents, wingovers and such, and gave up, trading altitude for airspeed as we headed back to the field.

With Younkin's consent, I made a fast, flat entry into the pattern carrying 20 in. and a solid 200 indicated, then leveled out at about 50 ft. for a pass down the runway, running the power back up to 30 in. and full fine pitch. We roared down the runway at a most conservative 240 indicated. I eased the stick back for a mild 1½ G pull-up at the far end and let the airspeed bleed off to 110.

Flap limit speed is 120 mph, with air pressure blowing them back up at anything above that. Later, Younkin told me he figured use of flaps cuts 5 mph off the stall speed. I turned base at 100 and let the airspeed dwindle to 90 on final.

"It's actually faster than that," Younkin pointed out, due to position error in the pitot installation. To shoehorn it into Blakesburg, Iowa, final approach must be at "no more than 90," since above that, the airplane floats. "At Atchison, I was on a two- or three-mile final with slow traffic ahead of me and I was S-turnin' it at 80," he said.

"If you use a power approach, you could get it into 1,500 feet. You might even get it into 1,200 feet, but you'd have to be pretty sharp to do it."

Sink rate on my Monocoupe is 2,000 fpm at 80 IAS, coming down final—and I felt right at home in *Mulligan*. Visibility down the side of the cowling was surprisingly good. Younkin called it "just about as good as a Staggerwing, I could see a little more over the cowling [in the Beech] than I can in this, but not much."

As we taxied in, angling across the grass toward Younkin's hangar, my main feeling was regret. Regret that I hadn't had a chance to really explore the airplane's performance envelope; not shot half a dozen takeoffs and landings in it; perhaps duplicated Harold Neumann's victory roll a time or two.

Jim Younkin, on the other hand, seemed mostly relieved. Ah, well, c'est la vie!

"Tell you what, Jim," I said. "Anytime you need a little hangar room, just let me know. I'll be happy to take *Mulligan* up to my place and store it for you. I'll even keep the oil stirred up in it. . . ."

Younkin grinned. "I've had a lot of offers like that," he said.

I'll bet.

Secretly, I resolved to be first in that line.

First printed in *Air Racing Unlimited*, Volume One, 1988.

Mulligan has a wing loading about like a Spitfire fighter, yet lands at a comfortable 64 mph. This version is also certified IFR, and if Jim Younkin ever turns his back, I'll steal it in a minute. When I do, I'll add a steerable, locking tailwheel—and oxygen, the lack of which caused a landing accident in the Rockies and kept the original Mr. Mulligan out of the 1934 Cleveland air races.

Chapter 4

Monocoupe 110 Special

The sure cure for boredom

The first Monocoupe 110 Special I ever saw was tied down on the ramp at Ottumwa Municipal Airport, more than a generation ago.

It was N15E, next-to-the-last Clipwing built by the factory in a twenty-year production span, then owned by airline pilot Don Taylor. With its big engine, stubby wings and burly fuselage tapering rapidly to an afterthought tail, it seemed to swagger just sitting there.

"Damn, I'd like to fly that airplane," I muttered.

I walked carefully around it, noting the total lack of visibility from the cockpit, the abbreviated dimensions, the hulking cylinders of the Warner, the long Aeromatic. I backed off and looked at it again, in totality.

"No," I said to myself. "I'd rather watch somebody else fly it!"

But that was long ago, and before too many years passed I came to regard the 110 Special as the ultimate in aeronautical desirability.

I haven't altered that opinion since, and if I ever get the chance, I'll own one.

I came steaming downhill into a wide right downwind for the 3,020 ft. turf Runway 25 at St. Louis' Creve Coeur airport doing probably 180 mph, the big Warner cranked back to 20 in. and the 96 in. Aeromatic showing 2000 rpm.

I was looking hard for traffic. So was Ewell "Bud" Dake, in the left seat. Fine; it looked all clear. Time for a low pass; show a little class to the kiwis lined up along the hangar line.

I dropped the nose and brought the power back up to 23 in. as I swung from base onto final and registered the airspeed zipping quickly past 220 before I concentrated totally on the pass.

I was conservative about it; never less than 50 ft. AGL, not more than 2 to 2½ Gs on the pull-up, no more power. Still, it was fun—and we were smoking as we passed; maybe 240 IAS. Rate of climb briefly passed 6,000 fpm on the way out of the box.

Now, *that's* Monocouping!

And NX1161 is the ultimate Monocoupe: a 110 Special, more commonly known as the Clipwing, with a seven-cylinder, 185 hp Warner radial, a tiny 23 ft. wing and abbreviated tailfeathers.

Actually, 161 is an ersatz 110 Special. It's really serial number 865, sister ship to my own number 866 and one of the eleven 90ALs built at Melbourne, Florida, in 1948 with 115 hp Lycoming O-235C-1 engines and hydraulic toe brakes.

But number 865 had had a checkered and largely non-flying career. It spent most of its years as a test airplane for plastic wing experiments that resulted eventually in the Windecker Eagle and lurking around the far corners of a Texas hangar gathering dust thereafter.

Finally it was sold to a fellow someplace down around Marfa, Texas, who restored it and flew it about five hours before he let a friend fly it. The friend promptly drifted into a mesquite tree on takeoff, hooked a wing and cracked the main spar.

That's when Dake bought it.

Bud Dake, current honcho of the national Monocoupe type club, already owned a very slick Lycoming-powered 90A Monocoupe (converted from a 90 Lambert-powered 1936 model), but like most of us he always lusted in his heart worse than Jimmy Carter. The object of his lust, of course, was the Clipwing, and he bought serial number 865 *intending* to turn it into a Clipwing.

Now, this is legal for long-wing 110s under what's called a "Group 2 approval," issued by some naive Department of Commerce official way back before Bud Dake was a gleam in his daddy's eye, but whether it also applies to the *very* similar 90As is a moot question, at best.

However, there once was a man named Ron Kendall who was both a hell of a pilot and the owner of a genuine 110 Special. He was also a practicing alcoholic, and when he passed out on the upside of a hammerhead over his girlfriend's house one rainy day, he woke up three days later in the hospital to learn that his Clipwing was badly in need of a new engine and fuselage.

Monocoupe 110s are not exactly as common as Cherokees, and Kendall couldn't find one for the rebuild. He did, however, find a 90A, and he used that in restoring NC2345. So the point is, there may be a bar sinister on NX1161's shield, but as lawyers say, there's precedent!

In any case, Dake works with his hands for a living, and his craftsmanship is simply flawless. So when he got through transmogrifying number 865, it was without doubt the finest example extant of the rare genus *Monocoupus 110 Specialus*—and there are more of them extant now than ever left the factory!

In a twenty-year production history, the Monocoupe factory produced or converted only seven of the fire-breathing Clipwings, but with NX1161, there are ten on the US civil registry.

Anyway, back to the pilot report.

I honked the airplane steeply to the right (a right-hand pattern, in case you haven't been paying attention), flew the downwind at 130 IAS, the base at 120 and final approach at 100, crossing the fence at 90.

About then, Dake couldn't stand it anymore and came in to lend a hand on the round-out.

He later said my problem was, I didn't get the nose high enough on landing. And he added, "You ought to ride with Bill Hutchins. He gets the nose up so high, you want to cover your head with your arms."

One thing's for sure: I understand why diminutive Don Taylor used to routinely wheel land N15E. He once told me it took him "300 feet for take-off and 3,000 feet for landing." I thought it was because he was short. It wasn't. It was because the three-point landing attitude scared the hell out of him.

However, with only 3,000 ft. of close-clipped grass in front of us, Dake was afraid we wouldn't be able to get it slowed down satisfactorily before we ran out of

The Monocoupe 110 Special is the product of both evolution and happy accident. Johnny Livingston kept trying to wring more speed out of his once-stock racer; he finally took it back to the factory and told them to "clip the wing to 20 feet" (from 32). Instead, the factory built a completely new wing, 10 feet either side of the three-foot fuselage. Later, others added the big 185 hp Warner and Aeromatic and trimmed the tail feathers. This is Little Butch, *arguably the most famous of the factory Clipwings.*

room and ideas, hence the help. Normally, landing roll on grass is about 1,000 ft.

The Clipwing has a tailwheel straight off a hospital gurney, a sort of oversized paper clip connector between rudder and tailwheel and mechanical heel brakes. It comes aboard at a rapid rate (like about 78–80 mph; I don't care what the specs say about 60 mph landing speeds), and the whole trick is to get it pointed right before you touch down, then just let it track straight ahead.

Dake told of landing 161 once at Oshkosh. It rolled straight down the runway for a hundred yards or so. "Then it hit one of those little humpty bumps and skipped; then it hit another one and another one and pretty soon it started off to the side. You should've seen those guys with the paddles take to the ditch!"

I understood perfectly. I saw Vernon Thorpe leave the runway once at Denton, Texas, and go helling out through the potato field at 80 mph in N15E, throwing dirt and shrubbery every which way.

Said Dake: "You wouldn't have any trouble flyin' this airplane. You just need to own one; get the chance to get out and play with it a little while; fly it the way you want to fly it."

I agreed. In essence, it's a matter of learning the sight picture out the narrow windshield and over the monster cowling.

Despite the care he took in maximizing the forward view on 161, this is the blindest airplane still in the sky since they retired the replica *Spirit of St. Louis*—and this bugger hustles along over half again as fast, even throttled back.

Furthermore, the thing comes down very much like a dirtied-up Bellanca Viking (that is, *very* steeply),

In the hands of Woody Edmondson, Little Butch *(so named as a play on Betty Skelton's Li'l Stinker Pitts) won the 1948 national aerobatic championship—largely because the 'coupe started at the bottom and worked up, whereas every other contestant had to start at the top and work down. Edmondson bought the plane during World War II for use as high-speed personal transportation, but soon began flying air shows.*

until it arrives in ground effect. At that point, it will float quite nicely: up to a couple hundred yards on an extra 10 mph.

The combination is demanding, to say the least.

Dake said in his own case, he managed to scare the hell out of himself every time "for the first 25 hours." In fact, he said, he still has to psych himself up to fly it—and it takes a while to "unwind" after the flight.

He definitely has a point.

I hated to see him cobble up a rare and genuine 90AL when he started in, but I have to admit, a Clipwing Monocoupe of any heritage is a sure cure for boredom.

With a length of 20 ft. 4 in., a span of 23 ft. 2½ in. tip to tip, a wing area of 95 sq. ft. and a gross weight of 1,620 lbs., it's obviously no trainer. Urged along by the big Warner and the 8 ft. Aeromatic, events happen very rapidly indeed.

The aforementioned Don Taylor, in fact, once told me it was "the most airplane I ever strapped on," and he had flown several World War II fighter planes.

John McCulloch, who for many years owned and flew N36Y, the famous *Little Butch* which won the 1948 world aerobatic championship for Woody Edmondson, always said much the same thing. So has every other Clipwing owner I've ever known.

The 110 Special uses a modified Clark Y airfoil, powerful 9 ft. long ailerons and zero dihedral. The 5 ft.

chord wing may have a slight angle of incidence, but if so the airplane doesn't seem to know it. The thing indicates 10 mph faster upside down than it does right side up.

As Dake remarked, the roll rate is such that "it'll cage your eyeballs." We timed a few, and arrived at 5½ seconds for a 360 degree roll; certainly fast enough for most people. And you can lift a downwind wing right off the ground in a crosswind takeoff.

This day, we had a thirty-degree right crosswind of maybe 7 or 8 knots. Being rather too gingerly about handling the airplane, I think, we traversed over half the 100 ft. wide sod runway before I horsed the airplane off the ground at about 60 IAS, let the speed build to 80 and rocketed out of there at 130 mph.

I had been surprised that the Clipwing taxied with such ease and precision, given the tiny tailwheel. Now, climbing out and doing little S-turns (both to learn about the airplane and to see what I was about to hit), I was equally impressed with the control harmony.

The Clipwing was *much* better harmonized than my own airplane, though the rudder is extremely light (even lighter than a Luscombe) and shockingly effective. I commented to Dake that it would take me three hours just to get accustomed to the control use on this machine.

You absolutely must use a little leading aileron to properly coordinate maneuvers in this airplane. Just a hair; anything else is too much, sending the ball racing from side to side—but it must be there.

The 110 Special does extremely nice aerobatics. We sampled barrel rolls; aileron rolls; a slow roll with a hesitation and a brief period of inverted flight, hanging off the belt; an Immelmann; a couple of loops pulling 4 Gs and dwindling to 80 IAS across the top. Dake remarked he got too slow doing a loop once recently and the 'coupe simply did a half roll on its own and flew off the top.

Despite the small rudder, the airplane slips very well, and Dake said he wouldn't agree with the frequent assertion that it needs more rudder. "More fin, maybe, but not more rudder." But if it had more fin, even, it would probably be *too* stable.

In fact, the 110 Special is *considerably* more stable than my own airplane. Let go of the controls and 161 stays pretty level, wandering off heading only slightly as the wings dip alternately to left and right. The nose bobs up and down maybe five degrees, but it shows no inclination to head for the ground at 300 mph, as mine does when left alone.

On the other hand, the Clipwing builds speed quickly, and it's easy to see 200 mph IAS if you let the nose drop slightly.

Speeds are excellent for the horsepower, but not exceptional by today's standards. A seventy-five-percent power setting of 25 in. x 2150 rpm produced 180 IAS, while 23x2000 yielded sixty-five percent and 162 IAS for a true of 175. Dake favors fifty-five percent: 22x1900 for 155 IAS and a block true of 160 on the average trip, burning 10 gph.

"I try to save my Warner," he explained. The Warners probably are the best small radials ever built, but parts for them—particularly the 185s—aren't as easy to come by as, say, a Jacobs or a round Continental or Lycoming.

Flying out northwest of St. Louis on a hazy, muggy, 80+ degree day, I cleared the area rapidly, eased back the throttle on the Warner and sneaked the stick into my lap.

Promptly at 80 IAS and with minimal warning, the Monocoupe nodded rapidly up and down, and on the second oscillation it fell off on the left wing—only to recover immediately as I relaxed back pressure slightly and fed it a small shot of throttle.

A power stall at 15 in.x1700 rpm brought the nose well up, to approximately twenty degrees above the horizon, and the Special hung on down to 68 IAS before unhooking with a sharp left wing drop. Dake, watching calmly, remarked that with full throttle "it'll hang on the prop at 60 indicated and just keep on climbin'."

Normal cruising climb-out at 130 IAS and full gross weight produces a sustained 1,500 fpm, and maximum climb with takeoff power will easily yield another 1,000 fpm at gross.

Listed service ceiling for the original 110 with a 32 ft. wing was 16,000 ft. Dake has had his Clipwing to 11,000, but says the short wing, the lack of a blower and the 6:1 compression ratio begin to tell on it at that altitude, and it's laboring pretty hard.

"The difference between this and the yellow airplane is that this one is good at certain things and the (90AL) is good at other things," commented Dake. "Both have their drawbacks; it's just that they're different drawbacks. This one just likes to fly fast."

Indeed it does—but that didn't stop Dake from flying formation on an Aeronca Champ paddling around just northeast of the field, out of the traffic pattern. Power was back to 19x1800, and the airspeed was down to 100-110 mph indicated.

The 'coupe's tail hung down pretty badly, but it felt rock-solid and responsive. "That's gonna look pretty silly, with the tail down like that," he muttered.

Dake also demonstrated the fact that the airplane needs either an extra 100-150 ft. or an extra 10-15 mph on the down line to recover from a hammerhead or any other vertical maneuver—a characteristic that's killed two pilots through the years.

We did not do spins. Dake didn't mention it, and neither did I. I will do anything else in my 90AL without hesitation, and I have done my share of spins, when I first got it, to get accustomed to its characteristics. But I do not entirely trust the airplane in spins—and neither do some other people whose opinions I respect.

I was just as happy to leave spin and snap maneuvers untested in 161, although if any of them is predictable, it certainly should be this one.

The Monocoupe 110 Special has a distinctive planform and a unique history. Under the so-called "Group 2" approval, many 'coupes can be converted to a Clipwing. This is NX1161, originally a Lycoming-powered airplane built in 1948 and the next serial number to the author's own. The factory produced seven Clipwings over a 20 year production span. All of them were destroyed at least once. There were 10 in existence in 1990 and several more under construction.

Discussing landings, Dake declared, "It's not a bad airplane on pavement" but it "absolutely" likes grass better.

Visibility is better in 161 than in factory 110 Specials, since Dake mounted the engine an inch and a half lower than George Owl originally calculated, and he cut the cowling deeper to allow for a 9 in. windshield depth. As a result, you can see pretty well in the air and on final; it's not until you flare for landing that everything forward of the sixty-degree line disappears.

The airplane is comfortable, with deep, soft leather seats and an excellent seating position.

Like me, Don Luscombe was 5 ft. 8 in., and the interiors of his airplanes all were designed around his personal dimensions. Therefore, it's always a bit surprising to me that Dake, who's 6 ft. 6 in., can fold himself into it successfully.

"It takes a little getting used to," he remarked drily. "It's like a lot of the high performance homebuilts they're building now, except that they're modern airplanes built with modern technology and this is an old-time airplane built with old-fashioned technology."

That's a good description. The PS5C pressure carburetor, for example, doesn't take kindly to rapid throttle movements and generally burps once as a shot of power is applied. Still, the airplane will clear the traditional 50 ft. obstacle easily in 1,000 ft. on a

*One of the most exciting airplanes ever built, the Mono-
coupe 110 Special has high performance, a high sink rate,
virtually no visibility and a low tolerance for errors. This
is N15E, next-to-last Monocoupe built. Last 'coupe off the
line was N16E, another Clipwing, in 1950. The buyer had
already paid for the airplane and took the incomplete
machine out of factory only hours before the sheriff pad-
locked it pending sale of assets.*

standard day; perhaps a bit less. And as for the
adrenaline-producing landing, the trick there is to
carry a little power, slip the airplane slightly to a point
right off the ground, flare out and wipe off the power
an inch above the runway.

Dake reported while he was building 161, John
McCulloch gave him two rides in *Little Butch.* "It was a
learning experience for me," he added. So was his very
first test flight in his own newly completed Clipwing!

He threw all the oil out of the prop hub, "and I had
to land this thing lookin' out the side. Very interesting!"

But, he added quickly, "it's an honest airplane."

And so it is.

It carries thirty-eight gallons of fuel—fourteen in
each wing plus ten in the baggage compartment—
providing a solid three hours' endurance and a still-
air range of 500 miles; certainly an average range
figure for 1950s and 1960s two-seaters.

It's short on baggage room, of course. *Very* short.
It's almost totally lacking in forward visibility (though
the way the airplane is meant to be flown, the big
skylight gives you an excellent view of whatever you're
about to turn into). It's powerful, fast, climbs like a
rocket and descends like a rock and has handling
exciting enough to thrill a Civil War statue. It's a
pussycat to fly. I even know a man confined to a
wheelchair who used to fly one with hand controls. At
the same time, if you get a little bit behind the airplane, it'll bite you in a heartbeat. Hard!

What more could anyone want? Any Monocoupe
is one of the flying world's ultimate toys. And this is
the ultimate Monocoupe!

If Dake ever turns his back, I'm gonna steal it,
ersatz or not.

First printed in *Air Progress*, March 1988.

Chapter 5

DeHavilland Dragonfly

Granddaddy of the Mosquito

It has been my privilege now to fly several different deHavilland designs, and the faint outline of a pattern is beginning to emerge.

* *Any deHavilland airplane will perform its design tasks in exemplary fashion.*
* *They will be an odd blend of the advanced and the old-fashioned.*
* *They will be totally honest flying machines.*
* *They will be fairly demanding of their aircrew.*
* *Insofar as design goals permit, they will all look like deHavillands: graceful rounded rudders and flowing horizontal tails, (usually) tapered wings, oval-section fuselages and smooth, flowing lines.*
* *If at all possible, they will incorporate some very clever woodwork.*

The Dragonfly, of course, embodies all of these deHavilland hallmarks.

Besides all that, it has a character as typically upper-class British as a mid 1930s Bentley. Withal, it's a handy and well-balanced machine that's great fun to fly.

"Sometimes it takes a little effort to get the engines started," remarked Mike Simmons as we settled into the comfortable red leather-and-fabric seats. He reached down and turned on the petrol cocks with his right hand, pulled the twin throttles closed with his left and nodded at his helper out the side window.

Outside, the helper reached into a hole at the rear of the port engine cowling and pulled a chain, thus opening a valve allowing gasoline to the fuel pump. He reached through the opened access hatch farther forward and pumped vigorously at the engine-mounted primer lever. It took him some time. Finally, he moved on forward to the airscrew and pulled it through several times. Naturally, it even turned the wrong way. "Okay," he said.

Simmons hauled back on the Johnson bar brake lever in the far forward left corner of the cockpit, cracked the throttle, flipped on the magnetos and hit the starter button.

It took four rounds of this treatment before the engine fired obediently, blurring the polished wood airscrew into invisibility.

The helper moved to starboard and we went through the same drill, a little quicker.

Depend on the British to be different! Most folks would put the engine starting necessities in the cockpit, where the pilot could get at it—even in 1935. Not the English.

Perhaps there was a shortage of mechanic's jobs in England at the tag end of the Depression and a consequent plague of unemployed clerks.

In any case, it took some time for the British to learn the right place to install primers, and a number of their 1930s and 1940s airplanes have them accessible only to a cooperative ground crewman. deHavilland was particularly bad about it.

Granted, the DH 90 was not the most modern airplane on the block fifty years ago. After all, it boasted fixed, spatted landing gear, fixed-pitch airscrews and long, graceful biplane wings. Construction was almost totally wood and fabric. The brakes were cable-controlled mechanical expander units. There was absolutely no provision for communicating with the world in flight.

On the other hand, this was designed as the progenitor of all those business twins now scooting about the world carrying everything from board chairmen to tech reps to the occasional load of illicit crops or funny chemicals.

Since the sun never set on the British Empire in those days, one would expect them to do a slightly better job of making their machinery reasonably self-sufficient. At least, I would.

I had a quick mental vision of a proper British pilot (ex-RAF, of course) trying to explain the correct procedure for priming a 130 hp Gipsy Major four-banger to a handy Hottentot on some dusty landing strip in the African bush. I know the English have a reputation for muddling through, but I'll bet that tried some men's resources considerably!

On the other hand, it's clearly even tougher for the pilot to do it all himself—which, I'm sure, was the case many times during the roughly thirty-four years G-AEDU (alias N190DH) spent flying hither and yon across the Dark Continent.

With both engines running, Simmons eased the Dragonfly carefully out of its parking place directly in front of the crowd at the annual Antique Airplane Association bash just outside Blakesburg, Iowa, and pivoted it toward the flying field.

He was very cautious about how he did it—and not just because of the people around. They were used to airplanes.

But this was one of only two surviving Dragon-flies, of sixty-seven produced between 1935 and 1938—and the only one still licensed and flying. Furthermore, the airplane had certain known weaknesses, most of which Simmons had discovered the hard way over some 230 hours of flight time in the last three years—including an Atlantic crossing. Not only that, it wasn't his.

Once aimed in the proper general direction, he handed the big red and silver biplane over to me, and I trundled slowly across the grass, steering with the powerful rudder and reaching across Simmons' chest to apply differential throttle.

Within 100 ft. or so, I managed to drop the right wheel into one of Antique Airfield's concealed depressions, impressing me with the Bentley-quality ride imparted by the rubber-and-steel doughnuts in the main gear compression struts.

Visibility over the short, pointy nose was excellent, though the ground angle and the considerable distance from pilot seats to instrument panel blotted

One glance at this machine and you can see the famous Mosquito coming! Designed as the first business twin in the United Kingdom, this DH 90 of 1935 unfortunately had to *compete with a variety of far more efficient American airplanes, including the superlative Beech 18.*

out everything directly ahead. The windscreen framing provided a handy index of direction.

Near the run-up end of the runway, I handed back to Simmons, who swung about thirty degrees to keep from blowing debris all over anyone behind us, and went through a quick check of the controls, trim and magnetos. There wasn't really much else to check on.

We rolled into position, facing uphill, and Simmons eased the throttles to the stop. The elderly deHavilland picked up its skirts and began to trot. Soon she was bounding gazelle-like from bump to bump across the rough Iowa hilltop.

The tail was up before 50 mph on the airspeed indicator, and at 65 we were airborne in roughly 1,100 ft. of ground roll, on turf and partly uphill on a hot mid-August day in Iowa, a thousand feet above sea level. We were maybe 500 lbs. under the airplane's two-ton gross, so climb-out was 750 fpm at 85 IAS.

I noticed there was considerable fore-and-aft movement in the odd control column during takeoff; a ritual that was to be repeated in reverse half an hour later during landing. The column presents a conventional mid 1930s modified Dep wheel to the pilot, but the copilot is not so well served.

Instead of a similar wheel on the right, a pivoting bar thrusts upward at two o'clock—a strange arrangement that works efficiently enough but does little to ease the task of flying a strange airplane effectively from the right side.

Truly, England's aviation industry in the mid 1930s was a place of wooden ships and iron men!

Simmons handed control over to me, and I essayed a few S-turns as we climbed to 3,000 MSL and leveled off, trimming for normal cruise at 2050 rpm and approximately 125 mph—roughly sixty-five percent. Just to see what would happen, I added 100 rpm (seventy-five percent), and let the airplane run for a couple of minutes to stabilize. We gained 3 mph!

Still, all this probably is a little better than the Dragonfly originally did, because the issue 130 hp Gipsys have been swapped for 145 hp Gipsy Major Mk 10s. . . .

Rolling the deHavilland as rapidly as possible from a thirty-degree left bank to a thirty-degree right bank while holding the nose on a point, I discovered the ailerons (top wing only) are heavy and relatively insensitive, reminding me somewhat of my own Monocoupe, while both rudder and elevator are quite sensitive and powerful.

Trimmed out (both flaps and trim are controlled by a pair of Johnson bars flanking the control column) and left to its own devices, the Dragonfly also is quite stable, though with a wing loading of 13.9 lbs. per sq. ft., it doesn't so much punch through low-level turbulence in the accepted manner of modern twins as it does ride over them, more like a light trainer.

On the face of it, that's a bit surprising, in view of the size of the airplane. The DH 90, after all, is a five-seat twin with an upper wingspan of 43 ft., a

Graceful tapered wings and beautifully sculpted tailplane are hallmarks of de Havilland airplanes from the 1920s into the jet age. So is the extensive use of wood. In the DH 90, the plywood monocoque fuselage construction left a weak point just aft of the passenger compartment. Several Dragonflys broke their backs in hard landings. Wheel landings are now standard.

lower span of 38½ ft., a length of 31 ft. 8 in., a height of 9 ft. 2 in., an empty weight of 2,500 lbs. and a gross of "approximately" 4,000 lbs.

However, all that wing provides 288 sq. ft. of area and produces the low wing loading—which puts it almost in the same class with the 13 lbs. per sq. ft. of the contemporary Cessna Airmaster out in the Colonies. The Airmaster climbed at 1,000 fpm and cruised at 143 mph on 145 hp while still offering a half-ton useful load—compared to the DH 90's 1,500 useful on (originally) 260 hp.

But the DH has its points. For one thing, it's very smooth and comfortable, as a good British machine should be. It's fairly easy to climb into and out of, though a smart pilot doubtless carried a portable step for the convenience of the Mawster and his lady.

It's also very quiet for a fabric twin; either due to good sound proofing or a result of the low horsepower and slow-turning fixed-pitch wood props (oops; I mean airscrews).

Finally, you can look at the airplane and see the Mosquito coming. Never mind the biplane configuration, the flying wires and the fixed spatted landing gear. Never mind the slow speed, the light wing loading and the fact that at times it demands a three-handed tennis player to fly.

It's a class act—and anybody can tell it at a glance. Perhaps that's why a sister ship (the only other survivor) was owned successively by a knight, a duke and a lord!

Despite the plethora of flying wires, fixed spatted gear, wooden props and a modest 290 hp (originally 260), the de Havilland is fairly speedy, clocking 128 mph at 75 percent power. It's also very comfortable and quiet. Very British, overall.

Designed by Capt. (later Sir) Geoffrey deHavilland, the DH 90 was derived from the DH 84 Dragon and DH 88 Comet racer and intended to provide relatively high performance on modest power in a simple twin. Price was low: 2,650 pounds; about $13,780.

Unlike the similar but larger seven-passenger DH 89 Dragon Rapide, its immediate predecessor, the DH 90, boasts a svelte, rounded monocoque plywood fuselage, made by gluing the thin wood sections and pressing them in special dies until they were cured. This, too, is a direct herald of the famous DH 98 to come.

Unfortunately, it also heralds the later airplane's propensity to break its back in a hard landing—which is why Simmons always wheel lands the blasted thing.

He says the British who checked him out on the airplane warned him that several Dragonflys were rendered permanently unserviceable in just such crisp three-pointers. There's about 17 ft. of empty space between the free-swiveling non-steerable tailwheel and the first fuselage bulkhead....

The wing leading edges and the whole tailplane also are plywood covered. The rest of the structure is typical deHavilland, with double spruce spars and an incredible number of different-sized jig-built rib pairs in each wing. The engines, landing gear and fuel tanks (which hold 102 US gallons) are slung from the wood cantilever lower center section.

N90DH is thus sort of a flying toothpick collection wrapped in painted linen; an aeronautical anachronism in an era of deep space exploration and satellite television.

But that's the point, don't you see?

This airplane is the design contemporary of Walter Beech's most famous biplane, the Model 17, which also carried five people, operated in and out of the same kind of airstrips and could cruise at 200 mph in its 450 hp Pratt & Whitney version. And, for that matter, of the three-mile-a-minute Boeing 247 thirteen-place airliners. And of the 200 mph cruise Lockheed 10 Electra, another twelve-place airliner that was Amelia Earhart's choice for her final flight.

All of them were not only much more efficient *airplanes*, they were designed for economical quantity production. And while none was a marvel of cockpit ergonometrics, they were at least intended to *help* the pilot at his or her tasks. The deHavilland, on the other hand, seems designed to *handicap* its pilot.

Where the American airplanes were revolutionary designs for their time, the Dragonfly was evolutionary. It was still only hinting at what it could become. And it was aimed in a different direction.

The hard-working Gipsys burn only 12 Imperial gph (about 15 US) at 2050 rpm, allowing the DH 90 a still-air range of 885 miles, while the generous wing allegedly provides a twin-engine service ceiling of 15,700 ft.

The modest power (13 lbs. per hp at gross) and fixed-pitch wood airscrews, of course, also mean a claimed single-engine service ceiling of 2,100 ft. at gross, and even that's likely to be a case of simply taking you to the scene of the crash.

At least you'll have plenty of control en route. Minimum safe single-engine speed is 75 mph, Vmc 72. You can drop the thirty-degree split flap (between the main gear only) at 85, and the big biplane stalls at an indicated 60–65 regardless of flap configuration.

I began with some 75 mph slow flight, both untrimmed and trimmed, and found the Dragonfly very smooth and responsive in coordinated turns up to forty-five degrees of bank, feeling as solid as it did at cruise.

Chopping the power, I found the elevator got mushy shortly before the break, but there was no airframe warning—an expected trait in an airplane of this vintage. At the break, the airplane consistently rolled very gently to the right, but recovered immediately as soon as I relaxed back pressure a tad. Even having to reach across Simmons to the throttles, my altitude loss was never more than 100 ft., sometimes half that.

Considering conditions at Antique Airfield, we agreed Simmons would make the landing and I'd follow him through on the controls. For one thing, the rudder bar on my side had no brakes (it's a typical British rig: pull straight back on the bar and you get both brakes; pull part way and tap a brake and that's what you get).

We came down final at 85 IAS with full flap and probably 1100 rpm to establish the proper attitude, and Simmons carefully set the airplane on the mains just short of the brow of the hill. He needed the help, he explained: "If I've got good brakes, I can get it stopped in 1,400 or 1,500 ft.—but not the way they are

When these photos were taken, G-AEDU was one of two survivors, of 67 Dragonflys built, and the only one flyable. It was totaled later in a landing accident. The mangled wreckage was repurchased by a British buyer and shipped *back to England, where it is reportedly under rebuild—a daunting task. The Dragonfly was a very complicated airplane to build, though surprisingly cheap to buy at the time.*

now." The brakes also are a necessity for directional control once the tail drops on roll-out.

Summing up, the corporate chief pilot said: "This is my first twin taildragger. I groundlooped it twice" learning to fly it in England in June 1983, where he picked it up for owner Charles A. Osborne, a Louisville, Kentucky, real estate developer.

But much of his initial difficulty was caused by an engine throttle linkage problem which prevented one of the Gipsys from turning up properly. Simmons' final solution was to hook a key chain to the throttle spring to get both to open up together.

By the time he had successfully ferried the Dragonfly from Southampton, England, to its new home at Clark County Airport, Jeffersonville, Indiana, via Scot-

land, the Outer Hebrides, Iceland, Greenland and Canada, he was an expert on quick fixes for the de-Havilland's vintage systems.

All told, the trip took thirty-three days and seventy-two flight hours and covered some 7,200 miles, during which he encountered various radio problems, a malfunctioning magneto and repeated doses of ice, fog and other weather phenomena.

The Dragonfly apparently took it all in stride.

Immaculate in its original silver-and-crimson factory color scheme, G-AEDU won grand champion honors at the 1986 AAA invitational fly-in.

You can't get much better than that!

First printed in *Air Progress*, October 1987.

Chapter 6

Taylor E–2 Cub

First of the Cubs

It is true that I love airplanes with a plenitude of power; machines that will go straight up and straight down.

But there's another side to aviation. The side where the soul resides: a place of grass-patch airports where the smell of the new-mown grass fills the cockpit at pattern altitude; where winds are gentle, the sky is a deep summer blue and the temperature is always in the mid-seventies.

That's the world where the Taylor Cub rules.

This is a lover's airplane, an aerial canoe with which one can paddle around the sky, elbow hung out in the breeze, watching the antics of the creatures below and waving occasionally, as they merit that favor.

A special beauty of an airplane like this is that one must plan ahead and stay out of trouble by utilizing thermal and mechanical lifting—for the little Continental A–40 up front lacks the muscle to keep you out of danger.

Rewards are equally unique: the quiet putt-putt of the engine, the sensation of floating like thistle-down over God's landscape. I hope I get the chance to do it in the twenty-first century—in a Taylor Cub.

Don't bet against it!

Very rarely, now and again, into everyone's life comes something nice. Unsought, unexpected; sort of a surprise reward for being in the right place at the right time.

For me it was NC15676, one of aviation's most significant airplanes, and one that sold twenty years ago for $85 and a shotgun.

Old 676 is an E–2 Cub, manufactured Nov. 25, 1935, at Bradford, Pennsylvania, one of 375 produced between 1931 and early 1936 by the Taylor Airplane Company, and the progenitor of an incredibly long and successful line of later Piper Cubs of varied persuasions.

The Taylor Cubs and the bathtub Aeroncas of equal vintage were the first, nearly the last and certainly the most successful of the true "minimum airplanes," and their survival rate was low—particularly that of the E-2. Today they are only slightly more common than unicorns, with fourteen left on the civil aircraft register.

I had flown a Monocoupe from Kansas to Burlington, Wisconsin, through haze so thick it was unbelievable, and as I taxied across the rich green sward to the waiting line of Cubs and other antiques, the very first person to greet me was a slight, merry gentleman who just happened to own 676, the star of this specialized fly-in.

I shook hands with Gene R. Chase once, years ago at an EAA convention at Rockford, Illinois. I barely remember it, and I'm sure he didn't recall it at all. But I knew about Gene Chase, late of Tulsa and now of Hales Corners, Wisconsin. Oh, yes, I knew quite a bit.

So it was a shock when, without warning and for no apparent reason, he invited me to fly his Taylor Cub!

Now, this is a bigger thing than perhaps most readers realize. For an antiquer to offer you a ride in his airplane is a mark of esteem. For him to voluntarily offer to let you fly it is the antiquing equivalent of the military's award of the Distinguished Flying Cross, at least. Such an offer usually is bestowed only upon those who have been personally observed by the owner at the controls of sundry (undamaged) other airplanes for many years, or those to whom he happens to owe money or some other great favor.

Gene Chase relates to the average owner as Barry Goldwater relates to George McGovern.

This is the man who refused to fly the late, lamented Grumman G–32A (two-seat version of the Navy's last biplane fighter) until he was provided a freshly packed parachute, and who demanded a second chute before he would hop passengers in it at Oshkosh. A fuel line broke and the Grumman caught fire in the air. It's gone now; Chase and his passenger are not.

But Gene Chase is a type hog, with some 188 different airplanes in his logbook. So am I, as he sensed immediately. He is also the soul of courtesy, as I am not. Hence, when I recovered enough from the shock of his sudden offer to respond, I told him I would be delighted, time permitting.

Time permitted. In fact, I delayed my departure just to make sure.

Then came shock No. 2.

I asked for a few minutes to round up another pilot and a J–3 to act as a photo plane to enable me to write a pilot impression. After all, E–2 pireps are scarcer than the airplanes. Chase said that was no problem, he'd round up the J–3 and fly it himself.

I demurred, pointing out I'd never been near an E–2 before. He shrugged. "If you can fly a Monocoupe, you won't have any trouble with the Cub," he replied. I objected that the 'coupe has brakes, while the E–2 does not. The 'coupe has a wing loading of 12.2 lbs. per sq. ft., the Cub only 5.5. I have a power loading of 10.39 lbs. per hp and a constant-speed Hartzell to get me out of trouble. The Cub's loading is 25 lbs. per hp, and the little wooden toothpick of a prop is not going to get anybody out of trouble.

Chase waved aside my protests, thereby confirming he is not only more generous than I, but braver, too. He pointed out the E–2's vital components.

Up front: One engine, four-cylinder, single-ignition, Continental A–40–3, nominal rating 37 hp, swinging the 69 in. prop at 2550 rpm.

Behind that: One fuel tank, nine-gallon, nearly full, as proved by Chase's handy portable plastic quantity indicator (a length of clear tubing with appropriate markings, dipped into the tank with a thumb over the top, pulled out and inspected).

Farther back: One instrument panel, containing one optional-equipment compass (totally obscured in

Ultra rare these days, the 375 Taylor E–2 Cubs were sold between 1931 and 1936. Along with the Aeronca C–2 and C–3, the E–2 kept flight schools alive in the desperate days of the Depression. The airplane grosses 932 pounds, cruises *at 55 mph and lands at 20. Climb is marginal under ideal conditions. Happy owner Gene Chase says he's always had a yen for minimum-powered airplanes.*

The single-ignition Continental A–40 has a nominal rating of 37 hp at 2,550 rpm swinging a 69 in. wood prop. It helps cool the pilot. Note lack of brakes, side windows. Cockpit is similarly spare.

a cloudy liquid), one tachometer, one large, oddly marked altimeter, one carburetor heat knob and one each oil temperature and pressure gauges; a narrow, canoe-like interior with two minimal seats, two sticks, two sets of rudder pedals, a magneto switch, a long bar throttle and a looped cord for an elevator trim.

To either side: Open air.

Overhead: A narrow glassine slit.

Chase took station at the nose of the aircraft and swung the prop smartly several times. "Ignition, and crack the throttle about one inch," he called. I flipped on the mag, cracked the throttle and called, "Hot, cracked." It seemed strange to omit "brakes." Chase gave a mighty heave. Nothing happened. He heaved again. Repeatedly. Still nothing. "Contrary little devil, the A-40," I remarked. Magneto off. Throttle closed. He wound backward a while. We tried it again, and this time the engine caught with a sudden spunky crackle from the four 6 in. individual exhausts.

Afraid I'd trundle right over the hospitable Chase in his own airplane, I yanked back the throttle, thereby causing the engine to come within a gasp of quitting. Hurriedly, I played the bar lightly as Chase stepped nimbly aside and vanished.

I needn't have worried. With 7.00x4 in. doughnut tires, the E-2 takes considerable goading to move on grass, and stops quickly. In fact, one man once told Chase he thought the wheels were binding. "Oh?" said Chase. "I hope not." With that, he reached up to the wing, tilted the whole airplane—and the wheel revolved slowly of its own weight.

The E-2 required about 2000 rpm before it began to move, and about 1100 to taxi, which I found encouraging. My last brakeless airplane was a Curtiss JN-4D, which stopped very well. But it had a tailskid, traditional all-purpose cure for both bad landings and short runways. The Cub's tailwheel steering proved very effective, and I never even missed the brakes during two right-angle turns and more than half a mile of taxiing to the end of the runway.

Wind was only about 6 knots, but it was veering slowly until it passed behind the wing. A sudden slight gust picked up the upwind wing as easily as a fallen leaf. Adrenaline pumping, I slammed in full right aileron. The airplane teetered briefly, left wing in the air, then dropped demurely back on its narrow gear—but it convinced me the E-2 would be very easy to scratch up. I asked Chase about that later, and he said he simply doesn't fly it in anything but a near-calm.

The A-40 showed a tendency to punctuate its healthy outboard popping with little breathless pauses, which I first ascribed to low rpm. Wrong

The Taylor Cub is an aerial canoe; a sort of certificated ultralight that enables the pilot to hang an elbow out in the breeze on soft summer days and sort of commune with nature. The only thing more basic than this is a Breezy.

again. The elderly Continental displayed the same behavior at all power settings up to full throttle, as it shortly demonstrated on climb-out.

With one fuel tank, one magneto, no trim indicator and no brakes, the E-2's pre-takeoff check is nonexistent. If the engine's still churning as you take the active, you're automatically in business.

Sighting down the side of the fuselage, I lined up on the asphalt and advanced the throttle bar. The popping up front took on an urgent note and the tachometer zipped up to a surprising 2550 rpm. We ran about ten yards and the tail came up of its own accord; another twenty-five yards and we lifted smartly off the paving, climbed briskly to about 40 ft.—and ran out of oomph!

It was hot, of course, with the mercury in the mid 80s, but even the staunchest Taylor Cub fan would have to admit climb is not one of its best features. C. G. Taylor advertised it would "climb 500 feet the first minute," presumably at its 932 lb. gross weight. Possibly he was optimistic.

Barring the occasional stammer, the little A-40 was banging away frantically up front, and the tachometer said the prop was setting new records. But, even with only 145 lbs. of pilot aboard, not much was happening. It's been a long time since I passed the end of a runway at quite that elevation. Eyeing the treetops with interest, I estimated that, charitably, I might be 200 ft. in the air. Two hundred in half a mile, solo. Yes, sir, it had been a long time.

Chase had warned me the carburetor heat had a tendency to turn itself on. Perhaps, I thought, that might partly account for the sluggardly climb and those heart-stopping little gasps from the A-40. Sure enough, the heat knob, far away on the instrument panel, was at full stretch. I tried full stretch myself, and discovered my arm wasn't that long. Loosening the seatbelt a foot or so, I tried again, and at maximum reach, managed to shove the knob home.

We were by now turning downwind, almost 400 ft. in the air. I dropped back in the narrow seat, retightened the belt, took pity on the engine and throttled it back to 2400 rpm. No help. The heat knob was hanging out again. Loosen belt. Reach forward. Push knob. Tighten belt. The third time this happened in two minutes, I decided the hell with it; there had to be a better way.

There was. I found with the belt only slightly loosened, I could brace my back against the seat, raise my left leg, extend my toes like a ballet dancer and shove in the knob quite easily. By the end of the flight, I was an expert.

Weather conditions, consideration for my host and his airplane and natural cowardice all combined to deter me from really exploring the limits of the little E-2's performance, but certain things became evident.

First, the controls are surprisingly heavy; much heavier than this airplane's grandchild, the ubiquitous J-3, apparently due mostly to high friction in the cable systems. Only the rudder is light and Cub-like. The wing loading is so light even minor turbulence causes enough wander to keep a pilot busy, but actual response to control input is quite good.

Second, it's great fun to motor around the sky in an E-2, your elbow dangling over the side as if you were out for an evening drive in your Model T. The Model T may be faster, of course. I would guess normal cruise for the little E-2 to be about 55 mph at 2300 rpm. The factory claimed a 65 mph cruise. Maybe so. At least Chase had a problem catching me in a stock J-3, which is good for about 75 at cruise. The actuality is unimportant; what is important is that it's the next best thing to an Arabian Nights magic carpet.

After C. G. Taylor's departure, the Piper family claimed an initial 400 fpm climb for the cleaned-up

and slightly more sprightly J-2. It's possible an E-2 might score as well on a standard day, though not necessarily at full gross. Of course, with 69 lbs. of fuel and oil, you only have 330 lbs. of payload anyway.

Normally, the big windshield keeps almost all the slipstream out of the cabin, with not enough wind to ruffle your hair, but if there ever was an airplane to teach coordination, this is it. Skid or slip a turn and you feel it not only in the seat of your pants but in the sudden breeze on your cheek—legacy of the wide-open sides.

Steep turns demand considerable back stick to keep the nose up, and there is quite a bit of overbanking. Stalls are nothing much, announced both by tail buffet and a lack of resistance in the last inch or so of stick travel. The big, square-tipped wing produces a bit of flywheel effect, and it takes a pretty stiff correction to bring up a dropped wing in the stall. I suspect it would do lovely slow spins, but since I never got over 800 ft. AGL, I never found out.

The wind, such as it was, now was aligned closer with a north-south turf runway than with the east-west paving I had used for departure, and discretion

The Taylor Cub is surprisingly heavy on the controls, with bags of adverse yaw. It climbs and glides at 40 mph, and wing loading and control factors are such that the airplane is not suitable for flying except in ballooning weather. Great fun!

seemed the better part of valor. Besides, this was a classic grass-patch airplane.

Pulling on the trim cord had proved both easy and effective in cruise, but seemed an affectation for landing, so I simply allowed the carb heat to sneak out and stay there, retarded the throttle and headed for the grass.

Best glide speed, like best climb, seemed to be about 40 mph, with the nose held appreciably lower than in a J-3. At this speed, everything seems to happen in slow motion. There's plenty of time to study individual posts in the approaching fence. With the engine throttled back to a polite rattle, the Cub floated over the fence at about 35, touched down at just over 20 and rolled to a stop in perhaps thirty yards, gently as a floating feather.

Sometimes it's best to quit while you're ahead.

Except for almost running down an advancing conga line of J-3s for lack of S-ing, the long taxi back to the parking area was uneventful, and the little E-2 stopped exactly in line with its fly-in neighbors. Regretfully, I reached up and shut off the magneto, watching the prop jerk to a halt.

Chase walked up. "Thanks," I said, clambering out and patting the E-2 on a wing strut. "I really enjoyed it." He grinned, a wide, wide grin, and replied: "I thought you would. I know I do. I've always had a thing for smaller, low-powered airplanes. To me, they're the most fun to fly of all."

Old 676 may be fun to fly, but it's gone through many owners and only 1,131 hours in its forty-year career, spending the last twenty of that making a circular route from Wisconsin to Chicago to Tulsa and back to Wisconsin. Ken Williams, a Portage, Wisconsin, EAAer, antiquer and restorer, bought it in nearby Poynette on Dec. 12, 1956, for the aforementioned $85 and a shotgun. It was in "terrible" condition, says Williams, and his wife adds, "I thought he paid too much for it." Williams proceeded to remedy that. He sold the ruined wings to another E-2 enthusiast for $20 and restored the rest. Then, in 1960, he traded it to another man for an L-2 Taylorcraft. Exactly a year later, he swapped the T-craft back in exchange for the E-2. "I got boot both times" from the same man, he says.

By 1966, the plane was in Tulsa, where Chase first flew it, and late that year Williams ferried it to the EAA Museum at Hales Corners, Wisconsin, where it remained on display as a "loaner" until 1970, when Chase bought it, intending to pick it up as time and weather permitted. Instead, he took a job with EAA and moved to Hales Corners himself in 1972, finally claiming his airplane. Since then, he estimates he's put about twenty hours on it, 4:45 of that in 1974.

The low utilization rate is understandable. The sharp limitations on performance mean equally sharp limits on when it can be flown safely. It is not a go-anywhere, do-anything kind of airplane.

But for pure enjoyment, it's hard to beat; a kind of bobbing wood chip in the ocean of the sky that's good for the soul of any pilot. And that, after all, is what flying should be about.

First printed in *Air Progress*, February 1976.

Chapter 7

Waco YPF–7

Tailspin Tommy's airplane

We look at an airplane like Joe Roselle's Waco YPF–7 and it seems rather quaint; a good-sized three-place biplane with wheel pants and biggish radial engine snug in an NACA cowling.

Bonanza and Mooney drivers tend to look down their noses. Why, a thing like that would be hard-pressed to cruise at 135 mph and probably burn more gas, to boot! Look at the built-in headwind. And how would you like to try to handle that in a gusty crosswind at Oklahoma City?

All those criticisms are valid. But we forget that in the early 1930s, when these airplanes were designed, most airports were only big grass pastures. True, some were airline-served pastures, but they were pastures nonetheless. And many of them weren't very big, either.

A friendly, big-wheeled Waco will take off and land from about any pasture you care to try—and do it safely. That's half the fun. Airplanes like this rarely operate from pastures these days, of course. They're retired from all that. They're in the magic business now: Dreams, on demand.

They really are time machines. They help aging boys recapture their youth. And there's nothing wrong with that.

A couple of fellows who'd ridden to Oshkosh, Wisconsin, with me had urged me to check out the beautiful open-cockpit Waco in the antique and classic area, but I'd been so busy I hadn't had time to do so earlier. Suddenly, in front of me was a gorgeous Waco F model, complete with big bump cowl, wheel pants and sliding canopy over the rear cockpit. Resplendent in silver and two shades of blue, it dominated that part of the field.

"Gee," I thought to myself. "I always wondered what Tailspin Tommy's airplane looked like. Now I guess I know." I'd read a lot of Big Little Books about Tailspin Tommy's adventures when I was a boy, and he always flew neat airplanes like this.

Striding toward me across the summer grass was a burly, genial gent in a wrinkled leather flying jacket and mustache who might have been Tailspin Tommy's flight instructor—but he wasn't. In fact, at that moment he had 184 solo hours, total.

His name is Joe Roselle, and he turned out to be an Oklahoma City lawyer instead of a flight instructor. He is, however, the proud owner of the only Waco YPF–7 extant, and 150 of those 184 hours were logged in that airplane—a most unusual circumstance. In case you missed the point, the YPF–7 is *the classic biplane.*

Wacospeak is an arcane language requiring considerable study, but basically, most Wacos are identified by a three-letter code followed by a number. The first letter denotes the engine, in this case a seven-cylinder Jacobs L-4MT, Type R-755, rated at 225 hp at 2000 rpm.

The second letter, "P" here, denotes the wing style—this one a single-bay biplane with rounded wingtips, a center section and four ailerons. The third, the "F," identifies a three-place open-cockpit airplane accommodating two passengers on a bench seat in the front, with the pilot bringing up the rear in lonely grandeur.

The digit, of course, identifies the year of manufacture. Thus, a -5 Waco was produced in 1935, a -6 in 1936, a -7 in 1937 and so on.

Wacospeak is subject to numerous exceptions, however, much like English, because the Weaver Airplane Company of Troy, Ohio, had a worldwide reputation for building just about anything a customer was willing to pay for. The YPF is a good example.

The YPF could be had either in three-place standard configuration or as a two-seater which could be flown from either cockpit. Each year's production was a little fancier than the previous year's (and a little heavier), and by 1937 the airplane was offered with a close-fitting hatch to convert the front cockpit into a streamlined, oversize baggage compartment as well as with the all-weather sliding canopy and streamlined wheel pants. All were, of course, options.

The very similar ZPFs (285 hp Jacobs), UPFs (220 hp Continental), CPFs (250 hp Wright) and DPFs (285 hp Wright) were all built under the same type certificate (ATC No. 586, issued Nov. 19, 1935) and offered the same options. When combined with rear cockpit heating and ventilation, the result was a fast, comfortable all-weather sport plane eminently suitable for year-round service by the well-heeled aviator. Indeed, the factory claimed a sea level top speed of 159 mph and a service ceiling of 20,000 ft. for the DPF-7 with the bigger Wright.

The YPF was said to be capable of a maximum speed of 150 mph at 1,000 ft., with wheel pants, canopy and cockpit cover; a seventy-five percent cruise of 135 at the same altitude and a maximum cruise (2000 rpm) of 143 at 6,000 ft., with a landing speed of 50, a ceiling of 17,500 ft. and an initial climb rate of 1,100 fpm at sea level.

Despite these performance figures, few YPFs were built. Waco authority Ray Brandly, in his book on the F models, shows two YPFs and a CPF built in 1935, two ZPFs produced in 1936 and three Zs and a Y in 1937. The Y went to Japan. None of those YPFs is on the US civil register today.

War was building in Europe in the late 1930s, and before long Uncle Sam developed a new pilot training program for college students called the Civilian Pilot Training Program. The government bought 600 suitably modified Waco UPF-7s for this new $6 million program. Since Waco had built only slightly over 2,500 airplanes total to that point, clearly the CPTP contract meant a lot to them. Even today, those UPF-7s are the most commonly encountered Wacos.

As delivered for the CPTP in 1941, the UPF-7 had become a two-seat trainer with two fully instrumented cockpits, a bigger center section cut-out to allow the instructor to climb in and out in heavy flying suit and parachute without dislocating his sacroiliac, a slightly beefed-up structure and a locking tailwheel. It had its own ATC, No. 642.

When Gary Miller of Grand Junction, Colorado, began building his Waco in December 1968, he started with a UPF trainer fuselage, a center section found near Greybull, Montana, seven original wing panels "that were good for nothing more than the fittings out of them" which he had collected while living in Ohio and detailed factory plans for a YPF-7.

The YPF is 23 ft. 4 in. long; 8 ft. 5 in. high; has an upper span of 30 ft. and a lower span of 26 ft. 10 in.; a 57 in. chord on both wings and a total wing area of 243.6 sq. ft., using a Clark Y airfoil common to most Wacos.

Construction, too, is traditional: a welded steel tube fuselage, heavily faired to a well-rounded shape; solid spruce wing spars with spruce truss-type wing ribs reinforced with mahogany plywood gussets and dural sheet leading edges, the whole fabric covered. Originally, the ailerons were metal-framed, but in the rebuild Miller opted to build them of wood for a better match with the rest of the airplane.

Gear is a tripod affair with a 101 in. tread, long-travel oleo-spring shock struts and 6.50x10 in. wheels with brakes and 7.50x10 in. four-ply tires and a 10½ in. pneumatic tailwheel.

The fabric-covered composite tail group is of wood and welded steel, with aerodynamic balances on rudder and elevator. Standard equipment included a starter, 15 amp generator, dual sticks and parking brake. The airplane has fifty gallons of fuel in two twenty-five-gallon center section tanks and can carry another 12.5 gallons in each of two optional auxiliary tanks in the root end of each upper wing. At 13 gph, normal range is 450 miles.

Empty weight is 1,694 lbs., gross 2,650, useful load 956 and payload with 48.5 gallons of fuel is 465 lbs. (two passengers and 125 lbs. of baggage, including 100 behind the pilot, 25 in the front dash panel). Early Ys had bump cowls, late ones did not.

Miller flew NC32077 for the first time on Mother's Day, 1975—the only YPF-7 on the register. "I built it up as a Y and it is certified as a Y," said Miller. "There'll always be controversy, but as far as the FAA is concerned, it is a YPF."

Unfortunately for Miller's future as a happy Waco owner, he took NC32077 to Oshkosh that year, where it walked off with Best Waco honors. Very shortly afterward, the airplane headed for the East Coast and Miller went home with $30,000 in his pocket.

By 1979, NC32077 had changed hands twice more, won a number of additional fly-in trophies and ended up in Virginia, where the airline pilot owner groundlooped it, damaging both wingtips. Immediately afterward, it was for sale again.

Enter Joe Roselle, who has always loved biplanes.

Roselle learned to fly in 1970 and amassed a total of thirty-four solo hours before allowing his flying to lapse. "I piddled around and got busy in my practice, and I went seven years without touching a plane," he said. He checked out in a glider, then went another three years without touching the controls of any kind of air machine.

All during the 1930s, the nearly endless series of open cockpit biplanes produced by the Weaver Airplane Co. of Troy, Ohio, typified the classic sport airplane of the prewar era. The PF series—three-place, single-bay, four-aileron biplanes with flush covers for the front cockpit, wheel pants, sliding pilot's canopy and a variety of engines— were particularly attractive. The only one on the current US register, this custom YPF-7 with 225 hp Jacobs is light on the controls, friendly, able to land anywhere—and great fun to fly.

"I finally concluded it was time to get my plane," he continued. "I had built planes when I was a kid; the biplane was always my dream of what a plane should be." Clearly, there was no choice. His first airplane *had* to be a biplane!

He began reading all the "airplane for sale" ads with great interest.

"I looked all over the country for a biplane," he continued. "I looked at Tiger Moths. I looked at Stampes, Stearmans, Travel Airs—and I'd still go back to the Waco. I even flew 'way up north one time to look at three airplanes that were supposedly immaculate.

"I finally saw this one in Virginia, and called the guy." The owner told him it had won at Oshkosh. "When I heard that, I knew it had to be good, so I went out there—and when I saw that plane, I knew I wanted it!"

The owner said another man had called earlier, also was flying in to look at it, and had first claim on the beautiful Classic Orange and Hershey Brown YPF-7. You might say Joe Roselle owes his airplane to a gallstone attack.

It turned out that first prospective buyer was taken off the airliner in Washington, D.C., ill, and spent the night in a hospital! "So the next day he called this guy, and I'd already bought the plane and left."

One of Roselle's early experiences in the airplane was even more daunting than that of the airline pilot in Virginia. Indeed, it would have been enough to discourage a lesser man.

He and his instructor were in the early stages of takeoff one day at Oklahoma City's Wiley Post airport when the Waco went out of control and, still under full power, collided with a nearby parked Citabria.

Both right wings were sheared off, the fuselage was twisted, the tailwheel was broken off and the nose case was torn off the engine. The insurance company, quite rightly, totaled the airplane. Roselle wasn't ready to give up. He called Miller in Grand Junction, Colorado. Miller came to Oklahoma, inspected the wreckage—and pronounced it rebuildable. Roselle promptly bought it back from the insurance company and handed it over to Miller, who trucked it back to Colorado.

Twenty five months later, NC32077 flew once more. This time, it was silver and blue—because Miller could not buy the earlier colors in the relatively small quantities he needed. That, of course, meant the interior of both cockpits also had to be redone in matching leather and fabric.

This time, Miller delivered the airplane to Bob Wagner, a West Milton, Ohio, air show pilot who flies a 450 hp Stearman for a living. Roselle took an airline flight to Ohio and spent four days with Wagner, learning to fly the Waco from the back seat. He's never been out of it since. Wagner even accompanied him on the long cross-country back to Oklahoma. Since then, Roselle's flown NC32077 three years without a scratch.

When I climbed into the YPF-7's front cockpit at Fond du Lac, Wisconsin, it was the first deep-cushioned blue leather biplane seat I'd ever strapped on. The side panels were upholstered in tasteful woven wool fabric, with inset panels of polished wood for various controls.

The sophisticated molded windshields do an excellent job of keeping the wind out of the cockpits. "The originals were made of several pieces," said Miller, but since the original materials were no longer available, "I decided to make it one-piece. After six or seven tries, I was able to produce a fairly decent windshield for it." The floorboards, sticks and throttles gleam like tableware at a fine restaurant. Unfortunately, the rudder pedals and toe brakes in the front cockpit were not engineered for use by normal people. I ended up with both legs splayed out like Kermit the Frog and my knees tucked up under my chin, with my feet bent back toward my shins.

There were, of course, no gauges in the front pit, either. I had expected none. After a while, you get used to flying airplanes by control feel and the sounds of wind and engine.

I taxied out to the runup area for Runway 27 (elevation 809 ft.), waited while Roselle checked the mags and locked the tailwheel behind me, and cautioned him to watch closely and tell me later what the instruments were reading in various maneuvers. When the signalman swept his green flag imperiously forward, I was ready. Quickly, I fed in the power with the throttle under my left hand. The 99 in. Curtiss-Reed fixed-pitch blurred.

The Waco's tail came up in about 50 ft., and within another 100 we were airborne, at probably 60 mph. My right hand hauled the stick back and the nose went up better than ten degrees as we climbed out at about 75 mph and close to 1,200 fpm. Since the air was a cool 62 degrees F. and we were down to probably thirty gallons of fuel, that tallied well with the manufacturer's claim of 1,100 fpm initial rate of climb at sea level.

Leveling off a thousand feet above the verdant Wisconsin countryside, I brought the power back to 1950 rpm with Roselle's help (the Jacobs develops its rated horsepower at 2000 rpm), and waited while the YPF-7 slowly accelerated to 115 mph IAS.

Waco factory claims notwithstanding, Roselle says at that power setting he gets 120–125 solo and 5 mph less with two aboard. Perhaps hyperbole is not a post-World War II invention. . . .

Heading out southwest to shake off most of the swarm of airplanes constantly buzzing around Fond du Lac during the EAA convention, I displaced the controls one by one and found the Waco expectedly stable, with a mild tendency to roll slowly into a descending right turn.

I cleared the area and ran through a quick stall series, Roselle reporting the power-off stall came at 61 IAS, while 1700 rpm kept the airplane flying down to 55 and full power held it to 42. Agreeably, the airplane's full-power stall was as gentle and wings-level as with power off.

Three YPFs were built at the factory, two in 1935 and one in 1937. The latter, the only true –7, went to Japan. NC32077 was restored from a collection of parts by Gary Miller of Grand Junction, Colorado. Miller started with a number of original wing panels, the fuselage from a wartime UPF-7 two-seat military trainer and a detailed set of plans for the ZPF-7. The airplane was thus certified in 1975, the only YPF on the register. Cruise is fast: 135 mph at 75 percent at 6,000 feet on 13 gph.

I took time for some mild whifferdills that just may have bruised the FAA's definition of non-aerobatic flight (to check control force gradients and control harmony, of course), and reluctantly headed back toward Fond du Lac. "Anything in particular you'd like to show me about your little airplane?" I asked Roselle. "I don't think so," he assured me cheerfully. Rats! Well, you can't win 'em all.

I deliberately held the airplane high enough that I'm sure Roselle thought someone was going to have to shoot us down, then pulled off the power and stood the Waco on the left wingtip, slipping earthward at what felt to be about 80-85 IAS and perhaps 2,000 fpm descent rate.

The wind was still about 10 or 12 knots and about 230 degrees as I leveled the wings, flared out and crossed the threshold at 70 IAS, touching down three-point at about 60. The landing roll was an estimated 120 ft., with mild braking!

I cleared the runway, taxied back to the ramp and shut down, handing Roselle back his airplane with a feeling of real regret. "I usually put in, oh, 30 minutes to an hour almost every day or every other day," said Roselle. "I'm crazy about it. It flies beautiful! It's everything you could hope for a plane to be."

Indeed. It's truly "the sportman's biplane."
First printed in *Air Progress*, November 1986.

43

Chapter 8

Luscombe Phantom

First Luscombe

The story is that Don Luscombe was sitting in a hotel room with just enough money left to get home when he decided to leave Monocoupe and found another airplane company under his own name.

The story goes that Luscombe was tired of wood and glue and nails, and had decided the future lay in all-metal construction.

In any case, for a designer he turned once again to Ivan Driggs, who had been responsible for the most recent Monocoupe.

For the most part, Driggs simply converted his D-145 design from wood and steel tube to aluminum—but he tried to slick up the landing gear, added some fancy little drag flaps and a few other touches.

The fact is, Monocoupe aficionados of fifty years ago never liked the "D." Some even go so far as to contend it's not a Monocoupe.

I've flown the D-145 and like it just fine, but I admit it has a big-airplane feel and an indefinable un-Monocoupish character. As might have been expected, the Luscombe Phantom is much the same—but more so.

Perhaps the best way to put it is, it's no trainer! On the other hand, Dr. Tschudi flew his all over the Middle East with no problems. . . .

I looked at the pretty little radial-engined airplane with its sparkling, cream-colored paint and bright-red trim, its mirror-polished metal propeller, its rare Watters tunnel cowl. Then I looked at its slender, youthful owner. Then I looked back at the airplane.

"I don't know," I said, "You've got me about half scared already."

Doug Combs grinned.

"That's what the airline crews I fly with say," he replied.

We were talking about 272Y, the last (and only recently) flying Luscombe Phantom. Don Luscombe himself once remarked that it was "easier to learn to play the violin than . . . to land a Luscombe Phantom," and nobody ever forgot it. After all, Luscombe himself once concluded a Phantom flight demonstration with a somersault on roll-out!

He may even have been right. Take 272Y, for instance. The airplane was the factory prototype and served as a shop "mule" for something like seven years, sometimes surrendering pieces to repair its damaged brethren. It was sold, finally, in 1941.

When Combs bought it, it had had eight owners and had logged 189 hours, total. It had been on its back four times, twice within twenty minutes of flight time! It had a $2,000 annual in *1958!*

But personally, I always wondered what was so impressive about the Phantom that the lady riding with Luscombe crawled out (no mean feat from upside down) and wrote him a check for one just like it. To me, that's part of the airplane's fascination.

I owned a Luscombe 8E for a long time, flew it over much of the United States under all conditions and always enjoyed it immensely. As a Luscombe lover, I naturally lusted after the rare and elusive Phantom, first and in some ways best of the breed. Somehow I never caught up.

Until now.

It's a long way from the ground to the gracefully curved lip of the Phantom's door, and I'm not quite so limber as I once was. Nonetheless, I managed to clamber into the right seat and settle into the rich red leather without major error, devoting some care to fitting my feet into the narrow available floor space. It even *smelled* rich inside!

Earlier, Combs had told me he had not quite 100 hours in the Phantom, wasn't yet comfortable in it and would feel much better about things if he retained the left seat—and the brakes. I said sure.

What escaped me, although I'd been warned in advance, was that the throttle on a Phantom is way over in the left corner of the instrument panel, so that I had to reach across Combs—and over his control stick—to fly the airplane.

In a letter discussing details of our planned session, Combs said, "I am well aware of your background, colorful experience and diversified exposure to planes of the Phantom's vintage. This comforts me some." Then he suggested a dawn flight for minimum wind, mentioned that he'd like to keep the left seat and added, "This may prove awkward for throttle use, but it's really not bad at all (the cockpit is not large)."

Actually, the cockpit is 42 in. wide—positively spacious, compared to some later side-by-side two-seaters. This, combined with the deep, spring-filled leather seat cushions, the skylight with its roller shade, the pile-carpeted floorboard and the obvious quality of all the appointments imparted an instant feeling of luxury—much as you might get from an immaculately restored V-12 Packard supercharged roadster, perhaps.

I was picked up by such a car once as a boy when I was hitchhiking home after a five-mile hunting hike. A yellow one, also with a red leather interior, a white top, cream dash and gorgeous chrome supercharger pipes exiting into the fenders. The Phantom's a coupe, but it reminds me a lot of that car.

It's not really very big. It only spans 31 ft., with a length of 21 ft. 6 in.—but it stands proud at 6 ft. 9 in., its stubby nose snootily upthrust, and it exudes class from every hand-formed aluminum panel. This one is both the Alpha and Omega of the type, its fuselage having started as serial number 1 and ending up as number 131.

It was sold as NC28779, but was re-registered several years ago to the simple 272Y of the prototype.

Technical details are easy enough to recite: NACA 2412 airfoil (same as my early-model Cessna 210),

A few months after I flew this airplane and manfully resisted the temptation to explore loops and rolls, owner Doug Combs wrote to report they'd just finished the annual. He discovered that the four bolts holding the horizontal stabilizer on the airplane had been installed upside down, and two of them were crushed! He observed that had I succumbed to temptation, the tailplane might well have departed the airplane. Upon such little things, now and then, do our lives depend.

with two extruded I-section aluminum spars per wing, stamped dural ribs, a 62 in. chord and an area of 143.25 sq. ft., the whole set at a three-degree angle of incidence to the fuselage, with 15 in. of dihedral at the tips. Each wing contains a 16.5 gallon fuel tank. A 3.75 gallon oil tank is on the firewall inside the fuselage. The semi-cantilever landing gear is of two oleo legs braced with streamlined steel wire and completely faired with metal cuffs and fillets.

The subtle compound-curved monocoque fuselage is of 0.065 in. aluminum riveted to 17ST bulkheads, and all the curved panels for the whole Phantom series were formed with a power hammer by a single talented workman, Nick Nordyke. Baggage allowance is 66 lbs. in a compartment behind the seats. Map pockets are in both doors, and the entire cabin is soundproofed. Payload with full fuel and oil is two FAA-standard people and full baggage.

And Combs was right. The throttle wasn't bad. Certainly not as bad as flying from the right with a

As an old Luscombe Silvaire owner, I'd hankered after a Luscombe Phantom for more than 20 years before I finally got a chance to fly 272Y. I still hanker after a Luscombe Phantom—but I don't think I'd want to have to plan on the Phantom as my go-anywhere, do-anything airplane. A dream to fly, it can be a nightmare on the ground, a legacy of design shortcomings in the the gear.

left-hand stick and center-mounted throttle, as I've had to do a few times.

Pride of place in the center of the panel goes to the engine primer, which is surrounded by five identical mushroom-shaped brass knobs, each about the diameter of a half dollar. Clockwise from upper left, they are the spark retard, mixture, carburetor heat, oil shut-off and fresh air controls, and their decor goes well with the brass spark plug insulators on the front of the seven-cylinder, 145 hp Warner Super Scarab radial peeking out from behind the snubnosed cowling.

I left the little group of brass mushrooms strictly alone. Even at 9 a.m., it was already pushing 80 degrees F. on the ground at Chandler, Arizona, and I didn't figure I'd really need carburetor heat. As for the rest, well, nothing looked too essential to me.

I planted a size 6½D shoe sideways over both heel brakes while Combs wound up the Armstrong starter and gave the shiny Curtiss-Reed propeller a single quick flip. Warners in general are well mannered, and this one was no exception. It caught instantly, settling immediately into a smooth mutter. "It really does have an electric starter," said Combs. "It's just that the battery's very cantankerous."

Apparently about half of the twenty-two Phantoms known to have been built between 1934 and 1941 had conventional steerable leaf spring tailwheels with limited pivot travel, located well aft. Later ones had a full-swiveling, non-steerable, locking unit directly under the rudder post.

272Y now has a sturdy 8 in. Scott steerable tailwheel, which alone should do much to curb any tendency the Phantom may have to dart for the weeds. But there are other problems.

The airplane's center of gravity is just behind the main gear—which is both tall and narrow, with a 6 ft. tread. The gear design is a sort of splint arrangement, which tends to flex, or "walk," fore and aft. Just because a shock strut is compressed doesn't mean the other is—causing the airplane to lean and encouraging ground loops. The mechanical heel brakes are sensitive and grabby. The high-set horizontal tailplane and prominent wing fillets also are blamed for the low rudder effectiveness in the three-point attitude—the reason Combs *much* prefers wheel landings.

There used to be another problem: excessive toe-in on the mains. Unbelievable as it seems, Combs swears that when he first flew the Phantom, the tire tracked inward 3½ in. *for every revolution of a main wheel.* No wonder the thing was squirrely on the ground! That's damn near in the uncontrollable category. Surely they didn't *all* leave the factory in that condition!

Despite all this, I'm hard-headed. If it were mine, I fear I'd have to sample its three-point characteristics, even if I flipped it too. . . .

I taxied out, S-turning slightly to clear the left front of the airplane, but found that in general the

Phantom provides excellent visibility for a mid 1930s radial-engined design. I never felt handicapped by the Warner, anywhere in the envelope. In taxiing, I found also that the brakes on my side worked, although you had to reach pretty deep to get them. Well, good. Now either of us could flip this puppy!

Run-up was simple enough, with the 89 in. fixed-pitch; a matter of checking the mags and carb heat, fuel (a four-way valve on the sidewall near Combs' left ankle), controls and trim and announcing our intentions on Combs' hand-held transceiver.

Acceleration was leisurely, and ground run was an estimated 1,000–1,200 ft. at 1550 rpm—a result of the much-abused Curtiss-Reed. The prop originally came off a Warner-powered Great Lakes, and had been repitched four times, a couple of them since Combs bought the airplane. He plans to replace it with a Hamilton-Standard ground adjustable soon.

Combs remarked that his first flight in the Phantom was inadvertent, when a bump and a gust combined to lift him off the midpoint of a 3,000 ft. runway during tail-up taxi tests. Electing to go around, he shoved the throttle in—and found that full power produced 2150 rpm and an initial climb rate of better than 1,500 fpm. The problem is, redline on the Warner is 2050.

"I came around and landed, and the only thing I could think of at that point was, 'You *bought* this son of a bitch!'" Combs said. He admitted he had "very serious regrets the first couple of days of ownership," but "there's nothin' that sounds like a round motor."

We didn't do as well as Combs, registering only 700 fpm—exactly half the factory claim. Ah, well, doubtless all it needs is a little tinkering—and the Hamilton-Standard, perhaps.

The Scott tailwheel, of course, gave excellent directional control three-point. Left to its own devices, the tail came up at about 40 mph indicated, and the airplane flew off at around 65.

I was immediately and pleasantly surprised by the feel of the airplane. The Phantom weighs only 1,320 lbs. empty (1,377 for 272Y) and grosses 1,950, but it feels more like a light twin, perhaps a Beech Baron. Unlike its daddy, the Monocoupe D-145, or its grandson, the Luscombe Model 8, the Phantom's controls are delightfully well harmonized—but equally crisp and responsive.

Similarly, the jack screw trim is *much* faster-acting than either the Monocoupe or Luscombe 8, and much more sensitive and powerful. Twirl it carelessly and you'll get a nasty shock!

Displacing each control in turn, I found cruise stability was excellent in all three axes, with oscillations quickly damped. Impressive indeed, even today, let alone in 1934!

We climbed to 3,000 MSL (1,764 AGL) and leveled off, with me doing my standard series of alternating thirty-degree turns to feel out the airplane. I set up 1750 rpm for a cruise run and let the speed stabilize. I was shooting for sixty-five percent, but Combs later wrote to say what I got calculated out to 84.1 bhp and fifty-eight percent.

There aren't many section lines in that part of the world, so we had to rely on the airspeed, which Combs assures me still indicates a bit low at the top end. We showed 122 IAS, at 1750 rpm, while 1850 (an estimated seventy-five percent) yielded 126 IAS.

I calculated a true airspeed of 130 mph at the lower power setting and 135 at the higher, based on 80 degrees F. at 3,000 ft. Combs figured us at 1,885 lbs. and 135 at the lower setting, which would've put us a whisker under 140 at the higher one.

If you think about it, all this compares very favorably with the factory's claim of a 144 mph sea level cruise. Combs pointed out the 8 in. exhaust stack extension and big tailwheel probably cut 8–12 mph off the cruise, while carrying the big ADF loop in the 8 cu. ft. baggage compartment and mounting it only for fly-in displays probably added 7 mph. In sum, he concluded, net cruise should be around 142–145 in factory configuration. "My guess is that Luscombe actually met his design speed goals," he said. Combs made no allowance for his lack of the 21 in. General streamlined tires that originally graced the airplane.

With the Warner burning 9.5 gph at performance cruise, the thirty-three gallons of gas available provided an endurance of 3.5 hours and a real-world still-air range of just over 500 miles.

Well, time to get down to work.

I climbed to 4,000 ft. MSL, slowed the airplane to 72 IAS, adjusted power and trim for that speed and did 360 degree turns left and right at thirty degrees of bank. The UrLuscombe tracked around the circle with all the solidness and stability of the Super Chief sliding into town. Hmmm. In the left seat, Combs was paying very close attention. In his pre-meeting letter, he'd said he hadn't tested the airplane's stall characteristics.—Double hmmm.

Pointing the Warner's nose at a convenient mountain, I eased the power off and the stick back, feeling for the stall.

Very Luscombe-like!

The Phantom flew right up to the stall and quit completely, with only the tiniest hint of elevator heaviness a heartbeat before. That first one came at 68 IAS, with a quick nose bob and a right wing dip, and we lost about 150 ft. of altitude before I caught it with a touch of throttle and relaxed back pressure.

I tried some more, recovering a couple of times in less than 100 ft. of altitude. I tried banked stalls, left and right. I tried power stalls, up to about 1400 rpm. All were absolutely no problem! Indicated airspeeds at the break ran as low as 58 and as high as that first 68. Behavior was always the same; gentler under power.

Finally, I went for the long full stall: power off, stick all the way back and hold her level with the rudder. I held it for only two cycles, in deference to the rarity and value of the airplane, but the second saw the airspeed down around 65 and I would guess the

Don Luscombe's first product under his own name, the beautiful Phantom was entirely of metal, unlike the earlier wood-winged Monocoupe. A single workman hand formed every panel in the 22 Phantoms built between 1934 and 1941. Expensive, the Phantom offered exceptional performance, cruising 144 mph and climbing 1,400 fpm with its 145 hp Warner turning an 89 in. Curtiss-Reed propeller.

third would have been well below 60. This was the only time the Phantom tried to bite. As I started to recover, a secondary stall struck like lightning at 70 IAS, with a determined *left* wing drop—doubtless produced by prop effect.

By now, it was hard to restrain myself. The Phantom was just *so* nice-flying, *so* precise and predictable on the controls that I dipped the nose and let the speed walk rapidly up the dial to around 160, brought it up and over in a big, hairy dive-bomber peel-off, followed up with a tight military-style lazy eight and a sixty- to seventy-degree banked 360 left and right, rolling rapidly from one into the other using a handy highway as the roll point.

God, it was fun!

When the itch in my palms grew nearly unbearable, I looked over at Combs and asked him if there was anything special he wanted to show me about his little airplane. He shrugged and grinned and replied, "You're more at home in it than I am," so we headed back to the field to shoot some landings.

I made a nice, conservative low pass down Runway 22 at about 30 ft. and 160 IAS to announce our intentions, pulled up and around at a tad over 2,000 fpm and handed it back to Combs to demonstrate his preferred Phantom landing technique.

He shot two, the second with flaps. The Phantom's flaps are neat little gadgets much like those on Cessna Airmasters and 190-195s, but a lot fancier. They're of stainless steel, with little folding U-channel actuators of the same stuff, worked by a jack screw and pivoting at right angles. They operate either elec-

trically or by a hand crank in the cabin ceiling behind the pilot's head.

Both times, Combs made a rather flat approach and kissed the asphalt with that gentle drag of rubber that leaves everyone in no doubt you're doing something right. The flaps steepened the approach angle and improved the view, but didn't seem to affect the touchdown speed, so I elected not to complicate my life by trying to crank backwards behind my head at the same time I was juggling a throttle in the far left corner and landing a strange airplane at a strange airport.

I fell back on my last favorite maneuver, instead: a slip to a landing, with a little power for better control (I cheat when it helps). And the Phantom surprised me again! It refused to slip as well as I thought it should; maybe 1,100 fpm at 85 IAS. With the Warner, I'd expected it to come down better. Slowing 272Y another 10 mph would have increased the descent rate, of course, but I didn't know the plane well enough.

The first landing went so well I couldn't believe it, so I pinned the nose with forward stick, advanced the power and roared down the 4,395 ft. length of the runway to do it again.

Once again I flew the downwind at 120, turned base at 100, came down final at 90 and crossed the threshold at 80, but this time I kept the throttle closed. I felt for the runway as I feathered the stick back, and we touched down at 75 with the gentlest "erk-erk" of the mains. Now, granted I was flying it on, but even so I wasn't far from the fall-out-of-the-sky point. The factory claimed a landing speed of 45, obviously three-point.

I'd have to see that done to believe it.

I held the tail up and let her roll. And roll. In fact, we rolled for probably 2,000 ft., prompting me to exclaim at just how well it rolled. Combs nodded. "Three thousand feet is the bare minimum I'll operate in," he said. He looked at me severely. "You know, you only had about two seconds there to make that landing," he added. "This airplane has a very narrow pitch envelope in flight; four degrees maximum." I nodded in turn. "I know," I said.

Combs said, "I figure I'm over gross every time I take off. I've got Linda and the banker and two insurance agents and all the people who care about the airplane." He figures he's responsible for it to all of them, and they'd never forgive him if he wrecked it. Consequently, he's very conservative about the way he flies it.

I can understand and appreciate that. This is a historic airplane in its own right: the first all-metal, high wing side-by-side cabin monoplane for the private pilot—and arguably the best. Certainly it's one of the most challenging.

Combs grinned and declared, "I'm convinced its reputation is deserved. You run out of control in all directions. There are so many engineering shortcomings on the airplane that it's obtuse even to discuss them."

He added, "This airplane is good for taking to fly-ins, and if you want to go out and get your adrenaline up a bit." On the other hand, on the record, since World War II and possibly before, nobody in this country has flown a Phantom as long and successfully as Doug Combs already has.

I let the airplane roll out, touched the tailwheel down gently, turned off on the taxiway and headed back to Combs' immaculate hangar, and as I did so I turned to him accusingly and said, "You were woofin' me! You had this tiger tamed long before we ever showed up."

And indeed he had.

An ATP, A&P and currently copilot on an airline Boeing 737, the thirty-four-year-old Combs has been flying for seventeen years, thus far amassing nearly 10,000 hours.

His first airplane was a Luscombe 8A. He instructed 1,000 hours in Luscombes; flew pipeline patrol in them. In trying to explain how he got interested in the Phantom, he said, "I guess I was probably 100 percent in love when I saw the one in the San Diego Air Museum. You walk up to it and your heart melts." He grimaced wryly. "Six weeks later, the museum and the Phantom burned up."

Then Fate took a hand.

Combs was restoring an 8E and looking for an engine when he called on Ross Funk, Phoenix area owner of a 150 hp Luscombe and a one-time Luscombe employee. Over Funk's desk was "a big, beautiful Phantom picture," and Combs naturally remarked how much he wanted one.

A few weeks later, 272Y was advertised for sale. Funk saw it and promptly called Combs to tell him his chance had arrived.

The airplane then was owned by Robin Collord, a former Air America pilot from Del Rio, Texas, who had put years of effort and much money into its restoration, farming out much of the work to specialists. Collord had been meticulous in his efforts, keeping copious notes that eventually filled a whole scrapbook, taking samples of the original paint, using the finest materials and so on.

"It was probably insane for me even to go look at the airplane," remarked Combs. But he did, not expecting much—and what he found surprised him.

He went home and sent Collord a deposit check the very next day, although it took five months and most of both men's patience to consummate the deal.

Meanwhile, Combs convinced his friend Linda Gamble (who operates the telephone system in Hampden, Maine, just outside Bangor) to go partners with him on the Phantom. A private pilot and the daughter of a naval aviator, Gamble already had been introduced to the Phantom display in the National Air and Space Museum by Combs.

The Phantom is one of those unique airplanes that's a part of aviation history more for what it represents than what it did.

Don Luscombe learned to fly strictly informally in France during his off-duty time while serving as a civilian volunteer ambulance driver, bootlegging instruction in whatever came to hand with whomever he could get to teach him. Once back home, he opened a public relations office in Des Moines, Iowa, and bought a war-surplus Curtiss JN–4D as his first "business airplane."

Soon dissatisfied with the Jenny, Luscombe used wood lath and old oil cans to build a mockup of an airplane cabin seating two people his size side by side. Then he hired young Clayton Folkerts to design an airplane around the mockup. Explaining that was all the money he had, Luscombe gave Folkerts sixty days to come up with the design.

The result was the "Monocoupe," a very successful basic design that was soon refined into several more advanced models. All shared the same steel tube fuselage, wood wing and fabric cover, the same layout and roughly the same size.

Luscombe left Monocoupe in the depths of the Depression and established the Luscombe Airplane Company, hiring Ivan Driggs—creator of the hot and curvaceous D-145 Monocoupe—to design the first Luscombe. The Phantom was the result.

For a personal airplane, it was revolutionary. The fuselage weighed 150 lbs., but was sandbag tested to nine tons. The wings were tested to 10 Gs. It was clearly fast, not to mention sleek and attractive. But from the first flight it was apparent that it was an angel in the air—and a devil on the ground.

It quickly proved to have a maximum level speed of 168 mph—remarkable for a machine of 145 hp—with a maximum dive speed of 240 TIAS. Service ceiling was 19,000 ft., and one overenthusiastic ferry pilot blacked out at 20,000 ft., exceeding an estimated 300 mph in his descent, before crash-landing.

Beginning in August 1934, at least serial number 1 and perhaps more were built in the leased factory of a defunct Kansas City airplane maker, but Luscombe soon moved his parts, jigs and hopes to West Trenton, New Jersey, where most were turned out.

Luscombe had hoped to make the fuselage panels on an experimental new hydraulic stretch forming machine developed by a Topeka, Kansas, airplane builder, but the machine ruined about as many panels as it made and finally was scrapped.

"If they'd used skin half as thick as they did, it would've worked fine," observed Combs. He has a point. But Luscombe and his helpers didn't know they really didn't need 0.065 in. skin panels.

Parts were made for at least twenty-five Phantoms, while the serials ran to 30—but known registrations include only twenty-one in the United States and one in Switzerland. The latter, HB-EXE, even

First sold in 1941, 272Y had had eight owners and logged 189 hours when Doug Combs and his partner bought it in 1987. It had been on its back four times, twice within 20 minutes of flight time! As of 1990, 272Y was the only airworthy Phantom—and Combs was the world's most experienced Phantom pilot.

made an extended flight through the Middle East in the late 1930s.

Combs says serial number 1 "was cannibalized periodically for parts to repair the continual flow of damaged airplanes returned to or bought by the factory for rebuilding. Finally No. 1 seems to have been left alone, and late serial numbers on the line were robbed of parts to meet this ongoing 'repair parts' need."

In 1941, the factory decided to use its last parts to assemble one final Phantom. Thus the old original fuselage was restored to its original configuration, redesignated serial number 131 and mated with whatever parts could be found. This is it.

"The owners of record rarely flew the bird as it went from one garage and accident site to another," says Combs. "In 1944 it suffered major damage and was returned to the factory, where nearly a year later it was returned to service, with a whopping 44:40 on the tach. It suffered minor damage in the hands of three successive owners from '47 to '52," when it was sold to yet another man who managed to fly it some fifty-eight hours before wrecking it again. He had it repaired and flew it six more hours before losing a dispute with a fence in 1958—apparently, the last time it was airborne until Combs' unplanned flight last year. "The logbook just reads like a shop history," he summed up.

The Phantom was sold to Collord in 1982 and trucked to Texas. Restoration was ninety percent complete when Combs bought it, but he says it still required 200 hours of work in Texas before it could be ferried to Chandler, Arizona, and another 500 hours after arrival.

The effort paid off. The lovely Phantom was named Contemporary Age champion in the Antique and Classic Division at Oshkosh 1988.

Ask Combs what he intends to do with 272Y now that he has it flying satisfactorily and he'll reply that he expects to fly it for the next four or five years. "He and I may get along a whole lot better with time," he says.

And if you ask Combs why he chooses to refer to 272Y as "he" rather than "she," as most pilots do, he grins slyly and asks, "Ever see an airplane with balls?"

And what will he do with it beyond that four- or five-year period? He shrugs. After all, he says, he has all the factory plans for the airplane. Maybe he can put it back into production.

A challenge for the 1990s!

Sipping iced tea after our flight, I looked at Combs and said, "You'll never know just how close we came to doing some aerobatics up there." He smiled quietly. "I know," he replied.

Whatever happens, Doug Combs says it's "highly unlikely" *he'll* ever dispose of the much-traveled Phantom. But he says when I get ready to spin test it, I may have to go by myself.

First printed in *Air Progress*, February 1989.

Chapter 9

Stinson Gullwing

Limousine

Not only are the gullwing Stinsons prominent among the classic 1930s airplane designs, they are remarkable in that they were built as aerial limousines—but most of them ended up as bush planes.

It is a tribute to their design and construction that they handled any role assigned to them with the same quiet competence.

If you have not ridden in one of these bump-cowled beauties, you should. With their roll-down windows, wood-grain appointments, rich fabrics and leathers, insulation, round engines and prewar elegance, they are a far different flying experience than a modern airplane.

They are not especially fast. Their climb is hardly rocketlike. But they will fly away with anything you can stuff into them, and haul it into or out of just about any cow pasture you care to try. They are built to last—and they have, fortunately.

Stinsons are thoroughly honest airplanes, moderately blind on the ground but easy to fly. So are lots of others. Where the gullwing shines is in its total ambiance—the unequaled ride, the elegance. It's kind of a Rolls-Royce with wings!

Suddenly, some part of me was a kid again, in a world where my folks drove Studebakers and lived on a paycheck while the stockholders smoked Havana cigars, drank bonded booze and wheeled around in V-12 Packards and Pierce Arrows and Lincoln Continentals.

Rumbling along a thousand feet over eastern Kansas, swaddled in top-grain cowhide, peering out at the world along the side of the big Wright's bump cowling and staring at the rich woodgrained instrument panel, I was transported back to those too-rare childhood experiences when some moneyed adult stranger actually gave me a *ride* in one of those long, sleek bubble machines.

It was that kind of feeling.

One thing the Studebakers and Packards shared was a mouse-gray mohair headliner—and the same stuff was sported by this snazzy 1937 Stinson SR-9E.

The Stinson Reliant series began in 1934, with the SR-5, a big four-place airplane with a straight, strut-braced high wing and a 215 hp Lycoming R-680 radial. Stinson then went quickly through the SR-6 and 7, and the SR-8—first of the "gullwings," appeared in 1936.

The 8 was bigger yet, carried five people and was offered not only with the R-680 in various strengths, but with the Wright R-760 in takeoff horsepower ratings up to 350. Just as importantly, it had a new set of wings.

Patterned after those used on the famous low-wing Stinson A tri-motor airliner, these retained the modified Clark Y airfoil section, but were unique double-tapered affairs that, in plan, swelled to a maximum eight-foot chord at the midpoint of each and tapered to 38 in. tips. Furthermore, they tapered inward to the root—though not quite so radically.

And as if that weren't enough, they also tapered in thickness, from a maximum of a foot and a half at the midpoint to maybe half an inch at the tips and, at a guess, probably 6 in. thick at the roots. They are not really "gulled," but this construction makes it appear that they are.

They are built exactly like a steel truss bridge, except they are made of steel tubing instead of solid metal, and are welded rather than bolted together. The wing truss is even heat treated from the strut inboard!

In other words, they're strong enough to hold up a house—and it's a good thing, because from the standpoint of size, the Reliants are sort of like Winnebagos with wings. Back up to a wheel pant on a Reliant, and you don't *have* to sit *down* to sit. You just sit!

But there are other peculiarities to the SR-8, 9 and 10 series Reliant wing. For one thing, the quick reduction in chord and thickness toward the wing root provides much better visibility to pilot and passengers than any contemporary airplane. For another, it's claimed that it diverted jolts and softened the ride due to the spanwise distribution of airflow from the center out.

I don't know whether that's true, but certainly it *is* true that a gullwing Stinson rides with the smoothness of an ocean liner and the stability of an iron bridge, as their buyers claimed. Personally, I always thought that was due to the fact that the thing grosses better than two tons, but maybe not.

In any case, that wing must have been a real challenge to build, because no two pieces are the same in any given wing panel—and they're all welded together! But those were the days when craftsmen still took pride in their workmanship, and when they were damned glad to have *any* kind of a steady job.

In those days, a dollar was really a dollar, and there weren't many of them around. The big SR-9E sold for $12,500 at the Wayne, Michigan, factory, at a time when you could buy a new Ford or Chevy for $700, a decent house in the Midwest for maybe $1,200. You could buy a good milk cow for $50—and it took the hides of five of those just to upholster the seats in a Reliant.

It still takes five, reported John Swander, the burly, bearded, low-key young owner of this outsized fifty-one-year-old classic.

He knows, because when he and his wife Jodi bought the thing, the interior was mostly exposed steel tubing and insulation. In fact, they flew it that way for more than a year, while they solved more pressing problems.

In a sense, NC17138 has been in restoration for nearly twenty years.

Sold originally to Dana L. Fuller, of the wealthy San Francisco paint family, 138 was one of several Reliants they bought. The year before, family mem-

Stinson built 496 Reliants, including this snazzy 1937 SR-9E with its 350 hp blown Wright R-760-E. The thing sold for $12,500 f.a.f. (fly away at factory) Wayne, Michi- *gan, in a day when you could buy a new Ford or Chevy for $700 and a decent house in the Midwest for maybe $1,200.*

bers had purchased a trio of SR-8s, one of them with the same Wright R-760E-2.

Fuller kept serial number 5209 for a couple of years and sold it. By the middle of World War II, it was in use by United Airlines as an instrument trainer. It passed through several other hands, and finally was damaged when a hangar fell on it.

Typically, it held up the hangar.

It ended up disassembled in a North Carolina barn. Then, in 1963, a Greentown, Indiana, pilot paid $600 for it, sight unseen. He and a couple of friends went to claim it in 1964—and he was disappointed at what he found. Nevertheless, they filled two trucks with parts and hauled them all back to Indiana—the beginning of a thirteen-year restoration effort.

Jim Lanning bought another basket case in Massachusetts to serve as a pattern, and had the engine majored. Slowly the airplane went back together. Eventually it was a licensed, flying airplane again, though Lanning never did get around to the little touches like the cabin interior.

Then he put it up for sale.

Meanwhile, Swander, an auto mechanic, motorcycle enthusiast and former dune buggy racer, began to take flying lessons. That was in the fall of 1978, and Swander—who's fifteen years younger than his airplane—didn't earn his private ticket for a full year.

Before he'd finished training, he sold a couple of motorcycles, bought a Stinson 108-3 and reworked that. He sold the 108 four years later, and by then "I was looking real hard at Reliants. I looked for two years."

He smiled through his bushy dark beard. "Of 496 built, there are 63 still registered. I turned down 90 percent of 'em." He figures he tracked down most of the remaining fleet and looked at many, from the Rockies to New York state.

Ask him why he was hung up on Reliants and he shrugs and says, "I liked their looks. That was the biggest thing. And I went for a ride in a V-77. I was very impressed" with the comfort and the low noise level. The brief experience with the V-77 quickly led him to the SR, and from then on he was a man with a mission.

He discovered 138 and an SR-8 both for sale, thirty miles apart. "We took off one Friday morning," and inspected the SR-8, but found that was "kind of a dog." He debated whether to look at the SR-9, but finally decided to do so.

At the time, the airplane hadn't flown for two years, and Swander told Lanning he was interested— but he wanted to ride in it.

Six weeks later, Lanning called to invite the Swanders back—and they went. They all went flying. In fact, they flew for three hours one Sunday morning, but "I wasn't so sure I really wanted it." Lanning landed, and invited Swander and his wife to take it on their own. They did, brought it back and found it was leaking oil from the front crankshaft seal.

Swander shook his head and backed off. But, he

The Reliants are big airplanes; sort of like flying around in your living room. They have roll-down windows, wood-grain instrument panels, real wood control wheels and mouse-gray mohair headliners. There's a classy quality about them that reminds one of a Packard or Pierce Arrow from the same era.

says, as he stood there watching Lanning hopping rides in it, "I knew I had to have it."

The next day he flew it home, the big Wright leaking a gallon of oil every forty-five minutes. "I nursed it home. Since then, I've been doin' nothin' but work on it."

He took it to a fly-in at nearby Atchison, Kansas, in the spring of 1983, and to the Stinson gathering at Minden, Nebraska, later that season. He was on final at Minden when the engine spat black smoke and quit. He dead-sticked it onto the runway in a strong wind. Pretty soon it ran up fine. He flew it home—and it quit again, on final.

It turned out there were pinholes in the carburetor float, and when Swander dropped his flaps and changed the pitch for landing, the float filled with gasoline and sank, flooding the engine. He'd flown it thirty hours that way.

He found when the float was fixed, fuel consumption improved dramatically. He got so enthused he had the engine majored—again.

The Stinson was covered with Stits fabric and polyurethane in 1978, as Swander was learning to fly, and was in good shape. The red and white paint scheme duplicated the original, but the colors were reversed on the horizontal tail, and when Swander redid them, the new paint reacted with the old and made a mess. The whole thing had to be redone.

He removed the Cessna T-50 expander tube brakes on the airplane and installed Goodyear multi-disc units, the same kind it had originally carried. He overhauled the stabilizer jack screw mechanism. Like

Gullwing Stinsons are so called because the wings look as if they're gulled. They're not; they just taper in both thickness and planform. The resulting spanwise airflow distribution gives the airplanes an unparalleled ride.

a Cessna 180/185, the big Stinson has an all-trimming stabilizer instead of an elevator tab. He found the 32 ft. continuous-splice trim cable was the wrong size, so he ran down a new one in Chicago and installed it.

The electrical system didn't work, and he had to replace that. A friend and fellow antiquer on the same field, John Krekovich, crafted new full-circle wooden wheels to duplicate the originals, again replacing Cessna T-50 control wheels. Together, they restored the instrument panel—including the shock-mounted center section with its distinctive bulbous whiskey compass—and carefully replicated the brown wood-grain paint of the mid 1930s. Swander even identified, located, overhauled and installed the original-style instruments.

New wood window frames were crafted, also. The only wood in the airplane is in the window and door frames and in the small formers and stringers used to round off the fabric of the airframe.

Using another totally original (and unrestored) Reliant 150 miles away as a pattern, Swander studied the headliner and the 38 sq. ft. of red leather he needed to restore the interior to the thing of beauty it once was.

He shook his head in disbelief, telling about it. "I've probably put 2,000 hours' restoration into it since

I bought it, and it was licensed and flyin' at the time," Swander exclaimed.

There are other compromises. The only hangar he could rent was marginally narrower than the Reliant's wingspan, so he has to shoehorn it into the building at an angle—and two tons of steel tube and fabric takes a lot of shoehorning!

Watching him preflight the airplane is a lot like watching a kid on a schoolyard jungle gym, involving much climbing and stretching and reaching around.

There's a lot of maintenance to it, Swander admits. "It's hard to keep up with it."

But it's all worth it when the big Wright bursts into life with a throaty growl and a little cloud of blue smoke, and goes grumbling out to the active, S-turning carefully through the lesser airplanes like a dowager in a red dress.

The SR-9 is a good-sized airplane! Span is 41 ft. 11 in., length 28 ft. 1 in. and it stands 8½ ft. high. Wing area is 258.5 sq. ft., gross weight wing loading 15.86 lbs. per sq. ft. and power loading 11.71 lbs.-hp.

The 52 in. wide rear seat accommodates three, while pilot and "copilot" occupy chairs as comfortable as anything ever bolted into a custom van, and there's headroom for anyone.

It's a long step up via the chromed steel ladders to

54

the access doors to left and right, and there are grab handles at the back of the outboard armrests on both front seats.

The curved semi-cantilever main gear has a 113 in. tread and uses Aerol (air/oil) shock absorbers that provide that Packard-equivalent ride, while the big 8.50x10 in. tires soak up any remaining shock. There's even an Aerol strut for the 10½ in. free-swiveling tailwheel!

Standard fuel was a forty-one-gallon tank in each wing root, but 138 also carries an optional twenty-four-gallon auxiliary, providing a total of 106 gallons and an endurance of just over 5½ hours at seventy-five percent (19 gph)—a maximum still-air range for this airplane of 825 miles, based on the book figure of a 150 mph seventy-five percent cruise at sea level. Normal tankage gives a quoted range of 600 miles; about standard in general aviation fifty years ago— and today.

Glass sight gauges jut from the bottom of each wing to give direct readings on remaining fuel in the mains, while an electric gauge on the instrument panel shows what's left in the auxiliary.

Factory figures listed an empty weight of 2,640 lbs., an allowable gross of 4,100 and a useful load of 1,460 lbs., but Swander says 138 is 200 lbs. heavier than standard, cutting useful to 1,260. Legally, all this means that a standard Reliant could carry full fuel and oil (five gallons) and 4.63 FAA-standard people, but that 138 could carry only 3.45 people. In neither case could the people carry a spare pair of socks.

A baggage compartment loaded through an external door just aft of the right passenger access accommodates bulky loads to 100 lbs., and another 50 can be stowed beneath the rear seat (75 and 30 in the case of Swander's machine).

Performance-wise, the big Stinson is no slouch. Indeed, though most of the gullwings were bought by the moneyed set, by corporate clients or by such entities as the New York Police Department and the US Bureau of Air Commerce, many of them ended up working for a living in the bush of Canada and Alaska—and were quite at home in harness, on wheels, floats and skis.

Factory figures say the blown Wright (mechanically driven supercharger, 9.13:1 ratio) and the 8½ ft. Hamilton-Standard controllable-pitch prop hauls the airplane off the grass in 800 ft., and initial climb will hit 950 fpm at full throttle (35.5 in.x2300 rpm, 1 min.), full gross, standard conditions. But Swander doesn't fly it quite like that. His engine turns up less than 35 in., and we were off the ground in more like 1,100 ft., climbing at 85 IAS and maybe 850 fpm on 30x2300.

Stinson listed a service ceiling of 17,500 ft. and a landing speed of 60 mph. We didn't check the service ceiling, but the gullwing does indeed come aboard at just about 60 out of an approach flown at 95–100 IAS, its vacuum-operated flaps and high drag in the three-point landing attitude bringing it to a halt with mild braking in 250 ft. of ground roll. It's no wonder the airplane was popular with bush pilots.

"You can work that airplane very comfortably out of a 1,500 ft. strip," remarked Swander.

In the air, the gullwing indicated 143 mph at 2,500 ft. and 26.5 in.x2000 rpm (seventy-five percent) and trued around 148, very close to the factory-promised 150, but Swander quickly noted, "I never push it that hard," chiefly because there are virtually no spares for the Wright. His usual power setting is 23.5x1925, "around 55%," for 130 IAS on 14.9 gallons of mogas per hour.

In-flight manners were impeccable, if rather deliberate.

The SR–9 is a big, heavy airplane—and it feels like one, with control pressures perhaps on the order of a Cessna 207 but better harmonized, due to the much lighter pitch forces.

There's a powerful trim crank for the stabilizer in the overhead, à la Piper, but no rudder trim except for a ground adjustable tab. Rather surprisingly, it didn't seem to be needed.

We had a couple of passengers in the back for a full load, so I confined my slow flight and stall work to some paddling around at 70 indicated (superb, trimmed; heavy, untrimmed) and some straight-ahead stalls with and without flaps, breaking at around 55–58 IAS.

I handed the airplane back to Swander with considerable discontent after a short familiarization period.

Someday, I'd like to get a chance to really feel out the big Stinson's performance envelope.

Who knows? Maybe with the next owner.

First printed in *Air Progress*, October 1988.

Chapter 10

Stout Bushmaster

The clone

The Ford Tri-Motor is so ugly it's beautiful. Its 1958 clone, the Stout Bushmaster, comes equipped with smooth skin, engine cowlings, internal control cables and a dorsal fin on the rudder, so it's not quite so ugly/beautiful.

Still, the two fly much the same.

The nice thing about operating one of these flying barns is that they're designed to go low and slow, grumbling along only a thousand feet over the fields and trees, looking at the scenery. This one earned its keep carrying sixteen paying passengers, operating out of a handkerchief-sized pasture that would give a Cessna 180 heart palpitations and had the tankage to fly ten hours at 95 mph.

Laurent "Frenchy" Savard was responsible for getting the Stout Bushmaster built and, finally, into the air in 1966. Two were built by 1990 and both were airworthy at that time. N7501V was in flying condition and on display in the Owl's Head Museum at Camden, Maine. N414H was still owned by Scenic Airlines and stored at Grand Canyon Airport, Grand Canyon, Arizona.

Long may they fly!

"We start the center engine first, because it has the generator," said Chuck LeMaster, reaching overhead with a muscular arm to flip the boost pump toggle switch.

The old Ford didn't have boost pumps. It didn't have electric primers, either, or aileron and rudder trim, or the elevator trim mounted on the pedestal right between us. The Bushmaster has all those things, and a few more—but it's still a pretty basic front office.

Matter of fact, the Bushmaster's flight deck actually looks more Spartan than the one on LeMaster's old airplane, a Ford 5-AT known throughout its life as "414." It took me a minute to figure out why. Then it hit me: The Bushmaster's cockpit is modern. It's got small gauges and toggle switches and insulated leatherette side panels. The whole effect is far removed from the Ford's happy clutter.

Even the control pedestal with its trio of levers for throttle and mixture has changed a bit. The Bushmaster boasts full-feathering constant-speed three-blade props. With the Ford, things were even simpler. It swung fixed-pitch props.

Aside from those things, though, I could have been back in the business end of 414H. There was the same narrow windscreen in front of me, the same incredibly fat wing stretching away to either side, the same view of engine to the right, engine to the left and engine straight ahead. There was the same 9 ft. distance from my eyeballs to the sward of LeMaster's private airstrip.

The right-hand R-985 whined, spat blue smoke and burst into a roar, followed smoothly sixty seconds later by the left, finally blending with the grumble from directly ahead. The trio sounded beautiful. They should. They're all zero-timed.

Differential power on the right-hand engine, a light touch of brake after we were moving, and the Bushmaster trundled into a sweeping left curve, headed downhill for the end of the runway. LeMas-

A (slightly) modernized Ford Trimotor, the Stout Bush-master flies identically—although NACA cowlings make it marginally faster, cruising at 95 mph. It boasts better soundproofing, a modern instrument panel, boost pumps, electric primers, full-feathering props, a taller rudder and a dorsal fin.

ter's proud of his turf. He takes care of it; doesn't appreciate divots gouged out by locked wheels. He didn't offer to let me take the airplane out of its parking place, and I didn't ask.

The FAA officially classes the Bushmaster 2000 as a lightplane, since its gross weight is listed at 12,500 lbs. But it's the biggest damn lightplane anybody ever saw. As the crow said to Dumbo, he'd seen a house fly. He'd seen a dragon fly. But he'd never seen an elephant fly.

Well, N7501V is about the size of a house. And some might say it's uglier than your average dragon. For sure there's something elephantine about its control response. But actually you'd have to say it has more in common with a barn than a house. A corrugated tin barn. A Butler building, maybe.

N7501V is a flying anachronism, an airplane completed in 1957, type certificated in 1966 and designed to a 1927 specification.

N7501V is the world's only complete example of a Bushmaster 2000—a modernized Ford Tri-Motor built by someone else. Technically it's still in production, though only 01V has ever flown. A. E. Moody, one of those involved in the project since inception, says airframe No. 2 is nearly finished and a third is in the jigs on the Long Beach airport. The work, he adds, is proceeding "very slowly." It is, he says, "the largest homebuilt going."

It's large, all right. The thing has over a ton of aluminum in its airframe, much of it in the huge wing, which spans an inch under 78 ft. and boasts an area of 851.7 sq. ft. It is 50 ft. 8 in. long, stands 13 ft. 5 in. and has a tread of nearly 20 ft.

For all that, it's pretty light. It weighs only 7,500 lbs. empty. In fact, the Bushmaster would probably fly quite happily with a useful load exceeding its own empty weight, if no one were looking—and I'll bet a C-note to a bottlecap it's done exactly that a few times

in the Arctic hinterlands. It may be too much airplane to push around the airport ramp just to keep in shape, but it's nothing much for 1,350 Pratt & Whitney ponies swinging 101 in. Hartzells.

It gets off like a scalded dog. Factory specs list a 600 ft. takeoff distance empty, 850 ft. at gross, and 01V will prove it at the drop of a $15 bill—the price of a ride in her. In fact, LeMaster says it will get off in 400 ft. on a 60 degree F. day at gross, and after flying it, I wouldn't argue.

We jounced to the bottom of the hill, turned around and checked the mags, cycled the props and were ready to roll. "Why don't you follow me through on this one, and then we'll come back and you can try it," LeMaster said in my ear. I nodded. He shoved the throttles home, pushed the control column firmly forward—and the tail was up almost instantly.

With only 180 gallons of fuel and 500 lbs. of people on board, we were nearly empty. There was virtually no wind, the mercury hung in the 80s and the uphill grade was maybe three percent. The big airplane waddled 100 yards, LeMaster eased back slightly and we were off somewhere around the 400 ft. mark, indicating 65 mph, climbing in a flat attitude.

The Bushmaster, like the Ford, is no skyrocket on climb-out. Even empty as we were, we were never able to get better than 800 fpm out of it, and that only briefly before it settled back to 700. But LeMaster says it'll yield the same climb at gross on a hot day in Denver, and I don't doubt it. The thing is a lot like a riding-stable nag—it only has one gait.

We climbed to a thousand feet above the eastern Kansas prairie and leveled out, reducing to normal cruise power of 25 in. and 1950 rpm. Trim is slow, requiring considerable winding of the wheel, but very necessary. Without it, elevator pressures on this airplane are extremely high.

LeMaster says all controls are heavier than the

N7501V was the prototype for the Stout Bushmaster 2000 series, which now stands at two airplanes. It seems there's not much demand for 95 mph airliners/cargo haulers that can operate in and out of 850 ft. of ground at gross weight.

Ford. Little input is needed for slight changes in pitch attitude, however—a typical big-airplane characteristic.

In my first ninety-degree bank, I discovered this airplane gives whole new pages of meaning to the phrase, "control coordination." The control heaviness in all axes means the pilot flies with a lot of back, shoulder and leg muscle, and as soon as the wing starts down the nose tries to follow—necessitating immediate back pressure to keep an intended turn from ending up as a shallow spiral dive. Then, leveling out, you reverse the whole procedure, consciously easing the control column forward in the transition back to level flight.

At cruise, the IAS quickly stabilized at 95—5 mph faster than the Ford and due, possibly, to the fact that the Bushmaster's engines were cowled. At the 25x1,950 power setting, the airplane burns 60-65 gph, giving a safe range of 550 miles on its 360 gallon, three-tank capacity. It is quieter than a Ford, a tribute to the inclusion of sound-deadening insulation in the side panels of the fuselage and flight deck of this modernized airplane.

It is easier to trim than the Ford, too, the old window crank on the bulkhead behind the pilot having given way to a pedestal-mounted wheel and, unlike the Ford, it has both aileron and rudder trim, as well. Control cables to elevator, rudder and ailerons are internalized, rather than left hanging out in the breeze to ice up and increase a pilot's problems. The fin and rudder are taller and there's a new dorsal fin, all giving a bit more directional stability in all flight attitudes.

Childhood and adolescence are always more fun than maturity, particularly in retrospect. Perhaps that's why it's such fun to peer out of the narrow, angled windshield of a Ford or of the Bushmaster and see a round engine outthrust, rumbling away, then glance to the right and left to see two more slung beneath the wings, humming in the same rhythm.

The big trouble with this class of airplane is that there's not a whole lot you can do with it except take off and land, fly around a bit and do some reasonably uncomplicated coordination exercises. A few minutes trying to rock the wings while holding the nose on a point convinced me that's about as much fun as lifting weights, any day. So I abandoned the maneuver in favor of flying low, slow circles over Ottawa, Kansas, to impress the civilians, then headed back to the LeMaster strip.

The airplane stalls at 58 IAS—a good, honest, straight-ahead stall after considerable buffeting and groaning and general protesting, and it can be brought to the stall only by application of a great deal of muscle. But when it *does* break, the nose drops determinedly, and there's not much the pilot can do about it. It flies out of the stall within 200 ft. of altitude and is ready to do it again, if the pilot insists, but this isn't much fun, either.

Landing, as I'd expected, was a piece of cake. Power comes back to 15-17 in. MP, props go to 2000-2100 rpm, approach speed is 80 mph and sink rate is 200-300 fpm, with a very flat attitude. Then it's just a matter of flying her onto the runway and chopping the throttles as the wheels begin to roll.

LeMaster was very good about the whole procedure, considering. He sat there and didn't do a thing until the grass stems were flicking the wheels, then came in on the control column to assist in easing his baby back to earth.

I glanced back through the big empty cabin—wider by a foot and a half than its Ford ancestor—and for a moment I could almost visualize it in other, harder-working days, jammed full of musk oxen and Eskimos, skimming over the Bering Strait for a little clandestine trading with the Russians.

"They told us there's a shortage of musk oxen in Siberia," explained LeMaster, "and since there are plenty of them in Alaska, they'd load 'em in the Bushmaster, fly across and land on the ice near one of the settlements on the offshore islands, trading for furs, I suppose."

The Bushmaster began its North Country career flying supplies to the northern end of the Alaska Pipeline, but when a strike shut down work it was sold to a Fairbanks investor who leased it to fly supplies to more than a thousand Eskimos living inside the Arctic Circle—fuel, medicine, ammunition, even prefabricated houses—and flying out barrels of fish.

"We weren't too popular with the Eskimos when they found out we were thinking of buying their airplane," LeMaster recalled, shaking his head. The Eskimos, of course, didn't have a chance. Fate was at work again, the same fate that's kept LeMaster linked with tri-motors for twenty years.

It started back in 1959, when he and a partner were busy spraying small towns with then-legal DDT for mosquito control. Looking for a bigger airplane, they bought N8407, a 1930 Ford 4-AT, from Bob Johnson of Johnson's Flying Service in Missoula, Montana, and quickly found that "everywhere we'd go, it was front-page. It even got to be embarrassing." So, at the end of the 1960 spraying season, they installed bench seats in the Ford and began barnstorming across eastern Kansas and western Missouri. "We had more fun. . . ."

Everyone, it seemed, either had had their first ride in a Ford Tri-Motor or wished they had, and a lot of them were willing to pay $5 for the privilege. The partners got so involved with tri-motors, DDT spraying and barnstorming that they bought another in 1963—the last example of the high-wing, fabric-covered Stinson tris.

That fall, the partners split. The Ford stayed with the other man, the Stinson was sold and LeMaster got the spraying business, although he occasionally still flew the Ford somewhere for his former partner. But LeMaster was hooked on barnstorming, and when in 1972 he had a chance to buy a bigger Ford, a 5-AT, from American Airlines, he did. He spent a year just refurbishing it at Tulsa, Oklahoma, before he even ferried it home.

That was N414H, currently one of the three 5-ATs flying, and an airplane with a past typical of the breed. First flown Sept. 4, 1929, it was a company demonstrator until 1931, was flown on floats at the Detroit River Boat Races and the Great Lakes Yacht Club, served two years with Pan American Airways, carried passengers five years in Central and South America, hauled chicle in Guatemala and sprayed grasshoppers in Wyoming.

With LeMaster, it moved to more glamorous duties. Neil Sedaka rode in it; pressed for the chance. Neil Armstrong, first man on the moon, flew it for ten minutes; said he took his first ride in a Ford.

The Ford was more than just an airplane, it was an integral part of the LeMaster family. Diane LeMaster knew nothing of airplanes when she met and married Chuck. He'd described the first Ford to her, of course, and once he even drove to nearby Lawrence, Kansas, so she could get a look at old N8407. It was parked on the ramp, locked up, and they could only peek in the windows like any other tourists. "I was surprised it was so big," she said.

Then LeMaster agreed to take it to an air show somewhere, and Diane went along. She recalls leaving the house at 3 a.m., flying toward the dawn in the old airplane, staring mesmerized at the blue flames shooting from the short exhaust stacks of the pod-mounted engines slung beneath the wings. It is, she says, "unreal." And when the sky began to lighten and she watched the sunrise past the bulk of the engine and the huge, fixed main wheel dangling beneath it, "it was like being in another age."

When 414H came into their life shortly afterward, Diane helped clean it, polish it and add the new interior. And on the barnstorming circuit she became the ground person, selling tickets and answering questions. Together, the three of them criss-crossed the country and flew even into Canada. For four years, they were inseparable.

It was a shock, then, when the Ford was sold.

That was in 1977, and LeMaster admits, "I couldn't believe it, either." The plane went to Scenic Airlines, flying out of McCarran Field over downtown Las Vegas at $12 a seat. In the words of the movie, *Godfather*, they made him an offer he couldn't refuse. LeMaster doesn't want to say how much it was, but "it was staggering." He took it—but he was almost weeping when he loosed the tie-down ropes beneath the wings.

And then, just sixty days later, LeMaster tracked down another tri-motor in Alaska. He'd known there was one up there, somewhere.

It wasn't *really* a Ford, yet it was.

Technically, it was, of course, the Bushmaster 2000, built in California from the original Ford plans and slightly revised and modernized under direction of William B. Stout, guiding hand behind the Fords. Stout died before the project was completed, but it was nevertheless pushed through to type certification, then slid into limbo.

LeMaster located the owner in Fairbanks and asked if the airplane was for sale. The man said he hadn't thought about it; he said it was leased to an operator flying supplies to Arctic settlements. Still, he added, he was running for political office and needed campaign money. The airplane was only an investment, anyway. He'd sell.

By coincidence, the Bushmaster was based at Bethel, Alaska, only 140 miles from the fishing camp where the LeMasters already had accommodations— which meant LeMaster could pop over for a quick peek before paying for anything more than a purchase option on the airplane.

Painted in peeling yellow and brown and liberally smeared with engine oil and exhaust stains, the Bushmaster showed evidence of a hard life. But the airframe had only 1,200 hours total time and seemed as sound as the day it left California. Only the engines were tired. Very tired.

The purchase contract called for the plane's delivery in Ottawa, Kansas. It took the ferry crew thirty days and some thirty-five flying hours, and when the Bushmaster was tied down at the LeMasters' in the fall of 1977, it was not to fly again until Independence Day, 1978. "We flew it for the first time on July 4. It was quite a celebration for us."

In the interim, the Bushmaster spent most of its time looking like the centerpiece in a salvage yard.

The old oil-burning engines came off and zero-timed different ones were installed at a cost of $10,000 each. The propellers were overhauled. Seats were scrounged from Scenic Airlines and installed, along with a new interior. And the day it flew, LeMaster delivered it to Mena, Arkansas, to have the old

Dubbed One More Tri, *the Bushmaster was barnstormed across most of the continent by Chuck and Diane LeMaster of Ottawa, Kansas, in the late 1970s. As of 1990, this air-plane was in a museum, but the second example was still flyable. Power is supplied by three 450 hp Pratt & Whitney R–985s.*

paint stripped from the corrugated aluminum airframe.

The day before the 1978 EAA fly-in at Oshkosh, Wisconsin, a painter from town came out to LeMaster's and wrote "One More Tri" in bold black script below the cockpit—a legend decreed by LeMaster's son, Tony. He also wrote, of course, "LeMaster, Inc., Ottawa, Kan.," for Chuck LeMaster is a man who believes in publicizing his hometown.

The next day, right on schedule, Chuck LeMaster swung low over Lake Winnebago and rolled the Bushmaster's wheels on the same runway where he had planted 414H a year earlier.

"For nine days straight, I sat in that thing about seven hours a day," he said. He logged sixty-five hours, more than fifty-two of them hopping passengers around the Oshkosh area at $15 a seat (inflation having boosted the price since 1959).

"We had just as great a reception as ever," he said. "If traffic hadn't been so heavy, we would have broken all records at Oshkosh this year." The fact that N7501V isn't really a Ford seemed to make no difference. Indeed, even the control tower operators called it a Ford.

At any rate, LeMaster is finding he's just as much in demand with the new tri as with the old ones, and he made several appearances last fall along the eastern seaboard. In truth, now that the LeMasters have it, other people seem to love the Bushmaster more than they. They have not yet given it their hearts.

"It's cold," explained Diane LeMaster. "When we sold 414H we never anticipated even seeing another one. Our heart went with it, so to speak. We seem to have Fords in our future or something.

"I keep telling Chuck, 'There can't be another one out there.' When we sold that other one, it was like a child. We cried."

Still, would-be buyers already are hounding him to sell 01V, LeMaster reports. They're making him nervous. After all, he says, there would certainly be no way to replace the Bushmaster.

Except—he recalls saying as much to one of his mechanics one night as they relaxed and sipped coffee. The mechanic promptly disagreed. Said he has occasional glimpses into the future, and could foresee another such airplane for Charles A. LeMaster.

"I sure don't know where that one's comin' from," says LeMaster, who can recite the present whereabouts of every Ford tri-motor known to man.

But if worse came to worst and someone made him another offer he couldn't refuse, you can bet that within forty-eight hours after saying goodbye to 01V, Chuck LeMaster would be back on the telephone, tracking down that faint smell of flying Ford.
First printed in *Air Progress*, August 1979.

Chapter 11

Douglas C–47 Skytrain

The best airplane ever built

What could I possibly say about the DC–3 and C–47 that hasn't been said before?

The truth is that this airplane, like the clipper ship, the steam locomotive and the automobile, is a symbol of human civilization. As an industrial artifact, it is nearly perfect. As an endlessly adaptable means of transportation, it is nearly perfect. As a design, it is nearly perfect.

As a useful tool, it is less than perfect, but that's not the fault of the airplane. Rather, the peculiarities of the DC–3 reflect the airplane builders' disregard for cockpit ergonomics in the mid 1930s. If you were a pilot, it was assumed you could cope with a few design eccentricities. It was also assumed you enjoyed being climatically uncomfortable.

Like every other airman I've met with time in the airplane, I have a great affection for the Gooney Bird. If I were the Sultan of Brunei, this is another airplane I would own and fly regularly around the islands, perhaps, visiting my harem. . . .

Bill Dempsay led me through the starting drill, and as the No. 2 engine came to life with a sudden roar and a cloud of blue smoke, I cocked an ear out the window. "There's something wrong," I said. "It sounds like a handful of rocks in a gallon bucket."

Dempsay grinned. "That's just the counterweights in the prop slidin' around," he said. "That's normal. It'll smooth out at around 1200 rpm. Don't worry about it."

I was skeptical. It didn't sound normal to me. After all, N808Z had been sitting out there in the Arizona sun for God knew how long. It had put in more than fifteen years' service with the military, nearly that long with the Atomic Energy Commission and then had been flogged nearly to death by the US Department of Agriculture before its old bones had even been put out here in the sun to bake. Who knew what kind of shape it was really in?

A ferry permit was one thing; airworthiness might be something else again. I watched that engine and the prop hub for more than an hour. They remained dry as the desert under us. No sweat, literally. In fact, we were freezing to death.

A combination of spring weather and mountains had forced us up to 13,500 ft. and caused us to detour straight eastward over Amarillo, Texas, before swinging back northward. It was late April, already hot in the desert but downright frigid at this altitude. And the heating system didn't work—a common complaint among C-47s, as I was to discover.

Fortunately, I carried a light leather jacket in my gear. I quickly put it on. Dempsay, desert rat that he is, had nothing but his short-sleeved sport shirt.

"I'll give you $100 for that jacket," he said.

I declined.

He got up, rummaged around aft a while and came back wearing a section of the vinyl flight deck headliner he had unsnapped and wrapped around himself.

Shivering in unison, the three of us droned northeast—me, Dempsay and the airplane.

I made my first DC-3 landing in the dark, on a ferry permit, with feet so chilled they were numb, from the right seat, with Dempsay handling the gear, flaps, power and props for me and calling out the numbers. There was a slight bump when she touched down, but it was an acceptable effort in anybody's league, and she tracked straight down the runway.

I was still to learn that the venerable "Douglas racer," as Dempsay called it (after the predecessor DC-2 which placed second in the 1932 London-to-Melbourne MacRobertson race) is a mistress of uncertain temperament.

I had had four hours of herding a USAF C-47 around the sky some years earlier, and in the six hours we flew northeastward in 808Z, I refreshed my memories of the airplane's behavior. Properly trimmed, she paddled along at roughly three miles a minute, burning 1½ gallons of gas in the same period, placid as a Jersey cow.

Like the cow she could not be left unattended, for while stable she was inclined to wander—the reason an autopilot was standard in the C-47. Like the heater, this piece of equipment had long since vanished from 808Z.

As it has been for generations of pilots, the C-47 was my first "heavy" airplane, that is, one with a gross weight over the FAA's magic 12,500 lbs. Indeed, the C-47's listed empty weight is 18,200 lbs.—and its gross is 26,200, or a shade over thirteen tons. The military, in fact, flew them to 33,000 lbs., and there are cases on record of a couple of flights inadvertently made at better than eighteen tons!

Fortunately, I had had brief acquaintances with a Ford Tri-Motor, its slightly updated successor the Bushmaster 2000 and a Boeing 247 before I came to the Gooney Bird, so I knew something of what to expect. Predictably, she is no Piper Cub on the controls, though she is a contemporary of that aerial canoe. The long ailerons alone boast a total of 102.8 sq. ft. of area, the elevators 83.5 sq. ft., the rudder 46.65. The stabilizer spans 26 ft. 8 in.—more than some lightplanes I have flown—and has a root chord of 80.8 in.

Since controls are manual (cable-actuated units just like the Cub) forces tend to be heavy, and the airplane takes muscle to maneuver, though it is not so ponderous in roll as the Ford and Bushmaster. Surprisingly, required input seems not much heavier at its 178 knot (204 mph) redline than it does close to the stall.

Despite the control heaviness, it is so delicately balanced in cruise that the weight of a 100 lb. passenger moving from tail to nose or back again will force the pilot to readjust the big elevator trim wheel on the control pedestal to prevent the nose from rising or falling.

And, perhaps because of the 15½ degree sweepback on the leading edges of the wings outboard of the engines (for CG reasons), there is the slightest tendency for the airplane to wallow as it pads along. With 95 ft. of wing from tip to tip, that's a lot of wallow!

No matter whether climbing, descending or simply cruising along, a DC-3/C-47 (the two are identical, save for the reinforced floor, cargo door and paddle props on the latter) never departs far from a level attitude—unless it's stalled, and stalls are something not lightly practiced in this airplane. Not only does the nose pitch down determinedly, but it can drop a wing very smartly indeed. Recovery takes between 500 and 1,500 ft.

Because of the size of the airplane and the altitude needed for recovery, full stalls aren't practiced in crew training. Instead, the plane is flown only into the approach to a stall, then recovered. Stall speeds vary with weight, power and configuration, of course, but range from 68 knots (78 mph) at 27,000 lbs., clean, power off, to a tad over 50 KIAS (58 mph) at 21,000 lbs. with full flaps and power. Warning is a comparatively mild buffeting of the horizontal stabilizer, and is less in clean configuration or with power on. In turns, stall speed can exceed 87 knots/100 mph, and banked

Sometimes it seems every pilot in the world has flown the DC-3, and every story that can be told about it has been. All are affectionate. Quite simply, this is the best airplane ever made—and the most famous. Cramped, drafty, barely capable of 180 mph, it has no life limitation on the air-frame. Fifty-three years after its introduction, it remains the standard of comparison for all similar airplanes. At least 1,800 remain in operation throughout the world, and the airplane still was being used in combat in El Salvador in 1990.

stalls are not only more sudden, but the down wing drops rapidly. Ailerons remain effective to the stall. Gear position has no appreciable effect on stall behavior.

All that notwithstanding, maintain safe single-engine speed of 89 mph (77 knots) or better, and the airplane will perform medium banked turns into and away from the dead engine in excellent fashion and perfect safety.

In short, in the air, the DC-3 is a lady.

On the ground, however, she can sometimes be a bitch! In fact, it's been said that any monkey can fly it but it takes a pilot to taxi it—and there's a certain amount of truth to that. The gear tread is only 18½ ft., not a great deal on an airplane of this size, and the pilot's eyeballs are 12 ft. off the ground at rest—a shock to short airplane pilots. This means it's easy to find yourself taxiing faster than you think you are, and that's usually bad news. There's an awful lot of mass following you around!

For that reason, all DC-3s are equipped with a locking tailwheel, and normally they are taxied with it locked except when turning. In fact, mild taxi turns can be made with the lock still engaged, by use of rudder. It is a great mistake to try to take off or land with the tailwheel unlocked. I know a C-53 owner (VIP version of the C-47) who tried it one time, went off the runway, into a ditch and bent his airplane very expensively.

DC-3 pilots have three means of ground control: rudder, differential power and brakes, and they should be used in that order. Big airplane brakes heat rapidly. They also can be worn out rapidly. That's expensive. In fact, nearly everything about a DC-3 is expensive! Last time I checked, the fuel tank caps alone were $90 each.

Brakes, flaps, cowl flaps and gear are hydraulic, and more than one DC-3 crew has found itself trundling smartly off the end of a runway when a line broke someplace and the hydraulic pressure went to zip.

The airplane has 45x17 in. tires and lovely, soft, long-stroke oleos, and it's possible to put it on the runway so smoothly the only way you know you're there is by the gentle drag of rubber on the paving. In such cases, your maiden aunt can drink tea back in the tail cone and never spill a drop. On the other hand, it's also possible to get a mighty bounce—often followed by a hair-raising swerve.

The DC-3 will three-point nicely enough, but tail-low landings on the mains are normal procedure. That's to keep as much weight as possible off the tailwheel, and it's accomplished easier with half flaps. Half flaps are available at 99 knots/115 mph, and full forty-five-degree flaps at 97/112. Full flaps require a mighty round-out. Once the mains are on, normal procedure is to shove smartly forward on the control column, holding the tail off until it quits flying.

Normal approach is 120-125 knots (140-145 mph) and approximately 20 in. manifold pressure on downwind, 105-110 knots (121-127 mph) on base, 85-90 (98-104) down final and 80-85 (92-98) across the threshold, carrying 10-12 in. MP. All this is accomplished by a good deal of jockeying of the elevator trim.

Normal economy cruise of 500 bhp (usually around 30 in. by 1700 rpm, depending on temperature and altitude) produces fuel consumption of 88 gph and endurance, on 804 gallons, of about nine hours (allowing a very small amount for climb) or a

It's sometimes said of the Gooney Bird that "any monkey can fly it, but it takes a pilot to taxi it." There's some truth to this. Also you'll make five landings in a row so smooth only the gentle drag of rubber announces you're down—and the sixth landing will humble you for weeks. Used as every possible kind of airliner, cargo plane, jump plane, bomber, attack airplane (Puff, the Magic Dragon), spray plane, executive aircraft and smuggler, Jimmy Doolittle called it "without doubt the most versatile fixed-wing aircraft ever built." Dwight Eisenhower ranked it along with the bulldozer, the Jeep and the 2½ ton truck as the items "most vital to our success" in World War II.

When the DC–3 was introduced, Walter Jamoneau was just rounding the wingtips and tailplane of the Taylor Cub. Mussolini's airmen were bombing Ethiopian tribesmen. Chrysler had introduced the Airflow, and Swing was the thing. And Mister Mulligan *had just posted its amazing speed record. The 10,721 DC–3s and their military derivatives were built, plus a couple thousand Lisunov Li–2s, the Russian rip-offs. Today, remanufacturing centers for the "Dooglas" are in operation in the United States, Poland and Taiwan. This amazing airplane is certain to fly on well into the twenty-first century.*

still-air range of around 1,500 miles. Climb power, it should be noted, consumes twice as much fuel.

Procedure is to feed the left engine off the left tanks, the right engine off the right tanks, and to run off the mains for at least the first hour to make room for return fuel, then switch to the auxiliaries. Since the airplane has effective three-control trim any imbalance is easily corrected, and both engines can be run off any tank. In an engine-out situation, the plane can be trimmed to hold the dead engine up five degrees and it will fly very stably hands off. In fact, the docile, thoroughly predictable nature of the DC-3 in flight simply can't be overstressed.

Twenty five years ago, a C-47 en route across the central United States one dark night tangled with a thunderstorm and lost its radios to lightning. The crew flew on until the fuel got low, then set the autopilot and bailed out over northern Oklahoma. The airplane flew on northeastward until the engines quit, then landed itself gear up in a field twenty miles south of my hometown. Because the gear extends from the wells when retracted, the only damage was a pair of bent props. A crew of local airmen went to the site, jacked it up, checked it over, hung a couple of new props—and flew it out!

The airplane's systems are just as simple and reliable as its performance. Our Combat Air Museum in Topeka, Kansas acquired two C-47s from surplus government sources, and has managed to keep one in the air most of the time for better than five years now despite a continual critical shortage of knowledgeable volunteer mechanics. I tell people that maintaining

an airplane this big and this complex is like maintaining a thirty-unit apartment house, and that's not far off the mark. Nevertheless, nothing critical ever seems to go wrong. Oh, we did blow a cylinder the other day—but that's more to be blamed on the three seasons of sky diving we did with the airplane and the way the pilot flew it than anything else. The same fellow burned up a couple of starter motors one winter when he persisted in trying to start cold engines against advice.

The 1,200 hp fourteen-cylinder twin-row Pratt & Whitney R-1830 radial has to be one of the most reliable aero engines ever built anywhere by anyone. Old hands swear if God had meant airplanes to have flat engines, P&W would have made them that way.

On the other hand, an engine that size has to be babied somewhat, because there's lots of metal mass flinging itself around out there on the wing, and power changes are best made gradually to avoid overstressing something important. In fact, it's a good idea never to go below square (manifold pressure versus rpm) until you're over the threshold. As for maximum power, 48 in. and 2700 rpm is allowable for takeoff, though we try to hold it at around 45 in.—no problem at the weights we fly.

Each engine has a twenty-nine-gallon oil tank, and twenty-five gallons is carried to provide for expansion room. All radials should use a little oil, and most of them will leak some, too. If it doesn't, old round-engine men begin to wonder.

Despite all that simplicity and reliability, the DC-3 shows its age in the complexity of the cockpit drill. An A-26 Invader from the same maker eight years later, for example, is stone simple to fly compared to a DC-3. The cockpit of a Gooney Bird is a busy place!

To illustrate, to start the engines, you must go from fuel valves (either side of the central pedestal) to props and throttles (atop the pedestal) to electrical master (overhead left) to hydraulics to magneto master (overhead and forward) to fuel boost (overhead right; one each engine) to inertia starter and primer (overhead) to individual engine magnetos (overhead forward) to mixture control (atop pedestal).

Hydraulic cowl flaps are operated by rotating handles on the right cockpit side panel; can be set at "open," "closed" or "trail," and must then be rotated back to an intermediate "off" click stop to relieve the pressure in the lines.

The gear has a down latch in the middle of the floor between pilot and copilot stations, and a long lever that controls hydraulic pressure, extending into the aisle from the bulkhead behind the copilot. To raise the gear, the idea is to flip off the pivoting latch lock with your thumb, pull up the latch, then reach back and pull the lever out and up. When the gear has cycled, the lever must be reset to neutral before the red gear light will come on.

Going back down, the procedure is reversed, except the hydraulic lever is pulled out and thrust down first. Then, when the pressure on the hydraulic gauge comes back up, the latch is pressed flat and the lock flips into place. To get a green light, put the hydraulic lever in neutral.

It's possible to fly this bird solo, from the right seat—except that, to work the gear, you have to bend down well below the level of the windshield to reach the latch.

Then, of course, there are lots of other things, like the tailwheel lock (underside of the pedestal), the throttle friction knob (pedestal left), generators, inverters (overhead), various lighting and radio switches and—well, you get the idea.

In the A-26, by contrast, everything "falls readily to hand," as the British say. The only thing you have to look around for there is a hydraulic sight gauge behind a panel in an aft bulkhead, and most of the time you don't even have to worry with that. As for something like the Ford, well, the only thing different from a Piper Cub is that you have three engines and three of everything pertaining to them.

And the DC-3 has a few handling peculiarities. For one thing, since there's very little of anything forward of the windshield, there's nothing much to align with the runway center line for takeoffs and landings, and it may take an hour or so to get square with the environment. For another, we've always been taught that when taxiing, you deploy your flight controls as if to climb into the wind or dive away from it.

Well, that last may not work in the DC-3! The ailerons are so long and have so much surface, it's possible to find them acting like sails when deployed—and taking you where you don't want to go.

There are times, too, when it's easy to forget there's 64½ ft. of airplane following you around. Remember that fellow who burned up the starter motors? I saw him swing the tail around just a bit one day—and knock a gas pump 8 in. out of plumb. And I was riding in the back one day when he and another fellow landed at a little strip in Texas (by mistake), bounced, swerved, went clear off the runway, up a hill and back down. And he's got something over 1,000 hours in C-47s, now.

None of that's happened to me yet. But I've only got 60+.

Despite all its faults, though, the old Gooney Bird grows on you. Like everyone else who was ever lucky enough to spend time in that cramped cockpit, I've learned to love it, and when I taxied past a graveyard of derelict C-47s at San Juan, Puerto Rico, a while back, it saddened me for hours. I fly the old bird every chance I get, and wish I had more. But at $200 an hour for gas and oil, it's not the kind of thing you play with on Sunday afternoon, just for sport.

One thing I'll bet money on: the DC-3 will still be flying, somewhere, in the 21st century!
First printed in *Air Classics*, Jan. 1986.

Chapter 12

Consolidated PBY Catalina

Adventures of the Amazon cats

The PBY is another of those airplanes you have to live with a while to learn to love.

This fifty-year-old design is slow, exceedingly heavy on the controls, awkward to maneuver and ungainly in appearance from nine-out-of-ten viewing angles. The cockpit shares the acoustic principles of a violin, and inhabiting it is a painful experience. It is downright dangerous in a crash.

Yet the Catalina is one of the more useful airplanes ever built, for it will drone along for fourteen hours or more on its 1,700–plus gallons of gasoline, operate from either land or sea and haul enough of a load to make the whole thing worthwhile.

Indeed, the US Navy never found a completely satisfactory replacement—and neither have its various civil users since. Perhaps that's why half a hundred are still around—in odd corners of the world—and why the price keeps inching upward.

As of 1990, sellers were asking half a million dollars for the old "P-boat." And after all, was that exorbitant for such an eminently satisfactory RV?

Besides, she's such a friendly old bird.

We were perhaps seventy-five minutes out of Belem, Brazil, 150 nautical miles from liftoff and one degree north of the Equator when 6509, 2,000 yards ahead and as far to our right, veered seaward and climbed to clear a building mass of clouds in our path.

David Tallichet swung a few degrees to the left and shed a couple hundred feet of altitude for the same reason.

It was the last we saw of 6509 that day.

The lead ship, 6551, had vanished in the haze ahead fifteen or twenty minutes earlier.

Our single radio had quit receiving fifteen minutes after departure from Val de Caeš International Airport, and we had just flown off the edge of our sole WAC chart (scale: thirteen nautical miles (nm) per inch) ten minutes earlier. We were left with a single six-year-old GNC chart I'd brought along—scale: 68 nm/in.! We had no clear idea where we were, except that we were somewhere over the drowned land just beyond the north bank of the Amazon River.

Perhaps it was just as well. The WAC chart had not been particularly comforting. It was dotted with legends warning, "relief data incomplete," and the longest of several emergency landing strips depicted on the huge Ilha de Marajo (nearly as large as New Hampshire and Vermont combined), which we had just skirted, was 900 meters—about 3,000 ft. Most were on the order of 2,000 ft., or less; hardly the place to try to set down a stricken sixteen-ton PBY Catalina!

Besides, I hadn't seen any of them.

What I *had* seen were God's own plenty of trees! I was to see a lot more. . . .

I had seen my share of jungle before, but nothing like this—endless miles of nothing but trees like the hairs on my head, interspersed near the coast by occasional reedy savannas where a few cows and horses at the rare *fazenda* grazed in hock-deep water, doubtless hosting numbers of fat leeches in the process.

The Amazon rain forest is the largest continuous jungle in the world, and the oldest vegetation. The result of 100 million years of uninterrupted diversifi-

First flown in 1935, the "P-boat" was considered obsolete by the outbreak of World War II, yet it proved to be one of the war's few indispensable machines. It was a PBY that found and tracked the Bismarck, seven months before the United States entered the war. It was a PBY that found the Japanese fleet before the battle of Midway. PBYs sank Japanese shipping in the Pacific and German submarines in the Atlantic, and rescued downed airmen from hostile waters.

cation, it consists of a bewildering assemblage of countless species of trees, mixed together so densely that perpetual darkness covers the forest floor. The trees average 150 to 200 ft. in height, punctuated by an occasional taller giant.

About two-thirds of the world's oxygen is produced by earth plants, the other third by plankton and sea vegetation. As much as half of all the plant-generated oxygen on earth may come from this greenbelt, certainly twenty-five percent of it.

Tallichet leaned over and shouted in my ear, "If you went down 10 miles inland, I don't think you'd ever find your way to the coast." I nodded solemn agreement, and shouted back, "There are things in there you wouldn't want to meet in the daytime, let alone at night."

The dank, swampy depths of the rain forest harbor an incredible variety of living creatures, most of them hungry. There are stinging, biting, bloodsucking, disease-bearing insects, vampire bats, jaguars, poisonous frogs, bushmasters, *fer de lances* and the green anaconda, an amphibious tree-climbing constrictor that the Brazilians claim may on rare occasions reach 40 ft. in length and nearly 900 kilograms (about one ton) in weight.

As for the slow brown rivers, they are infested with crocodiles, alligators, caimans, the vicious flesh-eating piranha, catfish large enough to gulp a child, sharks, giant turtles and who knows what else.

Clearly, it was no place for a Kansan!

Flying a few hundred feet over that dense green mat, it was impossible not to speculate on our probable fate if we were to crash into it.

My newfound friend, 1st Sgt. Jorge Cantanheda Franca, who had spent 8,000 hours as a flight engineer in PBYs, had crashed six times during that career, including once over the jungle when both engines quit simultaneously after vibration jiggled a crossfeed valve and shut off all fuel flow. The pilot was killed, the copilot mortally injured (par for the course, in the PBY). Franca survived ten days in the jungle, alone—but he was half Indian, and grew up along the river near Manaus, hunting with bow and poison-tipped arrows. I doubted a prairie gringo could do the same—assuming I survived the crash, of course.

It reminded me of comments the day before by two of the Brazilians.

My escort officer, 2nd Lt. Roberto da Costa, and I had been sheltering in a hangar while Major Wuerzler was off someplace trying to dig up our lone WAC chart. We were watching a fine drizzle which reduced visibility to perhaps a mile. Suddenly Costa, a handsome, earnest twenty-four-year-old Belem native who spoke good basic English, turned to me and said, "I admire your courage."

Surprised, I laughed. "No," he said. "I'm serious. I really do! I admire the courage of all of you."

I smiled. "Well, thanks," I said, "but I think you spell that 'stupidity.'"

Later that night, again abruptly, Franca brought up the same subject.

"All of Belém admires what you do," he said, as we sat relaxing with a cold beer on a hotel patio at the jungle's edge. "Everybody here in Belém say that you are a crazy man to fly the Cat. They don't have the courage to fly the Cat as you did. All military men here admire you. I'm going to pray for you."

"Lt. Costa said much the same thing earlier today," I replied, "but I didn't take him too seriously. It's just a ferry flight to Florida; no big deal." I told him what Costa had said, and my reply.

Franca leaned forward earnestly. "It is true," he said. "There is not a pilot in the Brazilian Air Force who would do what you are doing. I admire you. All of

Brazilians operated these amphibian PBYs up and down the Amazon and other tropical rivers for more than 40 years. The Catalinas finally grew so weary the FAB feared to fly them and parked them at Belem. Years later, a crew of crazy Americans came along and flew them home!

you." And he gestured around the little group of Yankees.

Franca, of course, had been right in the airplane with us on that first test flight.

But I recalled now that the commanding officer had declined an invitation to make one last flight in the Cats, which after all had served his country faithfully for over four decades. I began to wonder if he knew something we didn't. I knew they'd taken the PBYs out of service over two years before, when only six remained (including one salvaged from the river bottom and towed to Belém), but I'd assumed it was because they'd been ordered to go to the new, indigenously produced Embraer *Bandeirante*.

Maybe they simply didn't trust the old amphibians anymore.

The Amazon is the world's mightiest river. It begins in the Andean foothills of northeastern Peru and flows some 3,900 miles eastward through the jungles of Brazil before emptying into the South Atlantic.

It drains an area two-thirds as large as the United States and contains more water than the Mississippi, the Nile and the Yangtze rivers combined. At its mouth, it is ninety miles wide and averages 100 ft. deep for 200 miles upstream, reaching a depth of more than 350 ft. in many places. Ocean-going vessels travel 2,300 miles upstream!

By now, I could see how it got so big.

In the five days we had been in Belém, it had rained every day, usually beginning just about noon and often lasting for an hour or more. Typically, it rained so hard visibility was cut to 100 yards for part of that time.

"Yep, that's a real frog strangler," remarked Bob Stirm one day as he and I huddled under a carport. "A gully-washer!" Colonel Stirm, a retired USAF fighter pilot, was no stranger to tropical rain forests. He spent 6½ years in the Hanoi Hilton after his F–105 was shot down over North Vietnam.

Stirm indicated a point near our feet. "The water's still rising, too," he added. I nodded agreement. "I asked Lt. Costa earlier if it rained like this all the time. He told me just this month."

Later, though, I learned the Amazon basin receives more than 60 in. of rain per year, and is usually flooded from November until May. The river level at Manaus, a thousand miles upstream, may rise more than 50 ft. during the rainy season.

At the other end of Julio Cesár Airport, within the confines of the Brazilian Air Force's Parque de Material Aeronautico de Belém, were the hulking shapes that had brought us here: four Consolidated PBY-5A Catalinas, twin-engine flying relics of World War II.

The US Navy came to Belém in 1942, to build a small base and mount coastal patrols out into the Atlantic. In 1944, they handed over the facility (now Julio Cesár and the Parque) and thirty-one PBYs to newly trained Brazilian crews and departed, leaving to them the job of defending the northeast coast from the encroachments of hostile Axis submarines and commerce raiders.

With peace, in 1945, the Brazilians stripped guns and bomb racks from the P-boats and used them to help develop the interior, bringing medicine and supplies from Belém and Manaus to remote settlements. For more than thirty-six years, the PBYs flew their humanitarian missions up and down the Amazon and its 200-odd tributaries. It was late 1981 when the survivors finally were removed from service.

One is already in a museum in Rio de Janeiro. Number 6525, the one salvaged from the river, was slated to go on a pylon at nearby Val de Caes. Los Angeles businessman and warbird collector David Tallichet and Maurice Skinazi, his partner in the enterprise, bought the remaining four and a warehouse full of spares.

We—eight US pilots—were to ferry them back to Orlando, Florida.

We hoped.

So far, events had not gone entirely according to plan. Skinazi, a long-time Brazilian resident who had returned some months earlier to oversee this enterprise, had reported the airplanes ready to go, down to signed ferry permits, and summoned us all to Belém. We found upon arrival that they were not ready, ferry permits notwithstanding. It took four more days and the efforts of all of us, plus the dedicated nonstop labor of some fifteen men of the *1st Esquadrão* de Transporte Aereo, even to launch them on test flights.

Batteries collapsed from age and overuse, and there were no spares. In 09 and 51, we finally substituted pairs of 12 volt, 180 amp diesel truck batteries hooked in series. "You could weld with that," remarked Republic Airlines senior captain Roy Degan with awe. "Yeah," replied Roger Phelan, a two-tour Vietnam veteran C-130 pilot and Tallichet's director of aviation, "and I'm afraid we will."

An electrical fire inside 09 during a test of a newly installed radio sent mechanics scurrying for a fire extinguisher and set things back an afternoon. Somehow, 6510 seemed to have an aileron that still needed recover. Three different engines suffered minor illnesses, all of which had to be traced and treated.

Things were complicated enormously by the fact that none of the crews spoke even rudimentary Portuguese, and few Brazilians speak enough English for any meaningful exchange. Fortunately, Jorge Franca was the outstanding exception. A one-time welterweight Brazilian Golden Gloves champion and veteran of twenty-nine years in the *Força Aerea Brasileira*, the forty-eight-year-old NCO had mastered fairly fluent English through self-study and a two-month exposure to two US mechanics who had worked on the airplanes before we arrived. Without Franca, the mission would have been incredibly difficult indeed.

As it was, four of the first five test flights ended badly.

Three were terminated by wobbling nose wheel assemblies as the airplanes accelerated down the runway.

The fourth airplane, 6510, was the only one with a good nose wheel assembly. It took off without incident—but during its first turn, the left propeller ran away and could only be controlled with the feathering button. During its second turn, a fuel pump drive sheared, taking the oil pump with it, killing the right engine. The electric boost pump revived it long enough to complete the traffic pattern and land, but metal shavings in the oil screen showed the engine was ruined.

We left that one where we found it.

There was also the matter of the bureaucracy.

The Brazilians believe in a great deal of paperwork, most of which can be done only by a clutch of officials halfway across town, none of whom comprehend any English at all.

We learned once again that it takes a great deal of gesticulating, sign language and document-waving to convey the information contained in a simple declarative sentence.

Nevertheless, eventually three airplanes were positioned on the ramp at Val de Caes, three miles away. They no longer bore the FAB numbers 6509, 6551 and 6520, but the US registrations N4582T, N4583A and N4583B respectively, on their tails.

They—and we—were going home.

Our flight plan was simple. For mutual protection, we would fly loose formation, keeping one another in sight. And we would keep to the coast, with the jungle under our left wings, the water under our right, so if anything went wrong, we could ditch on the beach. It was our only real alternative. No one searches for you more than a mile inland, and the Brazilians had warned the hull integrity of the old amphibians was compromised. They predicted we could expect them to float no more than thirty minutes before sinking. And we had been unable to obtain

Cruising at 115 to 120 knots, the PBY has an endurance of 14½ to 18 hours and a still-air range of 2,500 statute miles, making it ideal for long-distance missions. However, there are problems. The flight deck is like the sound chamber of a cello, and after 17 hours in the air, pilot and copilot vibrate so badly they don't know whether they're walking or flying. And in a crash, the cockpit usually collapses, killing both.

life rafts. Each man was equipped only with an individual life vest—which was never tested.

We lifted off into a damp, overcast morning and swung left over the Guama River harbor, a two-mile-wide offshoot of the Amazon system, heading northeastward toward the South Atlantic some thirty miles away. Twelve hours' flight time ahead lay Port of Spain, Trinidad, off the coast of Venezuela, and its Piarco International Airport.

Less than two hours later, we were alone, far over the jungle, with visibility down to perhaps a mile and the ceiling pressing us downward.

I cocked a wary ear at the twin Pratt & Whitney R-1830s singing a duet over our heads, reassured by their steady roar. I had already been back through the airplane twice, checking for oil and hydraulic leaks, fuel siphoning, smoke or other problems, and found none. Even the panel looked good—what remained of it.

The gyros had long since died in harness, of course, but that was to be expected. More serious was the lack of any cylinder head temperature indication, but oil pressure and temperature gauges all worked. So did the hydraulic pressure, manifold pressure and tachometers.

What did it matter that the fuel and oil quantity indicators lay stubbornly at zero? I had used the marked wooden fuel stick to measure the tank contents at Val, and knew we had departed with 1,700 gallons of fuel in the 1,750 gallon bladders. I had flight-planned a gallon per nautical mile, plus reserve. We had more gasoline than daylight. I'd had each engine brought up to sixty gallons of oil each, and from their dry condition earlier they seemed unlikely to burn more than twenty or so by Trinidad (I was right; they only used a gallon per engine per hour).

As long as the engines kept churning, I wasn't really concerned. I knew roughly where we were, knew the magnetic compass was fairly accurate and knew we had only to turn right and intercept the coast eventually. In fact, I was more amused than anything.

I had been in these situations before, usually with Tallichet, and I was already convinced he is not fated to die in an airplane. Once again, it was a case of, "Yesterday I'd never been in a PBY; today I are a PBY pilot." A skill to be picked up en route, of course, on a ferry permit, far from home, in an airplane with only the sketchiest of logged history. . . .

I lounged in the copilot's seat, watching the green jungle and the wheeling birds close below, and thought about PBYs. I'd never done so before; largely, I guess, because they never seemed glamorous. They are not pretty airplanes from many angles, and sitting high above a pair of them making passes at the crowd last fall at Harlingen, Texas, they had seemed more like huge, awkward, incredibly slow gliders than anything.

But they are hell for stout, as they'd have to be to survive forty-plus years in anyone's military transport service; comfortable and somehow friendly to an airman. I was impressed.

The subject of a 1934 patent by designer Isaac M. Laddon and first flown in 1935, the "P-boat" was considered obsolete by the outbreat of World War II, yet ultimately it became an indispensable tool for both the United States and its allies. First built as a flying boat, an amphibian version flew in 1939, and deliveries commenced the same month the Japanese attacked Pearl Harbor.

When production ceased at war's end, output amounted to more than 3,300, from three US factories, two in Canada and one in Russia.

It was a Lend-Lease British PBY (with an American "observer" as copilot) that found and tracked the German battleship *Bismarck* in May 1941, more than seven months before the United States was officially involved in a shooting war. A Catalina discovered and shadowed the Japanese fleet at Midway. Whole squadrons were used for coordinated multi-plane night torpedo attacks against enemy shipping at Guadalcanal, Midway, Santa Cruz and in the Aleutians.

"Black Cat" squadrons, operating in the Solomons and New Guinea in 1942 and 1943, were the most effective US weapons for interdicting the small Japanese resupply freighters active in those areas at night. With their 2,500 mile range and ready availability, they were invaluable for anti-submarine patrols. In fact in 1943, a FAB PBY-5 attacked and sank a German sub off Rio, at the cost of an engine and two wounded crewmen from anti-aircraft fire (if I did not misunderstand, our airplane, 6520, also was engaged in wartime coastal patrol). A USN Catalina pilot earned the Medal of Honor for rescuing a total of twenty-five downed airmen from Kavieng Harbor at New Ireland under hostile fire, in a single mission.

Those are just examples. The list of achievements seems endless. The PBY evacuated troops, hauled supplies, landed agents, scouted forward bases and so on. It's quite a service record!

Quickly phased out of US military duty after World War II, the PBY just as quickly found new roles hauling people and supplies in watery areas, fighting fires in forested ones, exploring remote corners of uncharted jungles and searching for ore deposits with MAD gear.

Nearly all the pure boats are gone now, but Gianfranco "Denny" Ghiringhelli, the remarkable thirty-year-old Californian who served as our check pilot on this trip (and, finally, had to return early via airliner to meet a job commitment) said ninety/PBYs still remain in license—and in service—throughout the world. He should know. A week before arriving in Belem, he was flying PBYs in Australia!

With its bowlegged stance, goofy frontal grin and huge parasol wing, the PBY-5A is an ungainly looking thing, 10 in. over 63 ft. in length, another 2 in. over 20 ft. in height and with a wingspan of 104 ft. It weighs around 9½ to ten tons, empty, depending on installed equipment, and the 1,400 sq. ft. wing lifts a normal gross weight of 33,975 lbs. (max 35,300). The twin P&Ws are rated at 1,200 hp for takeoff and 1,050 max continuous, and provide a normal economy cruise (weak mixture) of 115 to 120 knots, depending somewhat on the condition of the airplane. With full fuel, it has a cruise endurance of 14½ hours at worst and can be coaxed to about eighteen (rpm 1900 or less).

For a pilot it takes some getting used to, but after a while, he's likely to come to admire it.

The airplane is extremely heavy on the controls; ponderous, in fact—probably demanding as much muscle as any machine I have ever flown, including the Ford 5-AT Tri-Motor. Furthermore, ours seemed to have been one of those fished out of the river and refurbished, for it persisted in flying sideways, the ball three-quarters out to the left and the left wing still heavy despite full aileron trim. At the end of a day at the controls, my deltoid muscles were boil-sore from holding that wing up!

(In Belém, I had been introduced to Sub-Officer Eraldo Ribeiro Barbosa, the man who recovered a Catalina that had lain sixteen days at the bottom of the river, spent forty days repairing it, and sent it flying out, original engines and all!)

On the ground, the PBY sits at a negative angle of attack on its short nose wheel, and normal technique is to accelerate to 50-55 knots and apply enough back pressure to raise the nose about one to 1½ degrees above the horizontal, hauling it off the ground 5-10 knots later.

The book gives an initial climb rate of 600-800 fpm at 85 knots (also Vmc), but since no one had an airplane with working cylinder head temperature gauges, we took the Brazilians' advice and used a cruise-climb of 110 knots, at the good old C-47 power setting of 36in.x2350 rpm, which yielded about 500 fpm. Cruise settings ranging from 26 to 32 in. at 2050 rpm produce indicated airspeeds of 90 to 120 knots (104-138 mph).

A curious thing about the PBY is its sensitivity to angle of attack. A one-degree shift produces an IAS change of 8-10 knots, pretty much regardless of power setting. It is one airplane that's very important to keep "on the step." The PBY most definitely *has* a step, too!

Rudder and elevator trim controls are mounted on a dangling overhead quadrant, together with the throttle and prop levers, and are sensitive, powerful and easy to use. Strangely, the mixture quadrant is on the bulkhead behind the copilot. Aileron trim is located on the instrument panel in front of the pilot. In the case of 20, its actual effectiveness was hard to determine. It never did us much good. Degan complained that the elevator trim on his airplane was misaligned by six degrees—so perhaps it was as much a matter of who'd worked on it as anything else.

The PBY is a rudder airplane, demanding the pilot lead with large amounts of it rolling into and out of any turn to overcome the high degree of adverse yaw in the big wing. We never had a chance to full-stall the airplane in flight, but Ghiringhelli, who has, said it is gentle and straight-ahead, with no tendency to fall off on a wing.

Lacking flaps, and assuming the trouble-prone hydraulic gear system works as advertised, landing a PBY on a runway is the essence of simplicity. Downwind, the boost pumps are turned on and the gear extended as the airplane is slowed to 90 KIAS, carrying 15-20 in. MP. Eighty knots feels good on base and final, adding back pressure as you arrive in ground effect and touching down on the mains at 60-65 KIAS, throttling back as you do so.

At that point, it's necessary to add increasing amounts of muscle to hold the nose off as the airplane slows, until finally the elevator stalls out around 40 knots and the nose wheel thumps the asphalt. The big rudder is fully effective until the nose wheel is down.

Taxiing is easy, but only with both engines running. I tried to move 20 (alias 83B) at night on the ramp at Piarco with only the left engine running, and found I couldn't get it to go straight because the hydraulic pump was on the right engine, and residual brake pressure was inadequate for the task.

I had about fifteen minutes to think of some of these things, to watch the birds fishing in the swamps below, to stare back at two men who stopped poling their dugout to stand and watch, when Tallichet turned to me and said, "Want to fly?"

"Sure," I replied, and took the controls, picking up my already-planned compass heading. We ducked through a few light rain showers, avoided several heavier ones and finally struck the coast in improving visibility, probably not far from Amapa, the only paved airport in that part of Brazil—after more than an hour of flying over who knows where.

Originally, PBYs had a flat-topped bow turret and a pair of waist blisters, all with machine guns. Martial trappings were removed after World War II, and the airplanes spent most of their career flying emergency and supply missions into the wild green interior of Brazil. One airplane sank in the Amazon River and was reclaimed 16 days later by inflating many inner tubes. It flew out—and we flew it back to Florida, badly out of rig.

We thundered across the Rio Oiapoque and into French Guiana; past Cayenne, past notorious Devil's Island, trending ever westward as we rounded the shoulder of the South American continent. The land began to change. No longer was it all flat and sodden, within 50 ft. of sea level. Now there were hills, some of them quite respectable ones of several hundred feet, and stretches where files of green-clad bluffs stood dipping stubby toes into the faded khaki waters of the South Atlantic.

We passed Paramaribo, neat and European-looking from the air, and one of the few signs of human influence in Suriname; vaulted a long bay a few miles on the seaward side and found ourselves in Guyana, where Tallichet took the controls again and edged inland once more, over a genuine paved road through occasional roadside settlements to sprawling Georgetown, not too far from Jonestown of religious suicide/massacre notoriety. I slid back the side window and watched the passing panorama a thousand feet below, luxuriating in the closeness of some sort of civilization. I have rarely felt the need for the presence of others, but now, somehow, it seemed comforting.

I took the airplane again over the port area of Georgetown and angled across the broad island-clotted mouth of the Essequibo River, dodging white build-ups of afternoon cumulus and occasional rain showers as we skimmed low over jungle as inhospitable as any I'd seen yet—so thick a dead tree couldn't even fall down.

Rarely—perhaps an average of every 100 miles or so as we beat our way along the coast—we passed lonely farmsteads, usually about ten acres hacked out of the jungle along the bank of some minor river that, for us, shall remain forever nameless.

Island hopping through the Caribbean in a PBY is a marvelous adventure, but in this case the safety margin provided by an amphibian was illusory. The Brazilians warned that none of the four would float more than half an hour, and we had no survival equipment on board. Only one aircraft had a navigation radio. It led me to speculate on how many man-eating sharks there might be per square mile in the sparkling blue water.

A few, sited in scarce and slightly more hospitable Brazilian savannas, were of eighty acres or more, with up to fifty head of white cattle, as many as a dozen horses. All were cut off from the world and from other men except by water. And, in the past, except for the possible visit of what the Brazilians called *pata choca*, the spread-winged mother duck, as they dubbed the PBY. Now, as we approached, wrapped in the thunder of our passage, they often emerged to watch the airplane's last flight overhead.

As we flew along the massive, swampy delta of Venezuela's great Orinoco River, Tallichet, who had appropriated the GNC chart, waved me abruptly to the right. Obediently, I swung away across the open sea—more relaxed, now, after nearly eleven hours of perfect performance from the engines—and aimed the bow toward Trinidad.

We sailed across the low hills of that lovely island, split the VOR station squarely, and landed at Piarco after 11½ hours in the air, second of our flight of three to touch down. Immediately ahead was 09, crewed by Degan, Phelan, and Pat Epps, an Atlanta area FBO and Degan's adventuring partner in other climes.

Immediately behind was 51, flown by Stirm and retired Coast Guard Commander Art Perry. They had suffered a hydraulic leak that forced them to crank the gear down by hand. This is no small task in a PBY, but apparently it happened often enough to make mandatory the issue of a set of two special tools for the job.

The first, clipped to the hull at the flight engineer's station, is an over-center lever that must be placed with one end in a bracket inside the airplane, the other in a special dimple on the main gear outside, and thrust smartly downward, thus flinging the gear out and down into lock.

The second, stowed forward, is a hefty pole with a blunt point at one end and a locking collar and ratchet at the other. The idea here is to thrust the pointy end into a hole between the pilot's and copilot's seats and release the uplock, then crawl forward and in front of the copilot's rudder pedals, fit the collar over a protruding steel bar, lock it and ratchet down the gear with the cogwheel on the end of the bar. It takes a good, braced position and lots of muscle, all applied within a space of roughly 2½x3 ft. In happier days, it was a two-man job (PBYs used to carry a crew of eight or nine). Once the gear is believed down and locked, the ratchet collar is released and the pointy end of the pole is thrust into a second, angled hole farther toward the bow. It must go in up to a small sheet metal collar. If it does not, it's back to the cogwheel!

Poor Perry was almost a candidate for a Trinidad hospital before he got that nose wheel down and locked.

We had risen at 4 a.m. to leave Belém at sunup (departure clearances delayed us an hour), and we had a block time in the airplane of nearly twelve hours—but entry clearances, airplane servicing and other chores kept us at the airport until 10 p.m.

I unlocked the door of my hotel room about 10:30 and flipped on a light, to be greeted by a cockroach big enough to pull a pony cart, poised on my bedside table waving his antennae in greeting. I was too tired to care. I dropped my suitcase on the floor, turned out the light, locked the door and went for a long-delayed meal. Falling into bed about midnight, I slept like a log for 2½ hours. Then, rising, I went into the bathroom, hit the light there and discovered our host had invited all his relatives to a party on our bathroom floor. The bugs were so bad, in fact, that my roommate declined to shower the next morning, contending they were massed in there, waiting for him.

I shrugged, allowed at least I'd drown a few of them, and showered anyway.

But my cockroach friend was nothing if not determined. He stowed away in my suitcase sometime that night. Twenty-four hours later, stumbling bleary-eyed toward the lavatory in San Juan with my electric razor cord dangling, I felt a strange clinging to my right leg. I looked down. There was the cockroach, all 3 in. of him. I flung him fiercely into the wastebasket, doubtless to start a new hybrid breed in Puerto Rico.

We made a leisurely midmorning departure from Trinidad for the 6½ hour flight up the Lesser Antilles to Puerto Rico, for we were all still vibrating slightly from the nonstop resonance of 2,400 P&W ponies the day before.

In close formation, the three PBYs swept low along the beaches and verdant hills of Trinidad and headed almost due north. Just over an hour later, we roared in left echelon over the Grenada airport, where US Marines and Cubans had contested four short months earlier.

We hurdled Saint Vincent and saluted their fellow UK subjects at Saint Lucia's Hewanoora International Airport with a tight vic of three just to seaward, skirted Martinique's eastern shore and turned left to sail past Dominica. In line astern, we roared directly over Guadeloupe's Le Raizet Airport close under a threatening rain cloud, doubtless startling some Frenchmen with our passage.

Somewhere around Guadeloupe, we became separated from 09 again, and only 51 and 20 remained together for the run past Antigua. We spent nearly an hour on a satisfying low-level photo run from Saint Christopher through the Netherlands Antilles, dodging rain showers and rocks rising from the sea, flying over royal blue water and ermine whitecaps, through golden sunbeams and rainbows.

In line astern again, we flew along the rugged southern coast of Saint Thomas, dotted with the luxury winter homes of the rich, and took a close look at the jewel-like harbor with its cruise ships and a jetliner rising from Harry S. Truman Airport close alongside.

Again, we were second to land at San Juan; 09 had beaten us once more. Again, 51's gear had to be extended manually—but this time Stirm, taking pity on Perry, handed over the controls and did the job himself. Again, there were a fair number of chores—additional clearances to obtain, fuel to arrange, accommodations to secure. Again, it was 10 p.m. before I sat down to my second meal of the day.

Up early the third and last morning, we were delayed nearly 2½ hours by more officialdom, some last-minute repairs to the wing fabric on 20 (luckily, they have duct tape at San Juan, too) and the fact that this time, the electric two-way toggle switch that energizes the inertia starter and engages the clutch on the No. 1 engine went out of business.

Fortunately, Consolidated anticipated this, too. A PBY, in fact, carries all sorts of equipment, right down to a pair of folding boatswain's chairs that clip to the leading edge of the wing and dangle down on either side of an engine to allow repairs at sea. And clipped to the left side of the hull just aft of the long-suffering flight engineer is a much stouter version of the old Model T crank handle.

To use this, one good or two not-so-good men stand atop the wing, brace one foot on the engine cowling, lean over 20 ft. above the ground and insert the action end into a hole under an access hatch. Then they begin to wind. When the inertia flywheel is spinning as fast as muscle can make it, someone yanks a folding T-handle to engage the clutch. Sometimes it works. It worked this time on the fifth try. The other engine was started with a power cart, as it was on the whole trip, because the irreplaceable original equipment battery was dying in its casing and unable to do the job unaided.

We launched, finally, at 10:45 a.m. local, in close interval, directly into a rain shower moving rapidly in from seaward.

At 200 ft., I hauled the airplane into a left bank and headed north, peering through the rain to spot 51, half a mile ahead. 09 was as close behind.

Twenty minutes after liftoff, 09 was half a mile in the lead and 51 was at two o'clock, 200 yards ahead and level. Suddenly, the airplane's gear dropped and Stirm announced, "83 flight, Alpha's got a bad hydraulic problem. We're turning back to San Juan."

At the time, we had not quite cleared Borinquen.

Later, Stirm explained not only was the leaky hydraulic system spewing fluid, but smoke began to rise from under the copilot's seat. He used the last of his pressure to extend the gear and, wisely, turned back. He landed in Orlando, Florida, at 5 p.m. the

A simple, friendly old airplane to fly, the "P-boats" remain in demand in the 1990s because of their long range and their ability to go anywhere. In a sense, they're sort of the ultimate RV, and around 60 of them remained in service when this flight was made. Like the C-47, the PBY was copied and produced in the Soviet Union during World War II.

following day, having found half an airport full of volunteers at San Juan to help him—including several with extensive PBY experience.

The remaining two airplanes had 1,124 nautical miles to fly—and 8½ hours of daylight to do it. Obviously, our original plan of flying to Miami and following the coast to Orlando would require some modification, since ferry flights are daylight only.

Since 09 had the only ADF in the flight, I informed Degan he was now lead. We were unaware that his ADF had gone on strike, also. Degan didn't let it bother him. He simply dug out his E-6B "whiz wheel," stuck a matchstick into the grommet and applied an old bush pilot's trick, learned from an Arctic flyer.

He explained it to me later: "Take Zulu time and multiply by 15," he said. "Subtract the assumed longitude position from that result. Take the reciprocal of this number, put the shadow of the sun on that reciprocal, and north will be where north is. Add variation to your true heading and fly the result."

He re-filed in the air, direct to Herndon Field, Orlando, and informed us. Since our No. 2 tach quit 70

nm or so south of Grand Turk, southeast of the Bahamas, and since No. 1 prop governor tended to overspeed at full increase, we weren't looking forward to any more takeoffs. We quickly concurred, and the two PBYs headed out across the blue water.

We crossed a frontal zone somewhere around Silver Bank that forced us up to over 7,000 ft. and led to a thirty-mile detour around towering cumulus and occasional showers, separating us for about half an hour and bringing us as close to the trigger-happy Cubans and their Air Defense Identification Zone as I cared to go in this class of airplane, but we broke out and rejoined between Long Island and Great Exuma, not too far from Deadman's Cay!

The higher altitude brought a welcome tail wind, and soon we were making ground speeds up to 160 knots—really cooking for a PBY!

Tallichet took over the airplane to play at formation flying with 09, giving me my last excellent chance for air-to-air photos, and once that was done, I had little to do but sit and watch the Caribbean slide by and speculate on the probable number of hungry sharks per square mile. As an overactive imagination conjured visions of my ragged upper half finally floating to shore on some deserted sandspit, I began to wish for a return of the jungle!

We roared over Nassau in line astern, and I took the controls again, following 09 into thickening weather, colder temperatures and gathering gloom, over Grand Bahama and, finally, over the coast of Florida!

Letting down over Vero Beach, we watched the lights come on as we approached Orlando and, with the last glow in the sky, I eased the old PBY onto Herndon Field as Tallichet shined my pocket flashlight on the instrument panel. We were back!

There were some loose ends, of course! I still have 10 kilos of specially-ground Brazilian coffee floating around somewhere that I haven't been able to reclaim, and Tallichet still has an airplane in Belém.

But, before long, if things go right, at least two of these faithful San Diego products will be in US air museums. One will go into Tallichet's warbird collection, and the last of the four will be offered for sale.

As for me, I have some new friends, twenty-eight hours of unexpected PBY time in my logbook—and a full-color mental adventure movie I can play back anytime I please!

Who could ask for more?

Oh, yes, I sent Jorge Franca a note telling him his prayers worked.

First printed in *Air Progress*, August 1984.

Chapter 13

Vultee BT–13

Vibrator!

Back in the opening days of World War II, the name "Vultee" really meant something!

The fast, modern Vultee V–1 of the early 1930s had performed creditably for the Republicans in Spain, and several derivatives of that airplane had been developed and sold in small numbers.

Chance Vought had been a major supplier of airplanes to the US Navy since 1920, and when war broke out the company's SB2U Vindicator scout bombers, SU Corsairs and OS2U Kingfishers were serving with the fleet. Commonality was a big thing then, and several makers offered such "families."

Vultee also fielded a trio of designs all based on the same attractive airframe. These included the BT–13, the BC–3 and, finally, the P–66 "Vanguard," a pretty little 1200 hp fighter with a claimed top speed of 348 mph. One hundred forty-four were built, and the Chinese ended up with 129 of them. The remainder were used by the USAAF for "communications duties" in the United States.

Today, the only survivors are the handful of BT–13s—still pretty, and still great fun to fly!

Glancing around hurriedly, I pulled the airplane's nose about twenty degrees above the horizon, then rolled the old bird up on the right wingtip in a coordinated sixty degree bank and honked back on the sturdy control stick to peel off, loading the wing up to maybe 2.5 Gs.

Surprise!

The Vultee said, "Wham, bam, thank you, sir!"— and paid off like a broken slot machine, rolling strongly back to the left. The airspeed still read 100 mph!

Well, I'd always heard the BT–13 had a sharp, no-foolin' stall. In fact, I'd explored it at some length maybe an hour before and found the stories generally true. But I'd had no idea the thing would unhook quite that thoroughly and completely.

No harm done, of course; we were above the puffies over the south end of Lake Winnebago at 8,500 MSL after completing a photo mission. Bill Doty, Jr., in the front seat, didn't even twitch. He just sat there and enjoyed the ride.

Still, what impressed me was how much more *compressed* the stall progression was.

Few airplanes give more stall warning than the old Vultee BT–13.

That's why a lot more pilots called it the Vibrator than ever referred to it as the Valiant, its official handle. A BT–13 will shudder and shake so violently the whole greenhouse rattles in its tracks, the stick vibrates in the pilot's hand and I swear the wingtips flap up and down.

Normally, all this begins about 8 mph before the actual stall and progresses predictably until the airplane quits. Clean, the book says that's at 75 mph. It will pitch radically down at that point and lose 600–800 fpm, protesting to beat the band, and it takes quick and judicious light application of coordinated aileron and rudder to keep the wings level.

The military pilot's handbook also says an approaching stall is heralded by "slight buffeting and vibration" as well as "mushy" controls. I wonder what they considered a "heavy" buffet? Probably couldn't see the airplane; just a blur.

That same book says the airplane stalls at 65 IAS with flaps down at both thirty and sixty degrees (half and full flaps, respectively).

Well, maybe so, but the forty-six-year-old airspeed indicator in the rear cockpit of N213BD stubbornly insisted the Vultee quit at 60 mph indicated in *any* flap condition! The only difference was, by the time we progressed to sixty-degree flaps and 27 in. MP, the nose was probably twenty degrees above the horizon at the break.

I found all this fascinating, because I'd never even *sat* in a BT-13 before, let alone flown one.

I'd known all about BT-13s most of my life, of course, because back when the rest of the kids were memorizing baseball players' records, I was memorizing performance data on every warplane in the world.

When I was learning to fly, it was common to see anywhere from one to three or four decapitated BT-13s out behind the hangar on every airstrip, beheaded by cropdusters who wanted the engine and prop for another Stearman ag plane. There were even a few of them still flying, but somehow I never got a crack at one. And then one day I looked around and they were all gone.

Once there had been nearly 12,000 of them. They were used by both the Army Air Corps and the Navy, and did much to teach the vast majority of America's

World War II combat pilots the things they had to know. Today there are fewer than thirty still flying, says Doty; perhaps as many more still in existence somewhere.

And now here I was tooling about the sky in as beauteous an example as there is in the world.

Doty bought the airplane in 1976, in ferriable condition, with a low-time engine but needing more work. "I thought it would be a nice, economical warbird—but at that time avgas was 53¢ a gallon," said Doty. "It didn't seem like much."

Doty, originally from Fort Wayne, Indiana, turned it over to the A&P school at Purdue University for restoration as a class project—but somehow the project never got finished.

Finally he reclaimed it and handed it over to the Travelair Corporation, a Doty family company which includes his father, a retired USAF major and corporate pilot; his brother Jim, a Provincetown-Boston Airlines captain in Florida, and himself—a Northwest Airlines DC-9/Boeing 727 captain, also now from Florida. Since he still lives in Fort Wayne, Bill, Sr., finished the job, a task that took him two years.

They test flew it a week before the 1987 EAA convention began, and had logged only ten hours on the reconstituted Vultee when they showed up at Oshkosh—including the trip from Fort Wayne!

"It's not a trainer that you can just let go of, like a (Cessna) 150. But it's honest," opined the younger

The Vultee BT-13 Valiant—or "Vibrator," as it was known by tens of thousands of flight students—taught a generation of young men many of the skills they would need to fight the greatest air war in history. Once there were nearly 12,000 of them. Today there is only a handful. This one, restored by

former USAF pilot Bill Doty and his flying family, is one of the most pristine. By 1990, this ongoing restoration was complete with blind flying hood, since the airplane was used to teach instruments to budding military pilots.

Airline pilot Bill Doty, Jr., said N213BD was restored exactly as it appeared in service in California in 1944, except for the rudder stripes. The rudder was the first piece restored, and the stripes served as an incentive through the rest of a long restoration. Photos were taken in 1989. By 1990, the stripes were gone. Instead, diagonal red stripes were added to wings. This BT–13 was delivered to USAAC the month before Pearl Harbor.

Doty. Unlike his father, he had learned to fly without a BT-13 in his curriculum—but better late than never.

And the whole family was not only willing but eager to share a flying impression of their airplane with others.

Actually, the Vibrator is a straightforward airplane.

In common with other World War II vintage military single-engine types, the crew scales the side like mountain climbers, groping for hand- and toe-holds on the smooth aluminum skin.

Once inside one of the roomy cockpits, the airplane proves well planned and comfortable—but don't drop anything, because it will end up sliding around on the belly of the aircraft and the only way to get it back may well be a short period of inverted flight.

Most controls are duplicated in both cockpits, but in late-model airplanes the starter is a double toggle switch in the front only. Oil cooler shutter, carburetor heat, oil dilution and primer controls also are missing in back. Original drill was to flip the master switch to the "Batt." position, energize the inertia flywheel and, finally, engage the starter clutch, but

N213BD now has a direct-drive starter that simplifies things.

Meanwhile, it's a good idea to hit a few strokes on the wobble pump to bring up the fuel pressure—something that may be required again a time or two while taxiing out.

Fuel gauges are set in the floor in the front cockpit and situated to be visible to both occupants. Identical selectors give a choice of left, right or reserve, and normal fuel is 120 US gallons, 60 in each wet wing stub. (Yes, Virginia, they had wet wings even in 1939.) Takeoff normally is on the left main, but if that one's not full, choose the fullest.

Originally, Vibrators had hydraulically-controlled two-position Hamilton-Standard props, but N213BD now has a constant-speed unit. Conventional left-side throttle quadrants house throttle, mixture and prop levers, but beware! The mixture and prop levers are reversed from the normal arrangement, and prop pitch is controlled by the little, low-mounted inboard knob, not the middle one of the trio. It is quite sensitive.

Below and slightly aft of the throttle quadrant is a combined trim/flap control, consisting of a double-wheel trim (outboard very logically is rudder, inboard elevator).

A short crank handle projecting from the axis of the trim unit operates the flaps. Cranking the handle counterclockwise (aft) lowers the flaps, cranking it clockwise (forward) raises them. I always got it wrong—and the Dotys agreed they do, too.

Errors are of little moment, however, because at two degrees per turn the flaps are so low-geared it's easy to catch. There's an index-and-pointer indicator at twelve o'clock on the crank assembly, but it's easier just to glance over the side. Flaps go all the way down to sixty degrees, and I'm still trying to decide how much good they do.

There's also an aileron trim tab, but it's ground adjustable only, and one of the first things I learned was that N213BD was mildly right wing heavy. It had been since it went back together, and they just hadn't had time yet to do anything about it.

Rudder pedals are standard suspended kick-adjustable military units, and the hydraulic drum brakes are typical of the breed—never quite as good as one would wish. The steerable tailwheel is connected to the rudder via bungee springs, but free swivels beyond the rudder arc. With a wheelbase of 10 ft. 6½ in., the Vultee is stable and easily controllable on the ground—a good thing in view of the size of the fin/rudder assembly.

Visibility out of the back cockpit is nonexistent for about forty-five degrees of arc directly ahead, but excellent around the rest of the compass, and I found it's no great trick to take off and land from the back pit. Only thing is, you'd better S-turn while taxiing, or those expensive grinding noises you hear will be the 9 ft. Hamilton-Standard puréeing somebody's spam can out ahead.

The military metal bucket seat, designed for parachute use, is comfortable and easily adjustable vertically via a small handle on the right side. Noise level is high, a combination of engine, prop, slipstream and greenhouse racket—but that's part of the mystique of flying World War II vintage warbirds.

The fixed landing gear produces a ground angle of better than ten degrees, with rather stiff air/oil shock absorbers.

Doty, a tall, black-haired man with a serious manner, bunged me into the back seat, made sure I had my four-point safety harness secured, cranked down twenty degrees of divided plain flap (four flaps, totaling more than 25 sq. ft.), and launched us down Runway 18 at Oshkosh.

Once we turned east over the lake, he landed the Doty family treasure over to me and I climbed on up to 3,500 MSL, doing little S-turns en route.

I was flying the airplane strictly by feel, and was pleasantly surprised to learn later that the 90 mph IAS, 28 in. and 2100 rpm I settled on seemed to agree well with the handbook.

The BT-13 is a good-sized airplane, with a 28 ft. 10 in. length, a height of just over 12 ft. 4 in., a wing span of 42 ft. and an area of 239 sq. ft. All metal, it weighs 3,302 lbs. empty (this airplane) and 4,350 lbs. at FAA gross (the military operated it at 4,600). Obviously, it's not overburdened with useful load, prompting Doty to remark that "With two pilots and parachutes, you're not able to carry full fuel."

Nevertheless, it's not really a bad performer. The handbook claims a maximum level flight speed of 166 mph at 1,400 ft., with a maximum cruise of 140 at 5,000 ft. and an initial climb of 1,050 fpm from sea level to 3,000 ft.

That's a little better than we got, but not much. We weren't wearing chutes, but we had full fuel and were within a few pounds of civilian gross—probably on the far side. I didn't time it, but I estimated the climb at around 700-800 fpm; not bad for a density altitude hovering at 5,000 ft.

The problem with the Vultee is that it has a genuine symmetrical airfoil: NACA 0018-64 Modified at the root, 0009-64 Modified at the tip. With seven degrees of dihedral and 3.5 degrees of incidence, it's not a strong climber—but I bet it flies upside down just dandy! Controls are fine; well harmonized and with required inputs estimated at 8-10 lbs.

In deference to the traffic, the lack of chutes, the baggage in the aft compartment and Doty's feelings, I didn't try to find out—but my fingers certainly itched. Bill Doty, Sr., later told me they'd already looped and barrel-rolled it, but that was over their home field at Fort Wayne. Someday. . . .

At seventy-five percent power, 27in.x2000 rpm, I saw 125 IAS for a true of 134, while a sixty-five percent setting of 21x1850 produced 115 indicated and 123 TAS. Later, cruising down to Fond du Lac, Wisconsin, at 2,000 MSL to keep a date with a photo plane, I flew at 21x1850 for 105 IAS and 112 true in 88 degrees F. temperatures and sixty percent humidity, on probably forty-five percent power and 17 gph—again, pretty good for a genuine vintage warbird!

Doty, Sr., reported en route to Oshkosh, he trued 133 knots (150 mph) at 1800 rpm and full throttle on sixty percent power and 21 gph at 12,500 ft.—comfortably over the book maximum cruise figure. Considering it was straight out of restoration, no one can argue with that kind of performance.

Military redline on this bird was 230, but the FAA cut it to 217, for the usual obscure bureaucratic reasons, and forbade intentional spins, though the military allowed up to three turns (I have heard the airplane tends to go flat around the second turn, but responds nicely to positive recovery controls). Service ceiling is 16,500 ft., and still-air range is listed at 516 miles.

Elevator trim is quite powerful, and the airplane flew very stably in trimmed flight at 60 IAS, performing twenty-degree banked turns left and right—despite a prohibition I read later in the handbook against letting the speed drop below 85 in any turn.

Heading for the 3,600 ft. paved strip at New Holstein, Wisconsin, I made my approach at 100 IAS carrying sixty-degree flap (military flap limit speed is 120—111 civilian—and due to the low flap gearing, it behooves the pilot to get with the program pretty early) and 13 in. MP, chopped the power 100 ft. in the air and crossed the fence probably at about 90, touching down three-point within fifty yards. It all just felt right.

I was promptly rewarded with a fairly strong tailwheel shimmy, which did not diminish as we slowed. We were down and stopped in 1,200 ft., no brakes.

On takeoff, the tail was up at about 40 IAS and we lifted off in probably 1,000 ft. without forcing the airplane. Again, we were at gross, having topped the tanks.

Departing Fond du Lac an hour later into a 10 knot wind, I would estimate we lifted off in no more than 700 ft., and landing back at Oshkosh on Runway 27, again into a 10 knot wind, I put it on the mains and turned off onto the grass in perhaps 1,000 ft.

The pilot's handbook says sea level takeoff run at 4,600 lbs. is 750 ft. on hard surface, no wind, standard day; 1,400 ft. over a 50 ft. obstacle. Landing over 50 ft. is 1,300 ft., with a ground roll of 650 ft., both with moderate braking.

Bill Doty, Sr., later suggested—and I agree—that standard procedure probably is 120 on downwind, 100 on base with twenty-degree flaps and 90 on final with forty-degree flaps or greater. For takeoff, he added, "I've been lifting off around 70 and climbing at 90," retracting the flaps at 400 ft. and climbing at 100 mph thereafter.

The BT-13 was the first "big airplane" most budding military aviators were introduced to, and it seems to me it must have been ideal for the purpose.

It's stable in all three axes; therefore surely made an excellent instrument classroom. It was said at the time that the airplane was so stable in landing that the pilot could fill out the Form 1 on final. It's reasonably fast and has a decent climb rate, particularly at lighter weights. It's responsive on the controls and communicates well with the pilot. Certainly he'd have to be passed out cold not to recognize a stall!

At the same time, it is not an airplane to trifle with. It will bite an inattentive pilot, promptly and hard, and it's big and heavy enough to need several hundred feet for recovery.

Apparently, it does pretty decent basic aerobatics. I have a sheet of manufacturer's recommended entry speeds for solo maneuvers in the airplane, list-

Fully aerobatic, stable on the ground and in the air, the BT-13/15 series was possessed of such violent pre-stall airframe shudder they were dubbed "Vibrator" by those who flew them. Buffet will wake the dead—and should, because the airplane has a sharp, no-foolin' stall that can kill the unwary at low altitude.

The BT-13, with 450 hp Pratt & Whitney R-985, and BT-15, with similar-sized Wright, were one of three Vultee designs based on the same airframe. The others were the BC-3 and the P-66 fighter. The BC-3 went nowhere, but 144 of the pretty little P-66 "Vanguards" were built. Most went to the Chinese. These airplanes have truly symmetrical airfoils.

ing not only chandelles, lazy eights, barrel and slow rolls and spins but also snap rolls, clover leaves, Immelmanns, Cuban eights and a thing called an avalanche, whatever that is. Entry speeds range from 115 mph for a snap roll to 180 for the last three maneuvers.

In short, it *is* an honest airplane—and one that keeps a pilot honest. Except for fixed gear and much lower maintenance requirements, somewhat slower speeds and a noticeably more miserly fuel burn, it will do just about everything a T-6 will do. What instructor could ask for more?

No wonder the Dotys figure total production came to 11,537 over a five-year period. (It's a little hard to calculate, since the Navy took over some US Army Air Corps (USAAC) contract airplanes as SNV-1s, then ordered many more of their own.)

The original army contract for 300 Valiants was let in September 1939 and was the largest order placed for basic trainers; indeed, one of the largest buys for any aircraft type that year. Two much larger contracts were let in 1941, and production continued until the summer of 1944. Valiant variants included the P&W-powered BT-13s and the equivalent Wright Cyclone-powered BT-15s.

What was to become N213BD, Vultee BT-13A serial number 2514, Army serial number 41-11504, was built at Consolidated Vultee Aircraft in Nashville, Tennessee, and delivered to the USAAC Nov. 5, 1941.

It served exclusively in California throughout the war, being assigned to Lemoore Army Air Field until March 1943 and serving thereafter at Lancaster, Victorville and Gardner Field.

The airplane was restored in the markings it was believed to have carried in late 1944 when assigned to the 3034th Base Unit, Army Air Forces Training Command. "Except for the striped rudder," added Bill Doty, Jr. "That was the first piece restored, and we painted the stripes on it and hung it where everyone could see it as an incentive, so when we assembled the airplane we just left it that way. Actually, it would have been silver in 1944."

Incentives were needed, because it's hard to find airworthy parts for a BT-13 these days. "There are cast-iron fittings that hold the tail on, and those things rust and there's no replacement for 'em," said Doty. "Also the steel wing supports."

Regardless of how hard the task, it's clear the result was worth it. There were probably a total of thirty-five Mustangs at Oshkosh 1987; as many T-6s or more. Dozens of T-28s. Over a dozen T-34s.

There was only the one BT-13. And it was a stand-out, clad in its coat of fresh silver paint, with prominent black markings and a bright red cowling, complete down to the new GI zip-and-snap canvas baggage compartment, the first-aid kit fixed at two o'clock on the rear cockpit coaming and so on. Even the tires had the correct wartime tread!

Who could ask for more?

Let's see, now. I know where there's a basket case BT-13. If I stash the parts around the Monocoupe, maybe I can get 'em all in the hangar. Then it's just a matter of finding time to work on it.

After all, every boy needs a genuine warbird or two!

First printed in *Air Progress*, November 1987.

Chapter 14

AT–6/SNJ Texan

Super-Harvard!

Unquestionably, the most successful advanced trainer in history is the ubiquitous North American NA–64, better known as the AT–6/SNJ Texan or the Harvard. Big, sturdy, powerful, reasonably fast, fully aerobatic, reliable and moderately challenging to fly, the Texan seemed to lack nothing as the United States geared up for World War II.

Inevitably, the day came when some bright young men looked at the airplane and found it wanting. Wanting more performance. If 600 hp and a two-blade prop was good, 1,050 and a three-blade must be better—and it was. If forty-one ft. of wing was okay, then thirty-three ft. should be better. It was, too. Especially after the angle of incidence was reduced.

One thing led to another and pretty soon these tinkerers had an airplane that performed like a grown-up fighter and still carried two in the same old roomy greenhouse to which T-6 pilots were accustomed. And the thing still flew like a baby carriage!

Frankly, if you don't mind burning a gallon a minute for your pleasure, the much-modified Harvard in this report is almost unbeatable as a sport plane.

Kent Sherman is long in the leg, so when he hopped out of the front cockpit of NX1467 and I stepped in, my first task was to strap the seat to my fanny and haul the thing up as far as it would go.

With that accomplished, I looked around and discovered visibility out of this much-modified Harvard Mk IV actually was excellent, despite the big Douglas Dauntless engine and cowling grafted onto the front end. It was, however, big. Not much of the three-blade 10 ft. 2 in. Hamilton-Standard remained visible.

I looked out at the shortened wingtips, with their protruding endplates.

Stubby!

I looked at the ailerons. Clipped—radically!

Hmmm. Was this another one of those "What am I doing here?" situations?

I shrugged. Only one way to find out.

I coaxed the 1,050 hp Wright GR-1820-52 to life and taxied slowly out to the end of the 6,500 ft. Indiantown turf runway, familiarizing myself with the pilot's-eye view of the beast on the ground and wiggling the controls experimentally.

At the end of the runway, I set the white pip on the rudder trim wheel at the three o'clock position and the one on the elevator at noon, made sure the prop was full forward, checked the mags and looked around. No traffic. Well, we hadn't expected any. That's why we were here, instead of at West Palm Beach, this pretty black-and-white bird's current home base.

Following instructions from the back seat, I held the hyperthyroidal Harvard with the toe brakes and advanced the power to 30 in. of manifold pressure, then released the brakes and brought the power on up to 41in.x2350 rpm.

Believe me, when that herd of Wright ponies begins to gallop in the same direction, the whole *field* shakes! In fact, when we came back later to pick up some gas before flying on to Palm Beach, the airport operator said we'd rocked his trailer on every takeoff.

This beast used to be a North American Harvard Mk. IV, Canadian version of the ubiquitous AT-6 Texan. That was a long time ago. That's a 1,050 hp Wright GR–1820–52 and a 122 in., three-blade Hamilton Standard you're looking at, straight off a Douglas SBD Dauntless dive bomber. Hitch that to a much-modified Harvard airframe, and you have an airplane that's not only good for probably 300 mph at optimum altitude, but is really fun to fly!

Initial acceleration was close to 2 Gs.

We had 6 or 7 knots of wind from about 4:30, but with the kind of power this bird boasts, it made no difference at all. The tail came up almost immediately, and at about the 1,000 ft. mark, the super-Harvard flew off, indicating around 90 mph.

I tapped the brake pedals lightly, reached down and flipped the gear lever as the black brute accelerated quickly to 150 IAS, then reduced the throttle to 39.5 in. and the prop to 2300.

At the same time, I began hauling back on the stick to hold my cruise-climb airspeed. The airplane was perhaps ten degrees nose up and climbing at around 3,200 fpm, despite a temperature near 90 degrees F.

"The acceleration on this of course is what's the most fun," young Sherman said later. "It'll come off the ground in six seconds. We've drag raced the T-28B, the F4U and the P-51 and beat all of 'em to the end of the field. After that, of course, the -51 pulls away."

The way we were flying it, the Wright-powered Harvard probably was delivering a power-to-weight ratio just a hair over 5 lbs. per hp compared to 9.5 lbs. per hp for a stock airplane—no slouch in anybody's league, and particularly not in piston-engined airplanes. There's simply no substitute for brute force!

In fact, I got a bit carried away on my second takeoff and pulled 46 in. until I hurriedly backed it off, which *really* made the North American scramble! And made the service trailer bounce up and down.

That time, we were airborne in 800 ft., I held about 120 indicated and got an IROC of about 4,000 fpm. We never missed the 8 ft. of wing chopped off the airplane.

But the Super-Harvard will do more than just climb!

I zipped up to 6,500 ft. averaging 2,500-3,000 fpm in the warm, humid Florida air, and leveled out, feeling for the step.

It took about three minutes, but with 38in.x2300 rpm, NX1467 indicated 250 mph—a figure Sherman's father Dennis later corroborated. Denny Sherman said the day he tested it, that computed to 292 mph on 950 hp at 6,000 ft.

The senior Sherman added at 12,000 ft. and +8 degrees C., 770 bhp produced 211 IAS and 271 mph true on 60 gph. A 25.5x1700 cruise setting (525 bhp) yielded 190 indicated and 243 true on 37 gph, while 26x1800 (575 bhp) gave 250 TAS on forty gallons.

On up at 24,000 ft., 25.5x2350 yielded a computed 550 hp, 175 IAS and 278 true while 23x2000 cut the speed only to 270 true and 21x1800 gave 400 hp and 250 TAS.

Sherman said he'd never been able to get just the right (standard) temperature conditions in Florida to really check the airplane's top speed at its 16,800 ft. critical altitude. But, he added, "We figure it's about 300 mph."

I suspect he's very close.

A setting of 35x2000 gave me 205 indicated, while backing off to 30 in. (the normal cruise setting) only dropped the air speed by 5 mph. An economy cruise setting of 25x1700 produced 160 IAS, and Kent Sherman remarked that that power setting at 10,000 to 12,000 ft. will produce a fuel burn of 40 or 41 gph and "awful close to 200 knots true."

Clearly, this is a long way from a stock T-6!

At first glance, it *looks* pretty much like a stock T-6, except for the stubby wings and the massive Wright, but there are many other changes.

As Kent Sherman explained, the airplane was intended to explore just what could be done with a T-6 airframe. He led the way around the big North American on the ground, pointing out changes.

The heavier Wright rides a foot closer to the pilot's toes than the Pratt & Whitney R-1340 in the stock bird. The airplane uses T-28 main wheels and brakes, allowing the leading edge of the wing to be straightened where it joins the fuselage, à la P-51. The center stress panels beneath the aircraft are flush riveted, as are the accessory cowlings and some wing panels.

The tailwheel now is fully retractable and enclosed by its own set of doors. On the ground, it still works like a stock unit, but it pivots through only two thirds of the original arc, and the linkage between tailwheel and rudder has been geared down. The wing's angle of incidence has been changed. The stainless steel machine gun troughs have been removed from atop the former Dauntless cowling and new pieces faired in their place. The oil tank, battery and pre-oil pump were relocated aft of the rear seat.

"We made a lot of changes," said Cliff Branch, the original civilian owner and the A&P who did the work. "A lot of the changes were already tried and proven on other airplanes that we had in the shop. On that airplane, we put it all together and then added a couple. And it all worked."

Branch in those days was associated with well-known warbird restorer Dennis Buehn, and Branch's personal airplane was the second Harvard given the SBD treatment in the shop. But Branch only *started* with the engine swap. He even took some of the offset out of the vertical fin!

He reported when he stopped, empty weight "was within a few pounds of military," and "when we put it on the scales, we didn't have to do a thing. It was right in the center of balance."

Indeed. One of the surprising things about this super-Harvard was its delightful control harmony and quickness of response.

Any machine that weighs nearly 4,200 lbs. empty and grosses 5,300+ *should* feel heavier than, say, a Cessna 150—but this one doesn't. The burly black-and-white bird boasted such delicate balance and such flashing performance that it seemed more like, say, a Pitts than a "big iron" military trainer from the last great war—although Kent Sherman claimed it has a heavier "feel" than a stock T-6.

It didn't roll quite like a Pitts, of course, despite the shorter 34 ft. wing, clocking four seconds to the left, five to the right for a complete revolution from a 180 mph entry speed as I laid on the stick and Sherman timed us on his watch. But that's definitely good enough to keep you in the rat race.

You can enter 1,500-2,000 ft. loops as slow as 210 IAS, but 230 is better, allowing about a 3.5 G pull and a little positive seat pressure over the top.

Slow flight was an absolute pleasure. I reduced power to 15x2000 and trimmed the airplane for level flight at 90-100 indicated and flew quite stably, tail noticeably down.

The super-Harvard flew steady-state turns at thirty degrees of bank without a bobble. It did stall when rolled rapidly from a thirty-degree left to a thirty-degree right bank, but walked right out of it with a slight shot of power.

The stall itself was interesting. There was a good, sharp buffet in all configurations, but the stall progressed quite quickly, with a "Bam, bam, goodbye!" sequence that could catch the careless off guard. At the break, the airplane always fell straight ahead on the first cycle—but it got rapidly snarly if held in a full stall, rolling off violently on first one wing and then the other and trying hard to spin.

The break itself came as low as 65-67 indicated and as high as 90, depending on whether the airplane was clean or dirty and whether I was carrying power. With gear and flaps down and 20 in. MP, the stall was

Super Harvard uses T-28 main gear, allowing removal of the wheel bulge in the leading edge of the wing. Wing angle of incidence also was changed and eight feet chopped off the span. Tailwheel now retracts. At 46 in. of manifold pressure on a warm day in Florida, the thing was off the ground in 800 feet and climbing 400 fpm at 120 mph IAS.

more stable, but the airplane almost immediately registered a sink rate in excess of 3,000 fpm. Ailerons remained moderately effective even in the stall.

I was particularly surprised that the tiny ailerons, trimmed forty percent from stock, were as effective as they were. I wasn't so surprised at the power of the unmodified rudder and elevator—except that Kent Sherman remarked 467 was "much better" than an unmodified airplane.

I had no way to tell. This was the first T-6 I'd ever flown.

"I wish you'd had a chance to fly a stock airplane before you flew this one," said Sherman. "Then you could really appreciate it."

One thing *I could* appreciate was the way the airplane comes out of the sky.

At approximately zero thrust (you don't ever want to undersquare a geared engine if you can help it) and 140 IAS, this thing comes down at 4,000-6,000 fpm, with the nose down probably five or six degrees. "It comes down just like a Corsair or P-51 or T-28 or whatever," said Sherman. I'm not sure what the wing loading is, because I don't know the remaining area, but at a guess I'd say it's somewhere around 35 lbs. per sq. ft.—about like a Spitfire.

Just because I'd have regretted it forever if I didn't, I stuffed the big black beast's nose down and let the speed build to about 290 indicated as we dropped out of the sky, ripping across the Indiantown airfield at 100 ft.

At the far end, I chandelled to the left and as the speed dropped below 140 I flipped the gear lever. With

A real drag racer, the Super Harvard will come off the ground in six seconds and outrun P–51, Corsair and others to the end of the field. After that, extra ponies prevail on the big fighters. This airplane comes out of the sky at 6,000 fpm—but handles like a baby carriage. An outstanding custom airplane!

three greens smiling at me, I trimmed to 125 and added a little flap, shaving another 5 mph off the speed. Rolling onto base, I was carrying 15 in. and 110 indicated, sinking 700 fpm with thirty degrees of flap.

I reduced power a little more, crossed the fence at 100 and put it on the wheels at probably about 85.

A real sweetheart, the super-Harvard simply kissed the grass and rolled straight ahead until I could no longer hold the tail up with the stick. There was a slight bump as the solid tailwheel hit the ground, and I reached up to pop the cowl flaps open.

Adding power, I taxied on to the southeast end of the field, swung around, reset the trim and did it again. That's when I ended up with 46 in. in my fist!

This time, I stayed in the pattern. Vaulting upward at 120 indicated and 3,800 feet per second

Californian Cliff Branch, who did the modifications, hand selected all the parts for what was to be the world's fastest Harvard from a California surplus yard and spent eight years working on it. He even took some of the offset out of the fin. He intended to completely enclose the main gear, but sold it first. The plane was owned by the Sherman family of West Palm Beach at the time of the report.

(fps), I made a wide duster turn, another pass down the field and one last chandelle to a downwind.

Power back, gear down, trim, flaps, and the second landing was a repeat of the first. A real lady, this air machine!

Taxiing in, listening to the grumble of the geared Wright, I reflected back over the flight, considering. Later I commented to Kent Sherman that I was surprised at the ease with which the airplane tracked straight down the runway on takeoff, with no apparent leftward-turning tendency.

"It's there, all right; you just didn't notice it," he replied. "It's not as easy as you made it look," either on takeoff or landing. I'd been bragging about how easy the airplane was to fly, and he grinned and said, "I've been in the back seat with some guys who took me all over the runway."

He added, "If you can fly a T–6 right, I think you're an excellent pilot. I think a Pitts is an excellent pilot trainer, too."

Switching back to the virtues of the super-Harvard and summing up, he said, "You usually do get awful close to fighter performance," although with only 140 gallons of gas, it's a tad short-legged for a Yankee fighter machine.

The only time in the whole flight that the airplane was less than totally docile was when I unlocked the tailwheel a little too quickly going to the gas pump. The back end whipped around quicker than I had expected, calling for a rapid application of brake. The brake was just barely able to cope.

Denny Sherman, sons Scott, Kent and Terry and daughter Denise run a used airplane business on West Palm Beach Airport.

Because they're in business, they've advertised NX1467 for sale a couple of times, along with Stiletto, an F4U–5N, a Sea Fury (the only one they don't own), a DH Vampire and the like. But their heart's not in it.

Said Kent Sherman: "We really don't want to sell it. Everything else is definitely for sale. The price of fighters, we haven't been able to afford those *forever*."

At one time, the Shermans owned *both* the super T–6s produced by the Buehn-Branch collaboration. Both were powered by identical engines, but the other airplane is a stock airframe.

When the time came to sell one, there was no question which was the easier to find a buyer for. Or which the Shermans would rather keep around.

They've hiked their asking price on NX1467 to $175,000, just for fear someone will buy it.

Frankly, if I were walking around with that kind of pocket change, I'd probably buy it anyway.

Any airplane with this kind of performance is hard to walk away from. And the stubby North American has the added attractions of a second seat and an engine with a 1,000 hour TBO!

Let's see now, if I sell the house and the car and my wife's airplane. . . .

First printed in *Air Progress*, March 1989.

Chapter 15

Me 109

The Luftwaffe's deadliest weapon

Of all the airplanes in the world, the Messerschmitt Me 109 is the one I've always most wanted to fly.

There are several reasons for this. First, the airplane has the greatest combat record in the history of aerial warfare. Second, it is such a wicked-looking machine. Third, if the Messerschmitt is a superlative tool in the right hands, it is an indifferent one; it does not suffer fools gladly. Fourth, it has been my good fortune at various times to meet and interview some of the masters of the Messerschmitt: Eric Hartmann, Gerhard Barkhorn, Johannes Steinhoff.

In short, I've been queer for Me 109s since I was about six years old.

To date, I've never had the chance to fly one—not even the Merlin-powered Hispano version—but I haven't given up hope yet. I have gotten as far as sitting in the cockpit, taking the measure of the machine.

Meanwhile, years ago I sat down to try as best I could to reconstruct a typical test hop in a Gustav. This is the result.

The airplane lay on the truck bed, a battered, wingless thing. The three propeller blades were curled back, there were ugly gouges and a couple of tears in the smooth metal underbelly, and the rudder overhung the Kansas street.

Various people had scribbled their names in pen and pencil along its pale blue flanks and across the long engine cowling, with that unfailing instinct that impels men and dogs to mark their passing. The chains lashing it to the truck had bitten to the bright metal. It had suffered other indignities.

The curious mob surged around it, poking, prodding, furtively searching for a souvenir that could be ripped off without alerting the uniformed man with the microphone who was making the pitch for war bonds.

Despite it all, there was yet an aura of vitality, of lethal capability about the fighter. An acrid tang lingered about the oil stains on the belly. A faint whiff of cordite clung to the discoloration at the gun muzzles. There was still something challenging about the spotted gray-blue camouflage and the smudged yellow of the cowl.

It was an Me 109E-3, the first of the breed I had ever seen. It fascinated me. It still does; it, and all its clan.

The thing was a weapon; the cleanest, simplest, smallest package of winged destruction that could be designed in 1934 and still leave room for a man, guns and enough fuel to make it useful over crowded western Europe.

That was its downfall, eventually. There just wasn't enough stretch in the narrow airframe to stave off obsolescence forever. The package was too small. But it lasted longer on the job than any fighter in history—and posted a record *still* unapproached by any other warplane.

There was always something predatory about the looks of all the 109s. The first models somehow reminded one of a northern pike, or perhaps a barracuda, with their angular cowls and squared wingtips. There was no doubt about the later models. They were pure shark with wings, gray and mottled and rapacious.

They all looked ruthless and efficient, and they were. Despite their smooth flowing lines, even the later models lacked the subtle grace of their great enemy, the Spitfire. They were as direct as a bullet between the eyes. There were roughly 33,000 of them, all told, plus another couple thousand built after the war in Spain and Czechoslovakia—far and away the most-produced fighter in aviation.

They were the chosen mounts of the world's most successful fighter pilots. Specifications show lots of other fighters were better than the 109, but it was the backbone of the Luftwaffe day fighter force for eight long years, and many of Germany's top aces would fly nothing else. They never felt outclassed in a fighter-versus-fighter engagement right up to the surrender.

"I know the 190 was a better bird," former Maj. Gerhard Barkhorn told me. "It was faster, it could turn inside the 109—according to the book. But in fact, I could turn inside the 190s." His blue eyes twinkled mischievously, and he flashed an infectious grin.

With 301 confirmed victories, Barkhorn is the world's second-ranked ace. He scored every kill—plus probably seventy-five never confirmed—in the 109, and when he commanded a wing of "long nose" Fw 190s in Silesia in the spring of 1945, he and his wingman led them into combat in 109G-14s.

The world's three leading aces all flew with JG (Jagdgeschwader) 52 on the Russian front. They were Barkhorn, Maj. Erich "Bubi" Hartmann (352 victories)

and Maj. Günther Rall (275). All survived the war and all served until retirement in the reconstituted West German Luftwaffe. Hartmann and Barkhorn were colonels, Rall a major general.

Another man who preferred the faithful *hundert neun* was Lt. Col. Johannes "Macky" Steinhoff, who finished the war with 176 kills. Later Lt. Gen. Johannes Steinhoff, Luftwaffe chief of staff, he still prefers it. Steinhoff too served in JG 52, tallying 149 kills in Russia and twenty-seven against the Western Allies.

The 109 was flown by every major Luftwaffe ace, and there were ninety-seven of them with 100 or more air victories by war's end. Thirty-five had 150 or more, and fifteen broke the magic 200 mark.

Six of the top fifteen *Experten*, as they were called, served with JG 52 in the East for at least part of their career. Among them, they accounted for a final total of 1,580 planes, and despite odds of 20:1, five emerged alive. That alone says something for the airplane.

What sort of machine was this, that could inspire such loyalty among such skilled and successful pilots and so long retain its usefulness in hostile skies?

That's surprisingly hard to determine. There are only thirteen of the German-built 109s still in existence. None is flyable. And though Messerschmitt still is a name known around the world in aviation circles, nowhere have I ever found a straightforward, complete pilot report on just what the airplane was like.

Today, it's hard to learn. When I asked Colonel Barkhorn to close his eyes and put himself back into the cockpit of a 109, he looked at me and demanded,

Of all the airplanes featured in this book, the ME 109 is the only one the author has not personally flown—and the one he'd most like to fly, of all the airplanes ever built anywhere, by anyone. This pilot report was based on wartime evaluations and on in-depth conversations with some of the greatest of the Messerschmitt experten. *Probably the most*

famous fighters of all time, the Me 109 was in production longer than any other fighter. More than 33,000 were built—more than any other airplane type, until Cessna finally surpassed the mark with 172s, in the mid–1980s. USAF

"Can you tell me exactly what you were doing twenty-five years ago?" It was a good point.

But still, let's see if we can reconstruct a pilot report on, say, an Me 109G-6, the most-produced single model in the long family line. Ready? Okay, let's roll back the clock a quarter century.

The time: July 1943. The place: a Luftwaffe station somewhere in occupied Europe. The plane has just been rolled out of its "hangar" (a barn with the front knocked out); it squats on its little bandy legs in the summer grass. There is no runway, merely a large pasture. It is sufficient, for the 109 can and does operate from 2,000 ft. of turf.

The first thing you notice is the lively coloring. The undersurfaces are pale blue except for the yellow wingtips. The upper wings sport a splinter camouflage in two tones of gray—one dark, one medium. The fuselage sides, fin and rudder are spotted with vague blotches of medium bluish gray. The spine and top of the cowling also are gray, in a splinter scheme matching the wings and horizontal tail.

The huge propeller spinner is black and painted with a broad white curlicue that starts at the muzzle of the nose cannon and runs to the engine cowl—the *Burbelschnauze* used for recognition purposes.

The yellow wingtips and a yellow band around the fuselage forward of the tail mark this as one of the Ostfront machines. The black and white cross is flanked by a large numeral forward and a horizontal bar aft, both in red trimmed in white. The color and symbol identify the Staffel and Gruppe. On the engine cowling just above the exhaust is a black and red shield bearing the sword and stylized wings of JG 52.

The second thing you notice is the steep attitude of the airplane as it rests on its high, narrow, splayed gear. The idea is to allow a steep landing attitude for maximum lift and to permit hard braking just after touchdown, but you'll learn the 109 can be rather easily stood on its nose in the dirt.

This is a small machine, with a wing span of 32 ft. 6½ in., a length of 29 ft. 8 in. and a height (one blade vertical) of 11 ft. 2 in. Nevertheless, it weighs 5,900 lbs. empty and 1,663 lbs. of that is in the 1,475 lb. Daimler-Benz DB 605A-1 twelve-cylinder, inverted-V liquid-cooled engine.

With a wing area of 174 sq. ft. and a loaded weight of 6,950 lbs., our wing loading is an eyelash under 40 lbs. per sq. ft., hardly in the Sunday afternoon pleasure class.

Just ahead on the windshield, the engine cowling bulges with the twin blisters of the 13 mm MG 131 machine guns, giving the airplane its nickname, *der Beule*—"the Bump." These, with 300 rounds of ammo each, and the engine-mounted MG 151/20 cannon with 150 rounds, comprise the plane's entire armament. They have been standard since the G-1/Trop.

The first 109 still had the dual cowl-mounted rifle-caliber machine guns used in World War I, but a third was quickly added between the engine banks,

firing through the prop hub. The 109D-2 mounted a hub-firing cannon, but the MG FF usually jammed after a few rounds, and when it fired, the whole engine vibrated. The substitute wing guns caused aileron flutter and set the British joking about the "Flutter-schmitt."

These problems were ironed out in time to equip the E model—Emil—with the engine cannon, the two MG 131s and a pair of MG FF wing cannons, but the sleeker F model—Fritz—reverted to three guns. Later, pod-mounted MG 151/20s with 120 rounds each were slung underwing.

They were standard on our G-6, but have been removed because they cut 20 mph from the speed and the 150 lbs. under each wing crippled maneuverability in fighter-versus-fighter combat. Besides, they cause the 109 to porpoise at cruise speeds and above.

Most of the German *Experten* still rate the earlier F as the best of the 109s, even though the late Gustavs and the handful of K models were much faster. The G-10 hit 428 mph at 20,000 ft., and the Ks between 440 and 452, depending on the variant.

Both Steinhoff and Barkhorn say the F was the high point of the design; fast (373 to 390 mph), clean and the most maneuverable of the tribe. Barkhorn calls it "the best model I ever flew." He said, "It could turn, this bird; climb, everything." He liked the long-range hitting power of its high velocity 15 mm cannon and says while the book proved it couldn't turn with the Yak 3s and 9s, the Spit Vs., La-5s and the like, "in it, I could." Airacobras and Hurricanes were no contest.

Bigger superchargers, higher compression ratios, ninety-six octane gas and fuel additives boosted the Daimler-Benz's rated power to keep pace with ever-increasing combat weights, but flying qualities declined somewhat after the G-2, last bumpless version.

The most troublesome Soviet fighter was the Yak 9, says Barkhorn, who calls it "almost as fast as the 109," despite identical specifications of 310 mph maximum at sea level. "She was a very fast bird." To Steinhoff, the problem was the Spitfire, which he considered outperformed the Gustav from the Mk IX on.

He least liked the high wing loading, which enabled the Spits to turn inside him. Despite this, the 109 could outclimb and outdive the British fighter throughout the war, and Steinhoff still maintains the Emil was better than the Spit Is and IIs in the Battle of Britain. He most liked the fact that the 109 was "a very stable gun platform," and adds, "The cockpit outlay also was perfect for its job."

He agrees the Fw 190 required less skill on the ground because of the wide gear, had heavier armament and was generally easier for the novice to fly. But he says he never liked it as he did the 109. The Messerschmitt remained the pro fighter pilot's airplane.

It's time to learn why.

You clamber onto the left wing root, swing your right leg over the side and duck beneath the side-hinged canopy and its dangling slab of armor plate. You discover immediately that the 109 was not built for big men. In fact, most of the Luftwaffe's hot pilots are average size or smaller.

Your legs stick straight out in front of you, and you find you're lying on your pelvis in the bucket seat. It seems uncomfortable, but you'll learn it gives better leverage on the rudder pedals and helps resist blackout under high G loads. The rudder pedals have heel baskets and straps across your insteps, but are not adjustable.

Instruments are largely standard, except they're marked in kilometers per hour and meters, rather than miles per hour and feet. Temperatures are shown in centigrade. Flight instruments are center and left, engine gauges to the right. There is no manifold pressure gauge, but a boost pressure instead, reading atmospheres per square inch in kilograms. The Gustav has an artificial horizon and radio compass. The Emil didn't.

The magneto switch is a knife-blade affair in a vertical slot on the panel. Down is off, up is both, and M1 and M2 are left and right. Throttle and mixture controls are in their familiar place on the left side, but the prop pitch is on the panel and comes with an instrument showing in degrees the blade settings on the electric prop.

The windshield seems abominably small at first glance, but it makes no immediate difference because the long hood blocks forward vision anyway, as in other World War II fighters.

The 109 is often faulted for poor visibility, particularly to the rear. It's a matter of being accustomed to it. "I could see so much from the cockpit; in my opinion, the visibility from this bird was excellent," declared Barkhorn. "They got me only once for this reason, and that was an Airacobra—I was so tired I didn't look behind me."

The mechanic closes and locks the canopy—an almost impossible job from inside—and stands clear, thumbs up. If needed, he could crank the inertia starter from the right side, but today the battery can bring the flywheel up to speed.

Switches on, mags on, mixture full rich, prop at full increase, punch the starter and engage the clutch. The 9 ft. 10 in. VDM prop jerks, the engine fires promptly and jets of blue flame and black smoke dart from the dozen short, individual stacks.

You open the throttle slightly and taxi to the far end of the runway. With plenty of weight on the tail and the effective toe brakes, fast taxiing is easy, but the stiff gear delivers most of the bumps directly to your tailbone. It feels much like driving a go-kart. The narrow gear also means you must lead turns well in taxiing.

Run-up and cockpit check are standard. Both flaps and elevator trim are manual, controlled by two large, spoked trim wheels set vertically against the left side of the cockpit. Flaps go to twenty degrees and the stabilizer to takeoff setting. The two-position radiator flaps are thermostatically controlled and are already open. Both the movable surfaces tilt downward with the wing flap setting.

Ease the throttle open for takeoff and the 109 leaps ahead. You feed in full right rudder to keep it tracking straight. Acceleration shoves your head back against the armored rest. Forward stick pressure lifts the tail, and vision improves dramatically.

You hold the Gustav on until 115 mph, then let it fly off, slanting upward immediately at a steep angle.

This official USAF photo, taken at Wright Field on Oct. 5, 1945, are of a G–6 model, the most-produced variant. The engine is the 1,475 hp liquid-cooled Daimler-Benz DB–605A–1 inverted V-12, weighing 1,663 lbs. Bumps on either side of engine cowling house 13 mm heavy machine guns, while a 20 or 30 mm cannon fires through the hollow propeller hub. The Me 109 is a good example of a large engine closely followed by a very small airplane. Maximum speed is about 390 mph, clean. USAF

Flip the gear lever up with your left hand, wind up the flaps, reduce power from 1.42 ata (4.5 pounds/inch) to 1.3 (3.5 pounds) and bring the prop back from 2800 to 2600 rpm. Close the radiator flaps.

Fishtailing slightly to clear the airspace ahead, you are surprised by the fast, positive throttle response and by the lack of friction in the control system. Climbing at 160 mph indicated, the Gustav belies its weight. Rate of climb steadies at about 3,300 fpm— slightly above average due to the missing wing cannon pods.

Level off and try a few speed checks at 20,000 ft. Normal cruise (62½ percent) gives a true airspeed of 260 mph at 2,300 rpm and a range of 615 miles on the 110 gallons of eighty-seven octane in the cell behind your back and under your seat. Performance cruise (seventy-five percent) yields 330 mph true at 1.15 ata, but the range drops to 450 miles.

Full throttle and a squirt of MW 50 (methanol and water mixture) produces an indicated 535 km/h or 342 mph IAS, for a true of about 390, and you realize that, if the wing cannon pods were still in place, you'd be lucky to realize the listed 373 mph and equally lucky to get the promised 348 miles range out of it. You see why the Germans like to cruise this airplane at 218-224 mph, and why the average combat sortie is only seventy minutes in duration.

The DB 605 consumes 127 gph at takeoff power, and though it will cruise at 85 gph at seventy-five percent, while you're injecting the MW 50 into the supercharger and using a higher boost pressure, consumption goes to 169 gph. Obviously, your 110 gallons won't last long at this rate.

On the other hand, your MW 50 tank contains only thirty gallons and can be used for just ten minutes at a time, with a five-minute lapse between spurts. At this increased power, your plugs will last only fifteen to thirty hours, but this is of little concern because your brand-new engine probably will need a major before that anyway.

Early in the war, the DB 605 engine was good for 100 hours' operational use before an inspection was needed. Then it was flown at least another 100 before overhaul, and 300 to 350 hours was not unusual. By war's end, the Luftwaffe was replacing DB 605 engines regularly afer twenty hours, and no one was surprised by a five-hour service life. This was due to lowered production standards, overdevelopment of the basic engine for more power, and the more frequent— sometimes constant—need to pull war emergency power.

Service ceiling on this airplane is 38,500 ft., and absolute ceiling is 39,750. It is supposed to be 41,400. Normal speed range for the *Kurvenkampf*—the dogfight favored on the Eastern Front throughout the war—is about 100 to 280 mph, and the 109 is very stable, very responsive, throughout this spectrum.

A few maneuvers show the airplane has no bad flight habits. Pull off the power and ease the stick back, and at about 135 IAS clean, the stick in your right hand flops quickly from side to side as the automatic Handley-Page slats slam out. Buffeting starts at about 115 IAS, and the Messerschmitt begins to try to drop the left wing, demanding increasingly alert use of both aileron and rudder in large increments.

There is no actual stall break, but at about 105 IAS, the controls can no longer cope with the increasingly violent wobble. Flaps and gear down, there is no real change in behavior except the wobble is not quite so violent and the plane hangs on down to about 90 mph. Like all such machines, rapid use of full throttle on the back side of the power curve will flip the 109 into a left roll against full aileron and rudder, but there is no tendency to spin. It merely falls. The 109 is so markedly stable laterally that some pilots think it undesirable, preferring more skittish handling in a fighter.

Slats out, a strong-armed pilot brisk with his controls can haul the 109 around in tight vertical banks up to 4 G, often out-turning more reluctant enemies in planes theoretically more maneuverable.

Because of this, experienced Luftwaffe pilots liked to fight the Yaks and La-5s at speeds close to 150 mph. Knowing their 109s better than many men know their wives, they could out-turn the Reds even at the 6,000 to 8,000 ft. best altitude of the Russian fighters. But as the speed and G forces build, the Messerschmitt's ailerons and rudder get heavier until the Russian has the edge.

Above 20,000 ft., the 109's maneuverability is excellent, challenged only by the P-51 Mustang. Below 20,000, most pilots think the Focke-Wulf more agile, but the 190's performance falls off badly at altitude. Below 15,000 ft., either is more maneuverable than the Mustang.

Some Gustav variants have pressurized cockpits, but constant use of an oxygen mask is mandatory anyway. The canopy's double windows are prone to collect frost at extreme heights and are impossible to clear.

The 109 is a clean airplane with a rapid dive, and a favorite evasive tactic is to dump the nose or do a half snap roll and head for the deck. At cruise power, the Messerschmitt will accelerate through 450 mph in about ten seconds. Tough and well stressed, the airplane was inadvertently dived to 505 mph IAS as early as 1938, when a pilot passed out at altitude from oxygen mask malfunction. He wrinkled the wing skins pulling out, but the plane held together.

It hasn't always. There are a few recorded cases where pilots pulled the wings off a 109, and chordwise wrinkles are more common. But USAAF pilots have pulled the tails off P-47s the same way. Unlike some World War II fighters, the 109 is restricted only by the physical endurance of the pilot, and although it does not spin readily, it can be forced in and held there. It can also be snap-rolled.

As in all extremely clean airplanes, the first prob-

Only one Me 109 flies today with a Daimler-Benz engine—and it began as a Hispano Ha. 1112 Buchon, *just like this one. License-built in Spain, the* Buchon *(Pigeon) is powered with the remarkable Rolls-Royce Merlin. The Spanish Air Force disposed of these airplanes in 1968, and two dozen or so were imported into the United States, chiefly by Confederate Air Force pilots who flew in the British film* Battle of Britain, *released in 1969. Perhaps eight or 10 really flew in this country, and most of them have been wrecked in landing accidents.*

lem in landing the 109 is to get the speed low enough to drop the gear. Radiator flaps can be opened at cruise and cut the speed by 13 mph. The gear is lowered below 180 mph and followed immediately by the flaps. Since they are hand cranked, they go steadily down to full forty degrees deflection. Nose-up trim is applied at the same time.

Normal approach is 150 to 155 mph downwind, 140 on base, 120 down final and across the fence at 100, nose high and with power—almost a carrier approach. The 109 touches down at about 85. A flatter approach will produce smooth wheel landings, but the left wing gets heavy fast as the speed drops through 100.

Landing is the time for the 109 pilot to be most alert, for the airplane has been cursed with weak gear and a tendency to swing on the ground throughout its career.

Factory engineers tried to solve these problems by strengthening the gear attach points and using an automatic tailwheel lock linked to the throttle. Nevertheless, the troubles persisted, and some five percent of the entire 109 production was lost in such accidents.

It also can be pulled off the ground too quickly on takeoff and again drop a wing. Aileron will bring it up momentarily, but the ailerons snatch and it falls off again, at about 50 to 70 ft. Such crashes have killed a number of pilots converting to the 109.

The brakes are powerful and sometimes seize. In 1945, II/JG 52 fell back from Hungary to Austria and occupied a base with an asphalt runway for the first time in years. Used to grass or dirt, thirty-nine of the arriving forty-two Me 109s crashed on landing, victims of the strange feel of the hard surface and the oversensitive brakes.

There were other headaches. In 1941, the extensively redesigned F model had a tendency to shed its new, unbraced tail assembly—a fault traced to lack of enough fuselage stiffeners and sympathetic vibration at certain engine rpm. The early Gustavs were noted for sudden mid-air fires, a habit that caused the death of famed Capt. Hans-Joachim Marseilles, victor over 158 British planes in little more than a year's service with JG 27 in North Africa.

But as you taxi in, soaking up the pasture bumps with your tailbone, you can't fault the Me 109's longevity or its claim to fame.

One of the most adaptable designs in aviation history, it went in ten years from 610 to 2,000 hp (with MW 50 and overboost), from a top speed of 292 to 452, from a gross weight of 4,850 to 7,438 lbs. and from three rifle-caliber machine guns to two 15 mm and a 30 mm cannon. Climb went from 2,700 to 4,850 fpm and ceiling from 29,500 to 41,400. Only endurance declined, from ninety to fifty minutes.

It was the first major World War II fighter in production, in 1935; first in service, 1937; first in combat, same year; last in service, 1967; and it was used in combat by more air arms than any of its contemporaries.

British claims to the contrary, there are some folks around who think the ubiquitous 109 is unquestionably the most famous fighter of the Second World War. Some of them are aging jet jockeys in Germany who are still trying to find an airplane that fits their stick and throttle hands as well. That's why they're flying Lockheed F-104Gs now.

"The 109 and the 104 are the same," says Barkhorn. "It's a real fighter."

The rest of us will always wonder just what the dimensions of the 109's challenge and charm really were.

First printed in *Air Progress*, August 1969.

Chapter 16

Boeing B–17 Flying Fortress

Queen of the skies

The B–17 was one of the first American bombers I ever studied. Of course, it never occurred to me that someday I might have a chance to fly one of the last survivors of the great fleets that darkened the skies over Europe.

By the time I did, the Flying Fortress was no longer the huge machine of my boyhood. It hasn't shrunk, of course, but my perspective has changed—conditioned by years of Boeing 747s, Lockheed C–5s and, most recently, the Antonov An–225.

The airplane was forty years old when I flew it, and as we droned eastward across half a continent my thoughts varied from how sweet the Fort was to fly, to how cramped it was inside and to what a frightening place a B–17 must have been in combat—half the Luftwaffe bearing down, and no place to hide!

As strategic bombers go, the B–17 was pretty inefficient, delivering only 5,000 lbs. of bombs on a typical long-range mission from England into the heart of the Reich. Still, that was nearly twice what anyone else's bombers were delivering at the time it was designed in 1934. And it was a beautiful flying machine.

If you ever get a chance, go for a ride in one. You won't regret it.

We were an hour out of Chino, California, when I noticed that the oil pressure gauge on No. 3 engine stood at 45 lbs. It had always been a little low, but I distinctly recalled seeing 60 lbs. not long ago.

I eyed it suspiciously, and verified that No. 4—on the same gauge—still showed 70 lbs. and ran a quick check of the cylinder head and oil temperatures on No. 3. The first was a little hot but within limits, the second a little cool but likewise. Just as they had been since takeoff.

Carefully, I examined No. 3 nacelle. No real trace of oil; just a spattering on the cowling, and it had been there all along. The 1,200 hp Wright seemed perfectly happy.

I looked back at the oil pressure gauge. It showed 40 lbs. Bad news!

I was alone on the flight deck. David Tallichet and Brian Wandel were back in the B–17's innards someplace, puttering around. Oh, well. Flying Fortresses, I'm told, fly very well on three engines. I went back to watching the oil pressure. It was down to 35 lbs. Still no sign of distress from the engine itself. It was ginning along, doing its job. The two temperature gauges were nailed in place.

There was plenty of desert below, if it came to that. Offhand, I could see about twenty square miles of suitable landing area in gliding distance. Back to the gauge. It showed 30 lbs., and the needle was visibly easing very gradually down the scale.

Tallichet slid back into the pilot's seat and Wandel took his post behind us both. I gestured at the gauge. Right about then it expired entirely, making a fifteen-second drop on down to zero. We all looked at No. 3. It still showed no sign of distress. Tallichet's right hand wandered toward the throttle and prop controls, then fluttered to a stop as I pointed to the two heat indicators. "It may be the gauge," I yelled hopefully above the din of 4,800 galloping ponies.

He and I looked at Wandel. Wandel shrugged and said, "We had trouble with it before." We all went back

The war record of the Boeing B-17 "Flying Fortress" stretches from Pearl Harbor to V-J Day. A total of 12,696 were built, and in the massive thousand-plane raids of 1944, they darkened the sky over Europe. Yet today, only a handful remain airworthy, and the sight of that famous planform can stop traffic on an interstate.

to watching No. 3. After all, this airplane has not been fired up in 4½ years. Sometimes engines catch fire, and none of us was sure the extinguishers worked. The Brazilians even added a handy ID sheet to the Dash One depicting various types of smoke and what each means. Unfortunately it was in Portuguese—not among the accomplishments of any of us. The minutes dragged by on little turtle feet, and finally we began to breathe a little easier. Hallelujah! It was the gauge, after all.

That suited me fine. I had never been in an airborne B-17 before, and now I was barely launched on a 1,300 mile, seven-hour flight as copilot. I wished to trade none of it for emergency landing practice. Wandel had never been in a Fort either. He probably felt the same way. I knew Tallichet's feelings. After twenty-one missions as an Eighth Air Force copilot, he was finally aircraft commander on a B-17. He was enjoying himself.

Besides, it took us too long to get the thing airborne. I didn't want it back on the ground as long as we had any real choice. This could have been the old bird's final flight. She was bound for a new home in the Yesterday's Air Force (YAF) Kansas Wing Warbird Museum and may never leave there.

Originally, we were to have left Chino the evening before and flown across the mountains to Barstow, enabling us to take off at dawn and make the balance of the trip in a single day. Sunset caught us instead, and we spent the night in a nearby motel.

Predictably, the next morning was WOXOF.

It stayed that way until 1300 or so, when Chino tower began letting people out special VFR. Unfortunately, the B-17 was totally without radio. A thousand feet up the sky was blue, but ground visibility was no more than two miles, and they flatly refused to let us out on a light gun signal without a special.

By 1400, a local Cherokee Six pilot agreed to lead us out as a flight of two. By 1430 Bill Hamilton, lead

mechanic on the Military Aircraft Restoration Corporation ground crew, had Nos. 2, 3 and 4 in action, but No. 1 was stubborn. Sweat poured down his face as he played throttle and mixture controls like banjo strings while I flipped starter toggles and primers and Tallichet looked interested.

I leaned past Hamilton and asked, "What did you do in the old days when something like this happened?" Tallichet grinned and made a flat gesture with his hand. "We called it a day; went to the Officers' Club and had a round."

Finally, at about 1455, No. 1 reluctantly went to work. Hamilton hopped out, and he and Randy Barckley took station ahead of each wingtip to guide us out through the hangar rows, one of which had been built since the Fortress was parked there in 1973.

Inverters whirring, a dozen prop blades beating the air, the old bomber eased off the concrete pad where it stood so long and nosed its way between the lines of buildings. Clearance was perhaps 10 ft. on either side of the 103 ft. wing. Everything was fine—for 100 yards. And there it was: a Cessna 310, just ahead and parked where our left wing must go. It had been tied down and left, locked and with brakes set, sometime since we began our long engine-starting ritual.

Barckley and another man flung themselves on the Cessna's tail, dragging it down below the level of the Fort's wing, and Tallichet walked the brakes, trying to ease the Boeing past the obstruction. Hydraulics whining, he crept up on the 310, edging right to give plenty of clearance for No. 1 prop. Too far!

At the right wingtip, Hamilton flung up his arms in a peremptory stop gesture, then put both hands palms together to illustrate what had happened. We had just wiped off the right wingtip light on one of those new hangars.

Defeated, we shut down all four engines once again and began to round up several items: somebody to move the Cessna, a tug, some chain and a couple of suitable bolts. B-17s do not back up under their own power and there was, of course, no such thing as a tow bar for it.

All told, it took us 120 minutes to move the B-17 110 yards!

As we prepared to crank up again, the guy in the Cherokee Six walked over to report the field was now VFR and since we didn't need him anymore, he was going to repark his airplane and go back to work. I didn't blame him. With the usual perversity of machines, the Wrights started easily and we swung onto the taxiway, free at last.

As we sat at the end of the taxiway running up No. 3, I spotted an oil filler door flapping merrily in the breeze—one last glitch in the process. I unstrapped, ran back through the airplane with Wandel, boosted him up on the wing and watched him use a screwdriver on the loose Dzus fastener.

Referring to his hand-scribbled checklist, extracted three hours earlier from the pilot's manual,

Tallichet ran down the pre-takeoff section. We verified 1,000 lbs. hydraulic pressure, fuel valves positioned, controls unlocked with the handy floor lever, cowl flaps open and locked, battery switches and inverters on, generators on and functioning, intercoolers cold, carburetor heat off, turbochargers off, boost pumps on. I cycled the flaps, Tallichet wiggled ailerons, elevator, rudder and checked that all trim tabs were at zero. He set the altimeter; I hopefully set the ancient DG to the approximate taxiway heading. Since we had no magnetic compass, it would have to do. I set the brakes and he began the engine run-up.

All four throttles got to 1500 rpm with props at full increase, mixtures at Auto Rich, and Tallichet twiddled the central turbocharger dial all the way from 0 to 8, its automatic setting, and back several times to exercise the mechanism. Then, with turbos off, he cycled the props, checked the voltmeter for generator outputs and reduced power to 1000 rpm, advancing each engine in turn to full power.

As No. 1 ran up, the airplane promptly swung to the right—and both of us jumped on the brakes. On No. 4, it went back to the left, evening things out. At 28 in., mag drops are minimal, none over 75 rpm. The turbo control went back to 8. All engines produced the expected 2500 rpm, but manifold pressure varied from 41 to 44 in., indicating some differences in turbo functioning. None gave the book-specified 47.5 in. maximum. Aside from that, everything seemed fine. Fuel and oil pressures, oil and cylinder temperatures all were in limits. Actually, for such a large and sophisticated airplane, there wasn't much to it.

"Okay," Tallichet announced, "now, if we have to abort this takeoff, when we go out, we'll have to go through the top hatch back in the radio compartment or run all the way aft to the door—unless you think you can go out the window." He gestured at the sliding side windows.

I examined my window, which was perhaps 15 in. high, and thought of the 2,810 gallons of 100 octane in the tanks. I decided with that kind of incentive I could probably go right *through* the roof like a jack-in-the-box.

I estimated the speed I could make, flipping off the boost pumps, master switches and magnetos, and hoped Wandel could get the fuel valves turned off before we hit. These were mounted on a bulkhead four feet behind me. In a crash, they might as well be back in the hangar as for my chances of getting to them. Not for the first time, I asked myself just what I was doing there, and why I kept getting into situations like this. . . .

The tower gave us a green and we trundled onto the active. As soon as the aircraft was straight down the runway, I locked the tailwheel.

Tallichet squirmed his rear deeper into his seat. He issued instructions to Wandel—directly behind us—to call out the airspeed, warned me to maintain full throttle when he removed his right hand, and to raise the gear and flaps on command. I nodded, positioned my left hand half an inch above his right. He glanced around, and I could see him tighten up, preparing for the challenge. After all, it had been a long time—and his only other flight in this bird was as a copilot on the ferry flight back from Wright-Patterson AFB, with Jim Appleby in the left seat.

"Everybody ready?" he asked. We nodded. "Okay, here we go," he announced, his right hand going forward decisively. The Wrights burst into a full-throated roar and the old bird began to move—55,000 lbs. of men, metal and high-test waddling down the concrete. There was a peculiar sense of strain about the

The Boeing 299 first flew in 1935, and the airplane saw combat in both the Pacific and the European theaters of war during World War II. The B–17 later served briefly in the 1948 Arab-Israeli War. It served many years longer as a rescue and coastal patrol aircraft, carrying a lifeboat slung under the fuselage. This was the service to which the Brazilian Air Force put N47780.

whole takeoff that I do not recall ever experiencing before. Except, of course, that perhaps it was all in my imagination.

At 60, the tail was floating. At 80 she began to get light on her wheels, nose thrusting eagerly at the smoggy air, and at 100 she was ready to fly. At 110, Tallichet eased back the yoke and she was off and running free, in a long flat climb up the hazy sky. He called for the gear. I flipped the electric toggle switch and watched as the right main folded slowly forward into its well. "Gear up," I yelled. Tallichet made his first power reduction, to 35 in.; called for 2300 rpm. I eased the props back and synchronized the needles as we rolled into our first turn.

The power came back again, to 28 in.; the props went back to 2000 rpm. Airspeed in the climb stabilized at 120 IAS. We seemed to be in business. I knew from reading the manual that the B-17 was supposed to climb at 2300 rpm and 135-140 IAS, but the manual was intended for crews with a full war load (meaning, with this kind of fuel, 4,000 lbs., or 400 lbs. per crew member), and I guessed our present climb was much like that of an Eighth Air Force bird grossing maybe 62,000 or 63,000 lbs. The altimeter moved upward in little jerks, making any time computations meaningless, but it was obvious why the B-17s used to circle over England for an hour or more. Initially, coming off the runway at our weight, we probably got 800 feet in the first minute. Now, we were lucky to climb 300 fpm.

Off to the right, a red-and-white Cessna 150 rolled into a gentle bank, watching us struggle upward, and I was fleetingly glad he didn't choose to climb with us. It would have been the first time in a long while I'd been outclimbed by one of those.

Tallichet made a sidling approach to I-15, detouring around San Bernardino, California, and we slid through El Cajon Pass at a comfortable 5,000 ft., fifteen minutes after takeoff. He leaned back, happy as a pup with a new bone, and gestured at the controls, inviting me to take over.

"When you get to Barstow," he yelled, "fly over the runway and then just follow the highway east." He fished in his pocket, came up with a cigar and lit it, puffing expansively. It was the first time I had seen him smoke a cigar—but, then, this was a genuine Havana, one of several liberated on a recent Air France flight.

I reached forward and grasped the control yoke with both hands, sliding my feet onto the generous rudder pedals once again. The yoke was wrapped in rough cord, still bearing the crumbling remains of a heavy black paint which once overlayed it. Paint particles stuck to my palms.

I looked out through the narrow windshield, over the astrodome and into the Mojave Desert stretching away before me; glanced to the side, out along the broad wing; checked the faded cowlings of the four Wrights rumbling happily away and leaking a little oil here and there; ran my cross-check of the flight and engine instruments and experimentally wiggled the controls.

She was expectedly heavy in the hand but surprisingly, delightfully responsive. At first, I tried to trim it to continue a slow climb to 7,500 MSL, but soon desisted because the elevator trim was, if anything, even heavier than the controls. I found it easier simply to apply a shade of back pressure, for the big bomber is sensitive to the most subtle inputs.

I rapidly decided, in fact, that much of the control heaviness was due to three decades of dried grease, dirt and general guck in the control system. I suspected if the pulleys and cables were thoroughly cleaned, she would maneuver like a cutting horse, with due allowance, of course, for the effects of mass.

With a fuselage nearly 75 ft. long, all that wing and 15 ft. of tail fin, she develops considerable momentum in motion, and must be led a little to arrest it. This is a lot of airplane! Even empty, she weighs 38,000 lbs., and her bowlegged stance on the mains caused me some instant concern until I was assured she was supposed to sit that way.

Leveling out at 7,500, I was surprised to note the air speed builds to 150 indicated. The F model Dash One I had read says at an economy cruise setting of 28x2100, it will indicate 149, and we were flying at 100 rpm less by the aircraft commander's decision—a choice which had fretted me slightly in the belief it was responsible for our sluggardly climb. Apparently this was not so.

I flew to the Barstow airport, made a smart right turn and proceeded directly down the runway as Tallichet reset the weary DG, then hung the nose on I-40, eastbound, I tried the fuel gauges again, one at a time. They stubbornly indicated "empty," as they had since initial start-up, despite the 15,000 lbs. of 100 octane I knew was still in the tanks.

Flying N47780 is a unique experience for any dyed-in-the-chromate aviation buff, particularly so for one like me who entered the first grade to the nightly reports of besieged London during the Blitz by Edward R. Murrow. And especially now, when there are perhaps no more than a dozen airworthy examples left of the Flying Fortress, the most famous bomber in history. I know of only three others flying that still carry their gun turrets and bomb bays.

Product of a 1934 Army Air Corps requirement, the Boeing 299 first flew July 28, 1935, and its war record stretched from Pearl Harbor to V-J Day. A total of 12,696 B-17s was built, including 12,592 of the battle-ready E through G models. They dropped 540,036 tons of bombs on European targets, compared to 452,508 tons by the more numerous (and more efficient) B-24 Liberators and 463,544 tons dropped by all other aircraft.

I know little about 780's career, though I know she is a B-17G-90-DL, one of 8,680 G models built and one of 2,395 of that number built by Douglas at Santa Monica. Completed late in 1944, she was serialed 44-83663 and delivered May 1, 1945, to Patterson,

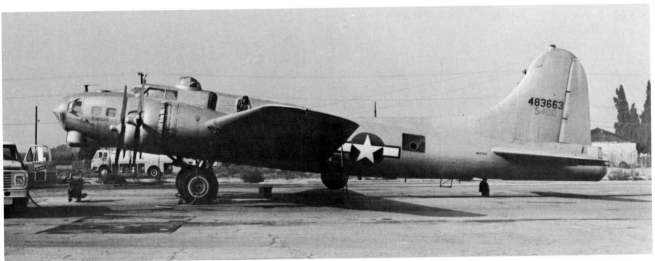

The world's first successful four-engine strategic bomber, the B-17 was really not very efficient, dropping a single 500 lb. bomb per crewman per mission in Eighth Air Force service over Europe. However, the airplane is easy to fly; a sort of four-breasted Cub. It is also, unquestionably, the most famous bomber in history.

New Jersey. Just over a month later, she was assigned to Garden City, Kansas, and the same December was handed over to AAF storage. In April 1951, she was assigned to USAF-Brazil and flown to Rio de Janeiro, where she was handed over to the Förça Aerea do Brasileira on May 4. Numbered 5400, she was the first of eleven acquired by the FAB and one of six still operated by them until 1968.

Since there are no logs with the airplane, I do not know her total time, nor her work in Brazil. But a letter from the Brazilian government details the number and type of missions flown by her kind, and I know that by the fall of 1966, a sister ship had logged more than 5,100 hours in FAB service.

Given back to the USAF by the Brazilians, she landed at Wright-Patterson in June 1968, and went on display at the Air Force Museum there. Replaced by a B-17F with a combat record obtained from Switzerland, she was made available on permanent loan to Yesterday's Air Force and flown to Chino early in 1973.

By the time we landed at the YAF's new Kansas Wing Warbird Museum, I had learned a little something about her character and condition. I know, for example, that she never failed to smack me a stunning blow atop the head at least once a day with the steel bottom ring of her top turret. It never got any softer. I know, too, that she is still basically a sound and airworthy bird, despite the minor ills of long inactivity and a certain amount of neglect.

And I know that she is an absolute 55,000 lb. pussycat to fly, a four-engine Piper Cub. Upon reflection, she had to be—for she was flown into combat by teenage crews with an average of 500 hours' total time and hurled into the greatest armed conflict the world has ever known. She emerged victorious. And more often than not, she brought her crews home, often under incredible conditions. Indeed, one crippled airplane even landed itself in England after the crew bailed out.

She is a gentle bird, stable and relatively forgiving to fly, although she is a rudder machine and demands coordinated use of the controls. With her weight, she is not bothered by thermal turbulence, and is comfortable but surprisingly cramped inside. There is not a spot in her fuselage where a man with outstretched arms cannot touch both her metal sides.

The bomb bay is only a few steps long, for this was the first of the real strategic bombers, and thus was designed as a flying machine first, a load carrier second. It is spanned by a narrow catwalk, a tight fit even for a slender civilian. I can only imagine what it must have been like for a hefty 200 pounder in an electrical bunny suit and a parachute.

The bombardier, of course, has the best view— and no doubt a frightening one on takeoff and landing. But pilot and copilot have very adequate vision out their narrow windshields. I noted the total absence of armor protection for those last three positions, and decided it was no fun to sit there and watch the Focke Wulfs barreling in for a head-on firing pass, four 20 mms and a brace of 12.7s hammering away.

It's much more fun to fly up Route 66 and watch the cars on the highway below. Often they slow perceptibly; now and then one will pull sharply onto the shoulder to watch us approach and thunder overhead, flashing that famous silhouette. Fun—and sad, too. Once it was not unusual to see a thousand of these aircraft darkening the sky in a vast aerial parade, shaking the earth with the thunder of their passage. Now a single airplane is an event rare enough to stop traffic on an arterial highway.

We flew northeast up I-40, then cut due east to pass south of Kingman, skirt Picacho Butte and flew almost directly over Williams and Flagstaff, Arizona, following US-66 to Winslow. We were nearing the last

Author flying the B–17. Droning eastward across the country, it was easy to imagine the Fw 190s boring in from 12 o'clock, wings sparkling with cannon fire—all aimed directly at me! The flight deck was a favorite aiming point *for German fighters; a frightening thought when there's no protection except a few thin sheets of aluminum and plexiglass and no place to hide. Air warfare took a lot of raw courage, on both sides.*

when Tallichet tapped his watch and made landing motions. He intended to RON there.

The Winslow field elevation is 4,938 ft., the runway 7,500 ft. long. No problem. We overflew the field, looking for a wind indicator. The wind was slightly across Runway 10, but near enough and mild. Below us, a Cessna trainer broke off its approach to Runway 23 and began a right-hand orbit south of the field. With Wandel calling off speeds again and me on gear and flaps, Tallichet greased the big bird onto the runway like a pro at 95 indicated, slightly tail low. We let her roll, eating up most of the runway before doing a 180 and taxiing back to the turn-off and what was obviously the shop hangar/airport office. We pulled up in front of the building, the Wrights grumbling, and stopped. There was not a soul in sight.

After a minute or so, a line boy appeared in front of the hangar door sixty yards away. Sliding back his side window, Tallichet stuck out his head and shouted, "Where do you want us to park?" The line boy merely stared, wiping his hands. Tallichet yelled again. The line boy loped toward us and, instead of stopping,

bounded up on the trailing edge of the wing. He was the first man I have even seen do that. It stands nearly 6 ft. above ground, slopes the wrong way and has no handholds.

He directed us to a corner of the ramp, dropped off and guided us into position. We followed, swinging around and shutting down—and before we could get out of the airplane, we were surrounded by eight or nine people, including some who had driven out from downtown. Also among them was the student pilot and his instructor, who promptly followed us down.

Similarly, upon arriving at the airport about 7:30 next morning, we found an even larger group on hand for our departure. They included World War II veterans, men and women in their thirties and even school-age children. Some had been there since 6 a.m. because they didn't want to miss it.

We almost disappointed them.

Tallichet wrestled futilely with the engines for a few minutes, then summoned Wandel from the ramp and took his place out front with the fire bottle. We tried another cycle or two with Wandel juggling the throttles and mixtures and me handling the starters, and got everything churning but the obstinate No. 1. With it, we got no place.

I decided on a last expedient. "Tell you what," I told Wandel. "Turn your mags off and give me full rich, full throttle. I'll crank her through six or eight times. Then give me idle cut-off and mags on, and when she fires go to auto rich." He nodded, and we suited the action to words. We cranked it through, I wound the starter flywheel as tight as it would go, opened the throttle to half, howled, "Now," and, as Wandel flipped on the mags. I jammed a finger down on the clutch, madly pumping the throttle. Blue smoke belched from beneath the cowling and the big Hamilton-Standard began to blur. There was a ticklish moment before the auto rich took, but with the starter still engaged, she held.

Creeping out onto the runway, a vicious juddering suddenly began somewhere aft. Tallichet stopped. Both of us were convinced we'd blown the tailwheel tire, which was low anyway. All of us were wondering where you get a B-17 tailwheel tire in the middle of Arizona, and how you get it changed even then. These people didn't even have an APU. Wandel made another lightning trip through the airplane and returned to reassure us we still had a tire. We resumed our creep, slower.

Tail in the weeds, we lined up on the runway, conducted our run-up and took another deep breath. No engine showed more than 41 in., the inboards less. There was no wind. The ground temperature was rising rapidly. It was probably already 75 degrees F. outside, we were nearly a mile above sea level and straight ahead of us, like a target in a gun sight, was what appeared to be a big alfalfa dehydrating plant with a huge tower rising in our flight path.

Ah, well, *c'est la vie*. We dropped one-third flaps. Again Tallichet's right hand went forward, pushing the throttles to the stop. Again I was right behind him with my left. At 100 indicated, he hauled her off and as soon as we were off the runway we started the gear on its sluggish path to the wells. Now there was nothing much to do but watch the tower get bigger . . . and whip triumphantly 80 ft. below us, with nothing ahead but falling ground for a hundred miles. We had the world by the tail on a downhill pull.

Except, of course, that we managed to get misplaced a little. Heading essentially cross-country to Albuquerque, New Mexico, we got established on our line in good shape, Tallichet reading the map and making hand signals to me while I flew. But then we relaxed and pretty well flew into the rising sun, dodging peaks en route. Trouble was, the sun as it rose veered well to the south and we ended up on a course ending somewhere in north central Mexico unless we got sorted out. We did, finally, approaching Albuquerque on a due north heading—a good 100 mile scenic detour that added an hour to our flight time.

Once across the Sandias, it was back to Route 66 and a strictly no sweat cross-country tour to Santa Rosa, Tucumcari and Dalhart, where Tallichet elected to land again due to the uncertain fuel situation. We all knew we should have plenty to take us to Topeka nonstop, but, with no gauges and some doubt about just how to get it out of the Tokyo tanks, he opted for discretion.

Runway 3 at the Dalhart, Texas, airport is 3,939 ft. above sea level and 9,000 ft. long, with beautiful flat approaches. In fact, it turned out to be an old wartime B-17 base, and old 780 settled in with a mild "erk" of the tires. But, once down, No. 1 got independent again. Advancing the throttle brought the manifold pressure up, but the prop remained at about 800 rpm. Only after some fancy throttle jiggling did the linkage catch and allow the prop to pick up again.

"What do you suppose is causing that?" Tallichet asked. He looked at Wandel. Wandel shrugged. He looked at me. I shrugged. What the hell, I just start 'em and fly 'em, I don't know how they work.

As we taxiied to the ramp, we were greeted by a line *girl* in a trig knitted jump-suit who kept motioning us to taxi close. I got nervous. "I hope they've got a tug," I shouted to Tallichet. "If they don't, we'll play hell ever getting this thing away from the pumps." He shrugged, and replied, "They must know what they're doing," and kept taxiing. Women affect him that way.

All told, we spent nearly two hours at Dalhart, which is why I didn't really want us to stop. One trouble with that class of airplane, when you shut it down, there are lots of things to do before you start it up again. For openers, we have to spend twenty minutes or so talking to all the old B-17 types, telling war stories and explaining who we are, where we're from and where we're going. Then there's servicing the airplane, which is a lengthy chore in itself. And taking time for a sandwich and glass of milk. And talking to the local press, and posing for a picture. And on and on.

Normally, I enjoy this sort of thing. But now we had something like 3½ hours of daylight left and a long way to go, and I really would have appreciated being back at my desk the next morning. I was already a day late.

Tallichet, of course, felt otherwise. As he remarked to one of the Flight Service Station guys who greeted us, "Maybe back during the war I was just a young punk kid lieutenant they wouldn't let fly the airplane, but now I've got it. I'm flying it, and those guys who were captains and majors are on the ground." The FSS guy, who was in the same category, nodded in understanding. "Now they're just another old man on the street," he said.

But the man in charge of this operation obviously knew his World War II-vintage aircraft, and in short order a big tractor pulled us a safe fifty yards or so from the pumps. He unhooked, waved the kid on the tractor away, then grabbed a big fire extinguisher cart and positioned himself in front of No. 2.

Tallichet disappeared into the airport office for something, figuring it would take us thirty minutes or

The B-17's fuselage is so narrow a crewman can stand amidships and touch both inside walls with his spread arms. Cramped, drafty, cold and often filled with powder smoke, spent brass and blood, the Fort was a tough old bird that often survived incredible damage and still brought her crew home. Nevertheless, in 1943 and early 1944, loss rate was such that a man's chances of surviving 25 missions were, statistically, slim.

so to get everything working. I had different plans. I'd already phoned Topeka with an ETA for Forbes Field, based on four things: known sundown, distance, cruising speed—and a departure ten minutes from now.

"Move over," I announced, shooing Wandel off the throttles and mixtures. "You give me hot mags when I call for 'em." This time, I gave all four engines in quick succession the treatment applied to No. 1 in Winslow. In three minutes flat, we had all four churning, and Tallichet burst from the office at a trot.

"Fooled you, didn't we?" I inquired as he dipped under the gun turret, danced between the seats and dropped into his place. "You sure did," he grinned. "I didn't expect that." I pointed at the waiting taxiway. "Let's go to Topeka," I said. He nodded, the throttles went forward and we trundled off down the runway.

Even our run-up now bore the speed and smoothness of practice. We barely delayed a Cessna 402 waiting behind us, and within five minutes more we were lifting off on our last leg.

We did not bother to climb much; we simply picked up 1,000 ft. AGL and drove up the highway. The Cessna flew formation a few minutes, 50 ft. above and 100 ft. off our left wing. Then it pulled sharply up and away, leaving our thirty-three-year-old relic snoring its way across the Great Plains.

We thundered across the Oklahoma Panhandle, drove over Liberal, Kansas—and the weather turned sour. After 1,000 miles of CAVU flying, I found myself plunging directly into a shallow but very solid overcast, just at my level. No matter. I was over home turf,

now. As long as the weather stayed at least marginal VFR, I'd follow the railroad track home.

I stuffed the nose down slightly to follow the receding ground, waved the map at Tallichet and quickly sketched with my finger a route to Meade, Greensburg, Pratt, Hutchinson, McPherson, Herington and I-70 via the iron horse, thence down the turnpike to our destination. Tallichet nodded, I tucked the railroad track under the right wing root and got to to work.

One by one, the little waypoint watering stations slid beneath us, nearly identical, largely anonymous. The murk thickened, and I was reminded of a similar situation six months earlier on the Atlantic coast of Mexico. So, obviously, was Tallichet, who leaned over to shout, "You didn't miss Pratt, did you?" I shook my head emphatically, stabbed at one of the little towns to the west and jerked a thumb below. Actually, I had no idea where we were, for sure. I knew only that Pratt lay ahead. Sure enough, five minutes later it sprung suddenly into full view below the nose. I grabbed a left, picked up the railroad track again and was off to the races.

The track twists and turns like a sidewinder in this part of Kansas, and I pirouetted the big Fortress like a polo pony. Technically, we were still VFR, but the combination of an overcast and a lowering sun had left us in miserable visibility. At this juncture I was not about to foresake those friendly steel rails, though I knew I could fly an approximate heading on the old DG and intersect the interstate and the Kaw River to lead us into Topeka. But there was a TV tower out there, somewhere. This way, there was never a moment's doubt as to my exact location, for I knew every landmark below me. This is classic pilotage in its purest form, and it has kept a lot of old pilots alive.

We roared past the little town of Herington, low enough to startle cows in the fields, and five minutes later picked up the moving daisy chain of lights on the pale double-strand necklace of I-70. I abandoned the railroad, which swings north to the river, and tucked the ruler-straight divided highway beneath my wing root instead.

At 7 p.m., fifteen minutes before official sunset, I brought one of the world's last flyable examples of aviation's most famous bomber over the capitol building of Kansas, "Air Capital of the World." Trooping the colors, I brought the grand old lady in a wide, sweeping turn over town, flipped a wingtip at the statehouse dome, and eased her down toward Forbes.

At 7:15 p.m. on the dot, right on her ETA, N47780 made an easy landing on the 12,800 ft. Forbes main runway, trailing her own special strobe light—a 3 ft. stack fire from the recalcitrant No. 1 carburetor. She was home.

Ferry permits, after all, specify daytime only.
First printed in Air Progress, March 1978.

Chapter 17

Consolidated B–24 Liberator

Waltzing with the elephant

The B-24J always reminded me of a warthog. Like the warthog, the airplane is deceptive. I always thought it would be ponderous and stable in flight. It is not. It reminds me more of the KC-135 than anything else I can think of. Give it five seconds and it will slide slyly out of your hand like a greased porker.

Nobody ever loved the B-24 at first sight, or even on introduction. But they learned to love it, for what the airplane would do.

The fact is, it was a better warplane than the B-17; probably a better warplane by far than anything the British were building at the time. Notice, I said warplane. *As an airplane, the B-17 had it beat, hands down. The B-17 is just a four-breasted Cub—a baby-sitter for combat aviators.*

But the B-24 is much more nimble, and the man who learns to fly it properly can accomplish feats of flashy airmanship and formation flying no slow-motion B-17 can ever hope to equal. The "Lib" also has a very comfortable flight deck and aft crew compartment. Avoid ditching, and it was a pretty good airplane to take to war.

The last time I made this trip in this class of airplane, cars stopped on the interstate below us just to watch.

But then we were in a Boeing B-17 Flying Fortress, and sometimes I think the whole world knows that famous silhouette. Now we were in the world's last flying Liberator bomber, and no one below seemed to care. At least, I saw no one pull off in 6½ hours of flight—and I tried to keep a lookout.

A pity.

The fact is, more Consolidated B-24 bombers were built than any other American World War II combat aircraft—somewhere between 18,188 and 19,000+, depending on your source. They flew more missions, dropped more bombs and did more damage to the enemy than any other aircraft in the war.

The B-24 flew higher, faster, farther and carried heavier loads than its stable-mate, the B-17, and those who flew it say it proved every bit as rugged when put to the test.

Yet the war still raged in the Pacific when the USAAF began phasing the B-24 out of service, and by the time the 1950s dawned, the airplane was a fading memory in most of the new blue-suited USAF. The very last B-24 in US service flew icing tests in 1953-54 and was relegated to the Lackland Air Force Base museum at San Antonio, Texas.

This airplane was luckier.

Built at Consolidated Aircraft's Fort Worth plant, 44-44272 was one of a batch of 100 B-24J-95s, one of 6,728 B-24Js produced (or 6,678, depending on your source) and one of approximately 2,500 Liberators delivered to the British.

Unlike most of its sisters, s/n 444272 wasn't pushed over a convenient cliff or melted down to make pots and pans after the war. Instead, it was one of a handful of Liberator B Mk VIs (B-24Js) passed on to the fledgling Indian Air Force when the subcontinent gained its independence from Britain.

Assigned to the IAF's No. 6 squadron, it allegedly was flown by the *same crew for eighteen years*, before the type was withdrawn from service. Purchased from the Indians in 1973 by Los Angeles businessman

David Tallichet, it was ferried from Poona, India, to England and, eventually, on to the United States, now bearing the name *Delectable Doris*, appropriate nose art and the markings of 250551, a Ford-built B-24J-1 operated by the 389th Bomb Group, Eighth Air Force, out of England in 1944.

At the moment, it is one of two Consolidated Model 32s still flying.

The other is the famous *Diamond Lil*, operated since 1967 by the Confederate Air Force. The eighteenth Liberator off the line, it was destined for the Royal Air Force as an LB-30A and earmarked for special duties, but was damaged on its delivery flight. Subsequently rebuilt by Consolidated, it spent the war shuttling from coast to coast in transport configuration. Therefore, while it *is* a Liberator, *Lil* is not technically a bomber.

Both planes were to appear at a celebration at Fort Worth's Carswell AFB, marking the fiftieth year since construction of the first Liberator, and *Doris* was inbound from March AFB, California, where she had been on display for the last year or so.

For two men aboard, the flight was a once-in-a-lifetime chance to say hail and farewell to an old comrade in arms.

Both had flown B-24s to bomb the complex of oil refineries at Ploesti, Romania. Maj. Edwin C. Baker took part in the famous Aug. 1, 1943, raid. Capt. Robert Gillman took part in the last, just over a year later.

Both Baker and Gillman think it's a crying shame that the Liberator is still overshadowed by the earlier B-17. So, for that matter, do Capt. Ray Gaston and 1st Lt. Harlan Price, both of whom flew in the Pacific. Gaston and his crew sank a Japanese cruiser and led the first strike on Manila in the campaign to retake the Philippines. Price was a Snooper, flying black-painted radar-equipped B-24s on long, lonely night patrols interdicting Japanese shipping in the Sulu Sea.

Not everyone liked the B-24.

There were its looks, to start. With its slender, high-aspect ratio wing, big, boxy fuselage, snub nose and twin tail, it always looked somehow unfinished. The later models with the nose and tail turrets, like *Doris*, remind one of a warthog.

Libs did not ditch well. The roll-up bomb bay doors tended to collapse under water pressure, producing an instant scoop. They were more demanding to fly. The B-17 virtually flies itself. The B-24, on the other hand, is always sliding off in directions of its own. It was claimed that sometimes fuel vapor would collect in the wrong spot and blow up the airplane, usually just after takeoff.

RAF Air Transport Auxiliary ferry pilot Hugh Bergel, for example, later wrote it "was the only American aircraft I came to dislike actively. Impressive in many ways though it was, it was so complicated, so difficult to see out of, so wholly unstable in flight and so heavy to control that ferrying it was tiresome and tiring."

Bergel called it "unnecessarily complicated" and "very unattractive to fly." He pointed out the Liberator flies nose up, restricting the pilot's view "until it com-

Denigrated as "the box the B-17 came in" and "a pig to fly in formation," the Consolidated Model 32 was built in greater numbers than any other US combat aircraft of World War II, yet it disappeared rapidly at war's end.

Today, it is one of the rarest of all warplanes. Two B-24Js (one newly restored, one never restored) and an LB-30 comprised the entire flying fleet in 1990.

pared unfavorably with a Spitfire," and added, "Even worse, the Liberator was unstable in all three axes—it would not fly itself for two seconds—and the controls were extremely heavy."

There's a certain amount of truth in what he says. For instance, the B-24 uses electric toggle switches to control the Hamilton-Standard hydraulic propellers, and it is not particularly stable nor easy to see out of.

On the other hand, Baker flatly calls it "the greatest aircraft that was ever made. It did all the work of the war at that time (1943). I don't say they were the prettiest, but damn, they were reliable! And we only are here today because that was one aircraft that stood up under the most brutal treatment."

Gillman tells of putting new pilots in the airplane and taking them through confidence-building maneuvers involving sixty- to seventy-degree banks, fighter approaches with a 360 degree overhead, a "bad weather approach" in which he would fly down the runway downwind, extend the gear and flaps, do a steep 180 degree turn and land—all without losing sight of the runway. And, of course, his humpty-bump, in which he would dive to pick up speed, haul the nose up and climb at full power until just before the stall, then push it over, drop the gear and flaps and stick the nose straight down, cleaning up the airplane and recovering before the speed got out of hand.

Gaston recalls his squadron got so good at the fighter peel-up and landing that they put six airplanes on the ground in less than two minutes, and tells of a test mission he flew June 10, 1945, when they were in the air 17:45!

"All the way home, we kept movin' people," he said. "The last two hours, the copilot was in the bomb bay and everybody else was as far back as they could get. Those props were so far back, you could count the blades. The engineer said we were out of gas. When we parked the airplane, we had 400 gallons left."

"I thought it was great!" he says. "I thought the damn thing would do anything you wanted, but you had to make it do it."

And Price calls the B-24 "Magnificent! My goodness, you wouldn't believe the beating that thing took." His crew was caught in a typhoon one night in which they saw the rate of climb pegged first at 3,000 fpm up and the next instant at the same rate down. "How in the world that airplane ever held together I don't know, but it sure did."

It's often claimed that the B-24 was a poor formation airplane because it is so lacking in stability, but Gaston says his unit in the Pacific (394th Bomb Squadron, 5th Bomb Group, Thirteenth Air Force) often flew formation so close they could—and occasionally did—deliberately stick a wingtip in the waist gunner's open hatch.

As an element leader for most of the war, Gaston's main task in formation was to fly smoothly and predictably, but he says when he did fly as No. 2 (deputy lead), it was "no problem" to maintain close formation in the shoulder-wing B-24, simply treating

The B-24 Liberator flew faster, farther and carried a greater bomb load than the B-17. It flew more missions, dropped more bombs and did more damage to the enemy than any other aircraft in the war, and it virtually replaced the B-17 in the Pacific Theater by late 1942. On occasion its missions lasted 16 to 17 hours.

it as you would a low-wing single-engine airplane. Normal step-down interval was about 8 ft. when arriving at the airstrip in close formation, and "you better believe" nervous waist gunners were ready to call out any deviation.

Price, of course, didn't fly formation operationally, since the three Snooper squadrons flew single-ship sorties. On the other hand, they got very efficient at coaxing the maximum range out of the airplane.

They also grew accustomed to flying the huge B-24J, with its 110 ft. Davis wing, its 1,048 sq. ft. wing area, its 67 ft. 2 in. length, its 18 ft. height, its 18¼ ton empty weight and 32½ ton normal loaded weight—like a fighter, going so far as to stand it on a wing.

Price recalled while he was acting squadron operations officer on Morotai, Halmahera, an island northwest of New Guinea, a full colonel named Knight approached him and asked Price to teach him to fly the B-24. For the next two weeks, he and Knight flew a brand-new Ford every morning. "We'd go down there and I'd take him out and we'd just buzz clouds and have fun. He said, 'I didn't know you can rack 'em around like that.' And I said, 'Sure, once you learn to fly it—but don't you try it for a while.'"

There was none of that on this trip. This, after all, was the last flying Liberator bomber, and its mission was simply to get from March to Carswell. Even that was not without incident.

The trouble started before the airplane ever lifted off March—a bent connecting rod in No. 4 engine. Once that was replaced, we were half an hour out when No. 3 propeller went into feather by itself. Since

The Liberator does not crash land well, tending to break in half at the bomb bay. Occasionally during the war, it exploded just off the end of the runway—victim of gasoline fumes and a stray spark, which is why B-24s took off with the bomb bay doors cracked. Visibility from the cockpit is limited, and there is little stability. Flying the B-24 is like waltzing with an elephant that keeps trying to lead.

No. 4 was running hot, the flight engineer recommended the airplane land at Palm Springs—which we'd just passed—and Tallichet acquiesced.

Doris wheeled around, returned to Palm Springs airport and landed, Tallichet standing on the brakes to make the first turn-off. We were met by no less than *three* $250,000 airport pumper trucks, manned by eager firemen in silver overalls, their services fortunately not needed.

"I tell you, it's kind of embarrassing," remarked Tallichet. "You work so hard, and sometimes you don't get very far." We repaired to his house for fresh grapefruit juice, vitamins and steak.

Minor repairs completed that evening, *Doris'* first engine fired at 0645 local the next day, and the airplane lifted off the runway at 7:10 a.m.

It had been over 110 degrees F. on the Palm Springs ramp the evening before, but the surface temperature was in the high 50s at takeoff, and it was chilly enough in summer clothing at 9,500 ft. to provide an inkling of how uncomfortable it must have been in the icy skies over Europe.

The B-24J has large swing-in waist hatches, each with a swing-out aluminum windscreen. Unfortunately, when those are deployed, it somehow creates a young gale as air is sucked through the bomb bay and sent blasting back through the aft fuselage. Fortunately, there's not much draft when they're folded flush.

Aside from the fact that they survived, the single most striking thing about the trio of Indian Air Force airplanes (one in England, two in the United States) is that they are totally original.

The walk-around oxygen bottles are clipped into place throughout the aircraft, the web ration bags still hang from their stations, the cartridge chutes still march into the gun mounts, the extra fifty-caliber ammo boxes are in place.

Even the SCR-269 radio compass, the three receivers, two transmitters, modulator and interphones are still in place, with their big ceramic posts, blade connectors and screw-in fuses—although of course they don't work, these days.

The half deck above the aft bomb bay, where most of the radio equipment is located, is both snug and spacious, but provides no external view. It is instructive to sit there and consider the quantum leap in avionics, one of the few real advances made in piston-powered airplanes since this airplane was built.

Fold-down tables, crew seats, canvas curtains, everything is just as the airplane left the factory.

True, a few of the portable oxygen bottles are gone, but the most important missing item is the Thermite bomb clipped to a bulkhead just aft of the bomb bay, where it could be used to destroy the airplane in the event of a crash-landing.

It was easy enough, in *Doris*, to half-close your eyes and imagine the Me 110s and 410s lurking on the flanks, waiting for a good shot with their W Gr 21 mortars or, sometimes, their adapted 50 mm anti-tank guns; the Fw 190s barreling in from twelve o'clock with wing cannon and nose MGs sparkling; the Me 109s zipping in from astern, punching out entire engines with their 30 mm nose cannon, their pair of 20 mm ripping off wing panels, puncturing fuel tanks, blasting away control surfaces. And, of course, ahead and below waited the flak belts—hundreds of fast-firing 88 and even 128 mm cannon, some of them radar-aimed.

There were no foxholes in the sky.

Ed Baker knows.

Nine aircraft from his 409th Bomb Squadron, 93rd Bomb Group (Heavy), 2nd Air Division, Eighth Air Force, took off from Berka Two, a temporary air base in the Libyan desert, at 7 a.m. that fateful Aug. 1, 1943. Three came off the target.

The 93rd was one of five B-24 groups marshaled for Operation Tidal Wave, a mass strike against the complex of seven oil refineries outside Ploesti, Romania, so vital to the Axis war effort.

They were to fly more than 2,000 miles, round trip, mostly at low level, strike their targets and recover—either by turning northwest, to England, or returning to Allied bases in Egypt, Libya or Palestine. Alternatively, they could divert to neutral Cyprus or, if things were really tight, to Axis-leaning Turkey.

They numbered 178 aircraft at takeoff, all told. One hundred sixty four arrived over Ploesti, and by that time things had gone to hell in a handbasket. The lead navigator's aircraft had crashed into the sea before they ever made landfall, and the backup navigator's plane dropped down to look for survivors, taking it, too, out of the formation.

The weather over Greece was horrible, and the three major elements of the formation broke up. The Germans, alerted by a thirteen-plane raid over a year before, had ringed the targets with flak and fighters—and they knew Tidal Wave was inbound.

The lead formation mistook the initial point, and turned in toward Bucharest. The rest might have followed, had not the 93rd's Addison Baker turned ninety degrees left and headed for Ploesti. The rest of Ted's Traveling Circus followed.

"We wound up bein' the first group into the target area," said Baker, then a twenty-four-year-old captain. They ran the AA gauntlet at 245 mph, some of the Liberators as low as 20 ft. above the cultivated fields outside Ploesti. "We got shot up pretty badly." They were even bombed, by the group overhead!

A B-24D is hardly a quiet place, with four 1,200 hp Pratt & Whitneys roaring away just outside the windows, with frenzied gunners firing fifty-caliber machine guns from the nose, from overhead, from the waist and from the tail. But today, forty-six years later, Ed Baker remembers the sound those 88 mm shells made whipping past his cockpit without detonating.

"You could hear 'em go by; kind of a swishing sound," he says. "Fortunately, nothing hit us. We did lose the No. 3 engine, from ground fire, I think. Then we went through the Balkans, up through the valleys, just a little above ground level."

Technically, it wasn't even his airplane. Richard Wilkinson was the aircraft commander. As squadron operations officer, Baker had simply assigned himself back to his old crew as an "observer." Doubtless sometime during that hellish twenty-seven minutes over Ploesti, he wondered why.

He describes how the flak gunners on the ridges tried vainly to depress their barrels enough to fire on the fleeing, twisting Liberator, scraping its wingtips on the valley floor. And you can picture young Ed Baker, sweating inside his leather-and-fleece flight suit, busy as a woodchopper on a January morning.

Of the three airplanes from Baker's squadron to escape the defenses of Ploesti, one made it all the way back to Libya, one landed in Sicily—and Baker's crew crash-landed in Turkey, where the airplane fetched up against a mountainside off the end of a Turkish fighter base.

In total, fifty-three airplanes were shot down or lost en route home from Ploesti, twenty-three more were forced down on auxiliary fields and eighty-eight returned—but of those, fifty-five had sustained major combat damage. Of the seven targets, two were heavily damaged, two were out of action at least six months, two sustained light damage and one escaped unscathed.

Interned in Ankara, Turkey, Baker spent a month sharing Turkish streets and shops with similarly interned Nazis and finally escaped, walking out

through Syria to Cairo. He figured if he could get back to England, he had accumulated enough combat time to rotate to the Z.I.—stateside.

He was wrong. His new CO figured experienced men were needed, even though by regulation he couldn't fly operationally in the European Theater of Operations again. So Baker spent another month or two flying a gaily-painted, war-weary formation airplane dubbed the *Striped-Ass Ape* out of Norwich, an orbiting signpost in the sky for the B-24 groups assembling over England before heading out across the Channel for Festung Europa.

He and Gillman spent an hour or two that evening comparing notes on the differences in the way their units operated.

Baker, a member of the first B-24 group deployed to Europe, flew nothing but glass-nosed D models. In twenty-five missions from England and North Africa, they always encountered enemy fighters. Gillman, on the other hand, flew his first combat mission Aug. 17, 1944, and took part in the last Ploesti raid the next day. Only once did he even see an enemy fighter, and that one had no time for him. But he was deeply impressed by the way the German flak got thicker as "Greater Germany" got smaller!

Gillman never took off or landed with crew members in the nose or tail. Baker always did. Gillman was a product of the military's multi-engine transition training program. Baker was not.

"There was no multi-engine training" when Baker was assigned to Pendelton, Oregon—and almost found himself on Jimmy Doolittle's Tokyo raid! They devised their own program; taught themselves to fly Douglas B-18s and B-25s, but at the last moment "I got bounced off the aircraft" as a copilot, and didn't make the famous raid.

Gillman enjoyed his three years in the military. Baker says there were no "good" combat missions.

Price remembers some of both.

Price flew 604 combat hours as a member of the 868th Bomb Squadron, attached directly to Thirteenth Air Force. "No wing, no group or anything. We were a 'Snooper' squadron. Fifth Air Force had one, and I believe there was one in the CBI. We all received our training at Langley Field, Virginia. We were supposed to go to the ETO, but we were pulled off and sent back for all this 'hush-hush' training," involving night radar bombing from 300 and 1,000 ft. altitudes, low-level flying and navigating by SHORAN and LORAN.

Early in May 1944, two 400 gallon tanks were installed in their B-24 and they took off from Fairfield-Suisun in California (now Travis AFB), bound for Hickam Field, Hawaii. "Those tanks remained in our plane, because as time later showed, all of our later missions were 13- to 15-hour missions."

In fact, that terrifying night in early 1945 when his airplane flew into the typhoon, they were aloft 17:20! "The last hour, we burned 80 gallons of gas. We landed with 20 minutes left, but they had to junk the airplane," due to airframe damage.

"We never took off in combat under 68,000 pounds, and on two different occasions, carrying four 2,000-pound bombs, we took off at 72,800 pounds. We'd take off after dark, about 8 or 9 p.m. It was usually rainin'. We wanted to be in the search area about 2 to 5 and be out of there before dawn. We didn't like daylight.

"I don't suppose there are too many American pilots left around anymore who've ever been in searchlights. That's the brightest, whitest light I've ever seen! I could thread a needle in that cockpit! Oh, my. It really gets your attention."

That was over Balikpapan, Borneo, one night, when "the radar-controlled searchlights got us, about 10 seconds before the bombs went away." Once they were out, they pulled the power, dumped the nose and dived for the searchlights. "She's redlined at 275, and the last time Chuck (Binford) or I saw the airspeed indicator, it was at 356. We were literally standin' on the left rudder and she was spiralin' out to the right, out to sea."

Price's unit flew many special missions, but their main task was to find and bomb Japanese ships around Brunei Bay in the early morning hours. Cruising at 150 IAS to save fuel, they would tip it over at 1,500 ft. and come downhill at 175 mph on a ten-mile bomb run, dropping 1,000 pounders with a ⅛ second delay a quarter mile out. "A hit would raise the air-plane up about 25 ft. And about 45–60 days after we got in the area, we had literally shut off the oil. We sank four ships, I'm confident. We got two in one bomb run. That was confirmd by the Navy."

He recalls his unit lost nineteen of its thirty-two aircraft, but only five fell to the Japanese. "If we lost anything in the first 4½ hours, there was no gettin' her home. We carried 27,000 pounds of fuel to drop 4,000 pounds of bombs. We could get her off at 125, but we needed 8,500 ft. of runway. It took us 45 minutes to climb to 9,000 ft." for the trip to the Sulu Sea. "We burned 500 gallons of gas the first hour."

One rosy dawn, ten miles northeast of Palawan, North of Borneo, Price's crew discovered a Japanese fleet that had been shelling Leyte. "We identified 'em, and then we made a big mistake. We turned and went into 'em to be sure we had the ID right, and why in the hell they didn't blow us out of the sky I'll never know.

"There were about 10 or 11 warships and a bunch of tankers, and then on down south, more destroyers, a couple of heavy cruisers and light cruisers. They all turned about 20 degrees, and the whole side of every ship turned an orange color about the color of a detour sign, and I thought, 'Oh, how beautiful' for just one second." Then he noticed water spouts were obscuring his view of Luzon.

"We turned around at 200 ft. and 225 mph," zig-zagging. "Chuck and I were both on the controls, tryin'

Most Libs were shoved over a handy cliff or broken with a handy crane and a sheet of steel, but 444272 was one of a handful given by the Royal Air Force to the fledgling Indian Air Force at independence in 1948. The same crew flew this airplane for 18 years, and when it was finally struck off the roles, it found a new home with California warbird collector David Tallichet, who has maintained it in airworthy condition since.

to increase roll rate, back and forth. The guys back in the plane estimated there were about 3,000 AA bursts, but they didn't touch us.

"In the next 24 hours, between the daylight B-24s and -25s, a couple American subs and the Navy Avengers, we sank a total of six warships. It was the last major loss the Japs had."

Gaston, too, had a bad experience with a Japanese warship in that armada, later that same day. He recalls he and his crew *saw* 16 in. shells being fired at their formation by the trio of battleships in the fleet. "They looked as big as a bathtub"—and did, in fact, knock down one B-24.

On the other hand, Gaston and his crew sank a Kuma-class heavy cruiser out of that fleet, all on the single thirteen-hour mission, that Oct. 26, 1944, in the Sulu Sea.

Gaston's people had a way of getting even. He tells of one mission when Zero fighters flew over their formation, dropping phosphorus bombs. One went through the right wing, but failed to explode. Then the Zekes pulled ahead, split-S'ed, and attacked with guns from twelve o'clock low. The B-24 shot one down!

A hundred miles west of Midland, Texas, Tallichet handed *Doris* over to me, and we began to get as acquainted as possible while holding a heading and altitude on an X-C flight.

At a power setting of 30 in. and 2000 rpm, the B-24 indicated 170 mph for a true of 200. She was delicately balanced, slightly more stable in pitch than in yaw and roll, but on the whole well harmonized. The controls were somewhat ponderous, but oiled and precise.

I could see why Gillman felt it useful to fly confidence-building maneuvers with new pilots. The B-24 is rather like dancing with an elephant that keeps trying to lead. You have to anticipate what the airplane's going to do next! But she responds quite well. Trim is excellent.

Admittedly, forward view is restricted, and as for the ugly label, well. . . . Let Gaston speak to that.

"I refused to fly a B-24," he says. "I was flyin' B-17s when they came around and told me I was bein' transferred to -24s. I said, 'I ain't gonna fly in that thing that looks like a railroad car! You can court-martial me!'

"And this guy said, 'Come on, take one ride.' So I did, and I said, 'Well, it flies good'—and that's how I ended up in B-24s."

The secret to the B-24's remarkable speed and load-carrying ability lay in its laminar-flow Davis wing, the patented invention of freelance aero engineer David R. Davis. The slight, bespectacled Davis had helped launch Donald Douglas in the airplane business and developed the first variable-pitch propellers sans mechanical controls before coming up with his new wing design, based on his observation of the shape assumed by falling water droplets.

He *gave* Reuben Fleet (founder and chief designer at Consolidated) the right to use the new airfoil, retaining only a royalty on foreign sales.

The symmetrical Davis wing turned out to be 102 percent efficient, both in wind tunnel tests and on the airplane—although a small accumulation of ice played havoc with its lifting ability. Ernest K. Gann once remarked, "It would not carry enough ice to chill a cocktail."

That's probably why they're not used today. Nevertheless, they graced more than 18,000 Liberators, not to mention the slightly later single-tail Navy Privateers and a handful of Consolidated flying boats.

They left an enviable combat record, now largely forgotten.

Price tells how another pilot, new to the squadron, made a dawn raid on Borneo's Miri oil field with his Snooper B-24.

"He dropped four thousand-pounders and made six strafing runs and brought back film of the results. Far East Air Force Bomber Command were ecstatic. They figured he destroyed 20% of the Jap oil production—one airplane on one morning. They came back in about seven or eight days and wanted to do it again.

"We said no. The element of surprise only works once."

Doris dropped easily down the sky just outside Fort Worth, swooped low over the runway at Carswell and touched down at 1:50 p.m. local time, 5:40 after takeoff from Palm Springs, perhaps 6:20 from March.

A swirl of USAF personnel surrounded the airplane immediately. One, quickly surveying the B-24, announced, "Technology hasn't changed that much." Another said, "Man, we could load this in nothin' flat," but yet a third pointed out, "I can't figure out where to put the alky."

A captain pulled up, took one look at the slightly grimy forty-five-year-old machine and snapped, "We can't display this aircraft in that condition. Make an appointment on the wash rack."

Somebody else told Tallichet there was no gasoline on the base; that he would have to fly *Doris* to a civilian facility to top the tanks, or arrange for a visit by a tank truck.

Things have always been like that for the B-24.
First printed in *Warbirds* September-October 1989.

Chapter 18

North American OV–10 Bronco and Douglas A–1 Skyraider

Mach nix!

In the mid 1960s, the United States was trying to fight a very old kind of war in Vietnam with space-age weaponry: heavy tanks and sophisticated supersonic airplanes designed to fight the nuclear Armageddon planned for in Europe.

Very quickly, it became apparent that most of it didn't work. The tanks bogged down anytime they tried to leave the trails, and using nuclear-capable Mach 2 airplanes to drop iron bombs was like going to the corner grocery in your Lamborghini Countach.

What was needed was a new arsenal of weapons, better able to cope with the elusive guerrillas scurrying around beneath the triple-canopy jungle.

It turned out that the Navy had part of the answer, in the venerable Able Dog—the piston-engine attack plane designed for World War II and used to such good effect fifteen years earlier in Korea. And the rest of the answer lay with a new design, produced to a specification that never really succeeded.

This is how they were.

"Four in hot—bombs," said Maj. John H. Hanna distinctly as he abruptly rolled the Bronco hard left. We were already inverted when the range controller's dry "Four" acknowledgment sounded in the earphones.

Hanna leveled the OV–10's wings briefly and pulled the nose straight down until the target vanished behind the instrument panel. Suddenly he rolled out into a "normal" sixty-degree dive, slewing the nose slightly until the target stood nailed in his reflector gunsight.

From 4,500 ft. MSL, the Bronco plunged earthward at 255 knots IAS.

Abandoning my efforts to frame No. 3 of our four-ship flight in the big 300 mm lens during his bomb release and pull-out, I swung the camera toward the target, trying to focus both target and at least part of the gunsight. The altimeter unwound like a clock gone mad as I struggled.

It beat me to the bottom.

In the front seat, Hanna pickled his bomb and yanked back the stick in one brief, practiced motion.

I couldn't really see him from directly behind, but I'm sure he was grinning from ear to ear as my own mass and momentum smashed me deep into the cockpit and the world grayed around the edges. The business end of the 300 mm sank toward the floor—and we vaulted back into the muggy Florida sky, the rate of climb shooting to 5,500 fpm.

It was the summer of 1970, and this was my introduction to flying in the woolly world of the USAF Special Operations Force, originally known as the Air Commandos.

Headquartered at Eglin Air Force Base, Florida, and operating mainly from nearby Hurlburt Field, the SOF flew some fourteen combat aircraft types ranging from the venerable C–47 to Cessna's sporty little A–37B, a Tweety Bird that took up weight lifting.

The Force's 1st Special Operations Wing there trained pilots from pink-cheeked youngsters just out of UPT (Undergraduate Pilot Training) to grizzled bird colonels with combat experience in three wars, and maintained enough men and airplanes in a ready status to deploy an instant reaction force anywhere in the world.

The training was in a variety of missions, many of them classified, but basically what they taught was bush flying in a combat environment.

Well, I'd set out to learn what it was like to go through the SOF's pilot training course, and now I was finding out. At least it gave me a real appreciation of the physical punishment the instructor pilots (IPs) of the 549th Tactical Air Support Training Squadron took in their OV-10s every day.

I accused Hanna later of getting even with untold generations of students through me. He denied it, but he couldn't keep the corners of his mouth from twitching. The IP, of course, normally occupied the aft seat in an OV-10, where the G loads are worse, and Hanna admitted he was regularly wrung out like a load of laundry.

Through mischance, we wound up flying on the scorable target range, which involved nearly an hour of a strictly roller-coaster routine instead of the full mission profile originally planned, and in all our time over the target I don't think we ever made a pull-out that registered less than 6 Gs. I don't know; Hanna had the G meter on his panel in front. But I do know there was a while when I wasn't sure I would keep down my five-hour-old hamburger, and I just don't get airsick—normally.

The action started at 1300. Four IPs, three students and I spent half an hour in a detailed briefing for the planned tactical mission, which was to include practice in almost everything except walking home (known to us combat types as E&E, for "escape and evasion"). Bombs, rockets, strafing, FACing—we were programmed for the whole nine yards.

Hanna tucked me tenderly into the back seat; then climbed into the front. Within sixty seconds I was bathed in sweat, for virtually the whole upper half of the OV-10 fuselage forward of the wing is plexiglass. It was sweltering, even with the right clamshell panels open. The surface temperature was in the mid 90s. So was the humidity. They said it was a good deal like Southeast Asia.

One of the major complaints about this airplane was its lack of air conditioning, for crew compartment temperatures frequently hit 120 degrees F. or more.

The OV-10 is a strange bird. There is nothing forward of the pilot but enough nose cone to house the panel instruments and a long pitot tube, and nearly all that is not plexiglass is fiberglass.

Generally, I much prefer a disabled aircraft to a parachute, but the OV-10 is an exception. This would be a very unhealthy place in a crash-landing, and I can understand why Bronco pilots are urged to eject.

In any case, I would have no choice. Pull the red handle in the front seat, and the aft seat rocket fires first. Four tenths of a second later, the front seat follows. "If I decide you go—you go!" Hanna assured me cheerfully.

There is one exception to this ejection rule, and it caused a problem or two for pilots flying the original tri-service version of the Bronco. That bird had a 30 ft.

In the summer of 1970 the USAF Special Operations Force—the Air Commandos—trained at the Eglin AFB complex in south Florida and flew 14 different types of aircraft, including the North American OV-10A Bronco, Douglas A-1 Skyraider, North American T-28B, Cessna A-37B, Douglas C-47, Helio U-10, and a variety of others. This is part of the ramp of the 1st Special Operations Wing—a fun place to be, back then.

The wing operated several models of the venerable Able Dog, all salvaged from the Davis-Monthan boneyard, along with the T-28Bs—commonly known as "half an A-1." The

OV-10s were a result of a declared need for a tri-service COIN (COunter-INsurgency) aircraft, and the rest of the grab bag was just added as a need surfaced.

wingspan, nearly all of it within the propwash. If an engine failed at low speed just after takeoff, that wing stalled and the airplane rolled so fast most pilots couldn't react before it was inverted.

The USAF Broncos have an extended 40 ft. wing, but it's still a tricky situation; so much so that commanders at Hurlburt frowned on the STOL-type takeoffs the bird was designed for, and that so delighted pilots' hearts.

But even with the long wing, loss of an engine in a full-power, low-speed configuration produced roll rates on the order of 270 degrees per second. The Dash One on our ship cautioned it "rolls and yaws rapidly toward the failed engine," and added, "Should engine failure occur at or near stall speed at altitudes below 1,000 feet above the terrain, safe recovery may not be possible depending on pilot proficiency and aircraft configuration."

There were other peculiarities, mostly dealing with the controls for the 710 shaft horsepower (shp) Garrett AiResearch turbines. There were no conventional throttle or propeller levers. Instead, there was a power lever and a condition lever for each engine, all neatly mounted in a console just under your left hand.

The first hurdle was in adjusting to the fact that the three-bladed, 8½ ft. solid aluminum propellers were going to turn 2000 rpm anytime the engines were running, no matter what the position of the engine controls and regardless of whether you were going straight up, straight down, spinning or just sitting on the ramp idling. Even in a whipstall, they'll turn 2000 rpm.

The engines, being turbines, are high-speed, low-torque units, rated in percent rpm because 100 percent is 41,730 rpm—too high for easy comprehension. Normal operating limits are 68.7 to 101 percent. There is a gear reduction system with several ranges, controlled by the condition lever.

The condition levers are marked "T.O./LAND," "NORMAL FLIGHT," "FUEL SHUT-OFF" and "FEATHER & FUEL SHUT-OFF." For normal flying, they are set in one of the first two positions. An inexact parallel would be the low and drive positions on a car's selector lever, since they select the engine power/propeller rpm response to the power lever setting. The last two positions are self-explanatory.

That leaves the power levers controlling everything else, including both fuel flow and propeller thrust setting (blade pitch). They are marked at "FULL REVERSE," "GROUND START," "FLIGHT IDLE" and "MILITARY" positions.

In practice, all this means you can cruise straight and level with the condition levers in "T.O./LAND," just as you can drive down a highway at 60 mph in low range. Unlike a car, you can take off in the "NORMAL FLIGHT" range, provided you've got plenty of runway, but it will take a while.

Because of the counter-rotating constant-speed propellers, the noise level does not change from ground idle clear through the normal speed range. Your ears are no help in flying this airplane.

Primary in-flight movement of ailerons and elevator is by aerodynamic action of spring and gear-operated boost tabs. Haul back on the short stick, and the action forces a long, narrow "trim" tab down, raising the elevator by air pressure. Electrically operated bungees move the flight control systems to no-load positions, as required.

The pitch trim system provides about 20 lbs. of stick force, nose up or down. There is a gyro-operated automatic yaw damper. Four rotating spoilers, shaped like pie slices, rise out of the wing with the up aileron and speed the roll rate. The result is a 10,000 lb. airplane that handles like a 950 lb. Pitts Special. It is particularly responsive in the pitch and roll axes.

The OV-10 has a cargo compartment that can carry internal loads of up to 3,200 lbs. and is supposed to accommodate six fully armed infantrymen. The rounded fiberglass pod end of the fuselage section is hinged to the left for compartment access, and surprisingly has no special effect on aircraft performance if it comes open in flight. "It just swings back and forth gently," explained an IP, moving his hand through about a thirty-degree arc to illustrate. "You'd think at the least it'd tear off at the hinge, but it doesn't."

The OV-10 is an odd-looking airplane, with something of the unfinished about it. From some angles its twin-boom, twin-engine layout reminds you of the World War II Lockheed P-38 Lightning, but there is none of the P-38's grace and beauty of line. The Bronco is well named. It is short-coupled, plank-winged, hammer-headed and ugly—but tough as they come, and great fun to fly.

The plane has 258 gallons of internal fuel in five foam-filled wing tanks and can carry either a 150 gallon or 230 gallon drop tank on the centerline. The twin turbines burn 83 to 93 gph. There are no moving parts on the fuel pumps, and the only way to check the fuel system is to crank an engine.

Starting is simple, but can be done from the front seat only. The condition lever usually is in "NORMAL FLIGHT," and the power lever must be in "FLIGHT IDLE." The starter spins the turbine, which lights off between ten and twelve percent rpm. The props are in flat pitch for starting, and must be unlocked before taxi by retarding the power levers into the reverse thrust range and returning them to positive. The air-plane wriggles slightly against the brakes as the props bite first aft and then forward, and you're ready to go.

The OV-10 has nose wheel steering, but taxiing normally is with asymmetrical thrust and even a little reverse occasionally. There is not a great deal to check before takeoff: trim, flaps, fuel feed, flight controls, canopy locked, gyros set, forward on the power, release the brakes and go. Takeoff is at 85 to 95 knots IAS, and you rotate five knots earlier.

Ground run is about 2,700 ft. at the 10,000 lb. normal gross on a hot summer day in Florida. STOL takeoffs can be made in 1,300 ft. at that weight, and with a 14,000 lb. airplane, the no-flap run can be up to 4,000 ft. Maximum takeoff weight is 14,400 lbs., and at 10,000 lbs. or less you can land on smooth runways with sink rates in excess of 850 fpm. Normal landing run is 1,000–1,200 ft., and STOL landings can be made in 600–700 ft.

Initial climb rate is 1,000–1,500 fpm at 130 knots, and the OV-10 will hit 10,000 ft. in ten minutes and eighteen miles across the ground. Stall speeds range from 42 KIAS with full forty-degree flaps, gear, power and an 8,000 lb. airplane to 105 at 14,000 lbs., no flaps, gear down, power off. Maximum allowable air speed is 350 KIAS, and maximum level flight speed is about 210 knots, clean. Full lateral stick rolls at 250 knots or higher produce roll rates nearing 170 degrees per second, with lateral G forces of about 2. Symmetrical G limits are plus 6.5 and minus 1.

Not surprisingly, the OV-10 comes down fast, covering about 9 nm per 5,000 ft. of altitude lost, clean, props feathered, at its best glide speed of 130 KIAS. Extended gear cuts the glide distance by a

The Super Spad is the biggest single-engine airplane the author ever expects to fly, and great fun. Furthermore, it's an outstanding weapons platform, capable of steady-state, controlled-airspeed dives at around 50 degrees and of pin-point accuracy. However, it takes a little getting used to. The beast exudes oil from every pore and overlays the oil with sooty exhaust. Its Wright R-3350 uses up to five gallons of oil per hour.

third. The gear extends in seven seconds, retracts in ten. Flaps retract in eight seconds. Maximum gear extension speed is 155 KIAS, twenty degrees of flap may be applied at the same speed, and full flaps at 130.

The airplane carries four sponson-mounted M60 7.62 mm machine guns in interchangeable pairs and has five external racks, including the centerline rack. It can carry up to 600 lbs. on each of the four outboard racks, and up to 1,200 lbs. on the centerline. Loads range from 20 mm gun pods through general purpose and cluster bombs to all types of air-to-ground rockets.

We were carrying the port side armed: two practice bombs, a canister of rockets and 100 rounds each in the two left-hand guns.

We were barely out of the Hurlburt pattern en route to the range when the left engine became ill, developing oil pressure fluctuations and rpm surge. We aborted—and, sixteen minutes after takeoff, we were back on the ground.

I unplugged, unhooked, unbuckled, climbed down and pirouetted gratefully in the cool 95 degree temperature, feeling the gentle breeze filter through my wet flight suit.

Not to be denied, we laid on a second flight at 16:30; one of those rare missions when the IPs got to do their own flying and firing—a semi-annual trip to the scorable range. There was much challenging and placing of bets in the squadron lounge. There was even discussion of a handicap for a pilot or two. There would be a pot big enough to be interesting.

The bird had been repaired. This time it functioned normally. And this time Hanna was eager. Suddenly he was 110 percent fighter pilot, no more

the soft-spoken, courteous officer he was on the ground.

He was making up for the two years he spent instructing in Cessna O-1s at Holley Field (near Eglin AFB) and for the nearly two years he had been in this program. And he was sharpening his skills for an expected second tour in Southeast Asia, for he hoped to be assigned to MAAG-Thai to advise the twenty-plane Thai OV-10 squadron just forming.

I kidded him, pointing out that as a Thai advisor, he'd likely get no chance at action himself. He grinned, shaking his head vehemently. "Oh, no," he said. He made a sweeping overhand cavalry gesture. "It's gonna be, 'Follow me!'"

We climbed to 4,500 and leveled off, skirting Holley Field. The height of our perch on this mission showed how FAC work had changed by 1970, responding to the increasing deadliness of ground fire in the combat theater.

Time was when a FAC skimmed along just above the trees, relying on their cover and his brief exposure time to avoid taking hits. No more. The enemy's use of AKs and light machine guns in barrage fire had forced the FAC upstairs. Now he flew at 4,500 ft., and tried never to drop below 3,000 AGL—effective range of vertically fired small arms—except for firing passes. At the higher altitude he was fair game for the light cannon, but he was still safer.

We dive-bombed, skip-bombed, rocketed and strafed. For all but skip-bombing, the sixty-degree dive angle remained constant. In the rear seat, hands off the controls, there was no sensation of the light practice bombs leaving the plane. There was a Roman candle "shwupp" from the rockets, a harsh bark from the machine guns. Hanna's concentration paid off, for

The OV–10A looks a little strange, with its twin booms, squared-off plank wing and bug-eyed greenhouse, but the Bronco is one of the most beautiful-handling airplanes ever built, due to geared servo tabs that take the work out of

maneuvering. Furthermore, props always turn at 2,500 rpm no matter what the airplane's doing, making power management simple.

This was the ramp of the 549th Tactical Air Support Training Squadron. Although the OV–10A is an exciting airplane to fly, its greenhouse-like cockpit is a real torture chamber in hot, humid environments like Florida and Vietnam. It was not uncommon to lose five pounds per mission from dehydration.

he won the pot, his total score edging out the other three pilots handily.

Ordnance expended, we rejoined, sliding into a tight echelon formation. It's easier to kill off airspeed in level flight than to gain it with the OV–10—a function of the turbine engines and the highly effective prop pitch control.

As No. 4 airplane, we had the toughest time, and Hanna jockeyed the throttles, maneuvering for position. We would drift back; he would add power. We would gather speed and come roaring up; he would flatten the pitch and we'd slow as if he'd tossed out an anchor.

We snarled over Hurlburt at 1,500 ft. AGL and the leader's right wing flashed up as he broke hard left. Five seconds and No. 2 followed. Then it was No. 3, raising a gloved hand in farewell, and we were alone.

Then it was our turn. Hard left, reduce power to arrive on downwind below 155 knots. The gear whined down, flaps following as the speed dipped below 130 and the Bronco swept around a curving base leg onto final, its nose well down. We eased down final at 85 KIAS and touched flat, the nose immediately bobbing downward as the power came off and the weight shifted from wings to wheels.

Then Hanna turned it over to me. I added power, the Bronco leaped ahead, eating up runway, and I rotated at a safe 85 knots. Nose up, we skated briefly like a planing motorboat, then sprang into the air. Lord, the controls were light!

The electric gear motor whined busily (it can be extended from either seat, but retracted only from the front), and the wheels thunked into place about the time we arrived at 500 ft. I banked left, the short wing snapped down and a little back pressure sucked the nose around as handily as a Cessna 150, with even less effort.

I broke out of the traffic pattern to the north, feeling out the airplane. It was quite neutral in stability, but the beast somehow stayed exactly where you put it. All controls were delightful, but the ailerons were unquestionably the best. I ached to try a few loops and rolls, some stalls, a hammerhead. But time was limited by both remaining fuel and the clock, and

Hanna wanted to get back on the ground and collect his winnings.

Okay. Here we go. Over the runway at 180 knots and break. I slapped the stick briskly to the left and booted the rudder, playing fighter pilot. The response was soul satisfying. Back on the power, slight back pressure, let it slide steeply down. The airspeed touched 155, and Hanna called, "Gear down."

Wildly, I looked around. No one ever took the trouble to brief me on the location of some of these rear seat controls. Below, the ground was streaming past. "I can't find it," I said. He hit his lever just as I located mine, painted the same basic airplane color and stuck in a corner, an obvious afterthought.

Base, and ease off on the power—slight back pressure—a little more. . . . "Get the nose down," Hanna said urgently as the speed dropped below 100 KIAS. Obediently, I dumped the nose as he came in with a little power. The Bronco was dropping out of the sky as if tired of this game, the sink rate flickering between 1,000 and 2,000 fpm. Then it stabilized at 500. We floated across the threshold 50 ft. in the air.

I let it descend briefly, then—unconsciously—brought the stick back, flaring the airplane, feeling delicately for the runway. We were perhaps 10 ft. off the ground, airspeed about 85 knots.

"No, no, no," screamed Hanna in my earphones. He came in on the controls, shoved the stick forward, drove the pretty little airplane brutally into the runway. I braced myself, expecting to arrive like a load of falling rock. Instead it was like jumping on a marshmallow. The wheels touched, the gear compressed, the nose whipped down. I came back on the power. All the way back—and we hung against the harness as the props reversed.

They told me later it was normal to slam this airplane onto the runway briskly; that it was designed to be flown that way. There is a scissors switch on the left gear that takes a healthy jolt to operate. Unless the switch is closed, the locking mechanism in the throttle gate keeps the props out of reverse, and you must lift up and back.

I was told, too, that in tests the OV–10 was hoisted repeatedly to the top of a large hangar and dropped. It withstood it without strain. And OV–10

Designed for use aboard Navy carriers, Skyraider has a small footprint, and the Dash-One warns if it even looks like the airplane might go off the runway, to retract the gear. Otherwise, A-1 is likely to somersault and land on its back, with a good chance of killing the pilot. Furthermore, repairs take less time if these instructions are followed.

pilots were shown a film of a Bronco landing on a tank test track, a rolling, wavy stretch of concrete so tortuous no tank can do more than 8 mph and a car goes out of control at 13. The OV-10 *landed* on the thing, completely under control, though the pilot's eyes were twin vertical blurs.

It still seemed a shame to treat $530,000 worth of airplane and equipment that way.

The Douglas A-1 was a totally different worm can. The big problem with the old former Navy *Able Dog* was in ground handling, and when I asked Maj. Dick Skeels and Lt. Col. Harry Dunivant about their problems in training low-time pilots, Skeels said quickly, "We cry a lot! It's a long process. We have to teach 'em how to fly an airplane."

Rudder trim on an A-1 changes markedly with a 10 knot change in airspeed, and Skeels admitted "one of the hardest things for them to learn is how to land the airplane. We try not to solo anybody until he's had at least 25 landings in it."

Nevertheless, Lt. Col. James F. Yealy, boss of the 4407th Combat Crew Training Squadron, pointed out proudly, "This is the only place in the world where they can get WWII-type fighter experience."

The venerable Douglas Skyraider was, then, the world's only remaining piston-engine tailwheel airplane in first-line combat, and Yealy said: "This bird really is one of the No. 1 choices for all the young sports that come in here. When these guys finish their tour in that A-1, they're gonna be real pilots! They're gonna be so far ahead of their contemporaries it isn't even funny."

The A-1, of course, was the famed Super Spad of Vietnam legend; first choice of pinned-down grunts when close air support was needed. Easily the most glamorous of the airplane types still used by the bush-hat boys then, it vied with the OV-10 and A-37 for the "flashiest" title as well.

It was undoubtedly their toughest airplane to transition into. The course took six weeks and sixty hours in forty-five sorties for USAF pilots. VNAF pilots got seventy-seven hours in fifty-nine sorties.

What did it take to convert a 240 hour UPT pilot into a combat-ready A-1 jock?

"First we teach 'em the basics," said Yealy, a small, tough fifty-year-old who had spent his adult life flying fighters. "You know: 'This is a propeller, this is a tail-wheel.'" Most had never flown propeller-driven airplanes, never seen a tailwheel, he explained. They knew nothing of the art of positive ground control, of torque rolls, of juggling levers for throttle, prop, mixture, supercharger.

The A-1 wouldn't take much crosswind; landing limits for a ninety-degree wind were 10-20 knots, depending on load and pilot experience, and many students tended to jam the stick forward on touchdown to plant the nose wheel that should have been there. That was always embarrassing. Former F-102 and F-106 jocks tried to steer with the ailerons—an action that produces opposite results in the A-1.

"Probably our greatest thing is directional control," noted Skeels. "It does get a little scary once in a while."

If an A-1 got off the paving, it was a sure repair job. The airplane has small main wheels set near the CG, and it stubs its toes easily in soft ground. Usually, it flips over on its back, killing the pilot and extensively damaging the airplane.

So the mandatory procedure, once an airplane wandered off the runway, was to pull up the landing gear. Capt. Jim Galluzzi, 4407th maintenance officer, said fewer than 100 man-hours were required to put an A-1 back into the air after it had been bellied in. A new engine, prop, gear knuckles and some sheet metal work were all that was required. If it flipped, it was a major rebuild—and the USAF had no airplanes to spare in 1970.

In fact, the A-1 was a vanishing bird. There were thirty-three then at Hurlburt. Those, plus perhaps 100 in Southeast Asia, were the last of 3,180 built. There were another seventy-five airframes in the boneyard at Davis-Monthan AFB, Arizona, but most were unusable. Galluzzi estimated perhaps twenty-five serviceable airframes could be reclaimed there.

"We need a thousand more of 'em," he said, noting in 1966 the USAF queried Douglas about putting both the A-1 and the B-26 back into production. Douglas offered to produce another 300 A-1 airframes at $580,000 each (the original cost was $415,000), and a small lot of B-26s at $1 million each. The USAF did not take the offer, and by 1970 the tooling had been destroyed or dispersed.

The SOF had some thirty-two B-26s until that year, when those and a few in Panama were phased out and retired from USAF service for the second time. But the planes are known to be still flying somewhere.

Galluzzi and others all agreed the A-1 and B-26 were the best aircraft types tried for Southeast Asia and for COIN (counter-insurgency) use.

"At the present time there's nothing to replace the A-1," said Yealy. "It's an old bird. We've run Davis-Monthan completely out of parts. I hate to see it go. I really do."

Going or not, the training program continued at full blast. Once the new students learned the basics of conventional aircraft, they learned to fly the A-1—an often challenging task. They learned to use it in instrument flight, aerobatics, gunnery and ordnance delivery. Finally they worked the tactical ranges under simulated combat conditions, flying both day and night missions.

A student in an O-1 or O-2 from the Holley Field FAC school spotted targets. On Sandy (rescue) missions, ground control teams from Hurlburt parachuted in, called for the A-1s to suppress fire and stood by while choppers came in to pick up the downed airmen.

"We go in first and troll for ground fire at low level," Yealy explained. "We do everything really that the Thud pilot does, and more. We do interdiction, armed reconnaissance, truck busting, close support. We can do just about anything, and we fly day and night." And he noted "they get lots of night gunnery, because most people have never ever flown ordnance delivery at night" when they arrive in the SOF program. From comments among the IPs, that phase got pretty sporty sometimes.

Yealy began his career flying P-47 Thunderbolts in World War II and, except for four years as a civilian before going to Korea, had been in the single-engine airplane business since.

In Vietnam, he was operations officer for the "Hobos" in his second (1968) tour there. He earned the Silver Star and four DFCs, the Bronze Star, eleven Air Medals and the Vietnamese Armed Forces Honor Medal flying A-1s.

It was a little strange to hear him speak of the A-1 as a fighter, though that's obviously the way he and other Spad pilots thought of it. Designed at the tag end of World War II as a Navy shipboard attack bomber, it was rescued from the dustbin by the Korean War and only gained fame at age twenty, in Vietnam.

If a fighter is an air superiority weapon, the lumbering old A-1 fell short in USAF hands in Southeast Asia, as it did in Navy service. But if a fighter is an airplane that hangs in there and slugs it out with the enemy, the A-1 indeed qualified. To borrow a British pilot's phrase to describe the Hawker Hurricane, the Skyraider was "a collection of non-essential parts flying in formation." And air superiority weapon or not, more than one MiG fell to the guns of the Super Spad in Vietnam.

Jim Yealy flew his A-1 to Khe Sanh daily for almost three straight months, supporting the besieged Marine bastion there. "It was just like watchin'

Despite its 50 ft. wing and gross weights up to 25,000 lbs., the A-1's 2,700 hp Wright and four-blade 13½ ft. prop will torque roll the airframe right around the engine against full aileron and rudder, as Jim Yealy, boss of the 4407th Combat Crew Training Squadron, loved to demonstrate to new sports.

a John Wayne movie," he recalled, shaking his head. "But the bird, Jesus, for that job there was nothin' like it."

Try to tell Jim Yealy the A-1 was not a fighter!

The Skyraider is a monster airplane; the biggest single-engine airplane I ever hope to see, with a 2,700 hp Wright engine and a maximum all-up weight of 25,000 lbs. It is so big the 50 ft. wing looks stubby.

You do not climb into an A-1, as you do most airplaines. You scale it, like a mahout mounting a half-trained elephant.

This is easier said than done, for the airplane lives on oil; swims in it, leaks it from every gasket. The fuselage is slippery with oil and grimy with exhaust residue. It is the only airplane I've ever seen with a "windshield degreaser" to clean the oil film from in front of the pilot.

It was also the only airplane I had seen with an endurance limited by its oil capacity. It is possible to hang more fuel on this machine than you can burn, for the R-3350 uses up to five gallons of oil per hour—more than the fuel consumption of the Luscombe I flew to Florida—and it carries only 38.5 gallons; enough for a maximum 7½ hour flight.

Except for the pull of the reel-type shoulder harness, the A-1E is a comfortable airplane, with a surprisingly good view out across the massive nose. It is better than most modern lightplanes, nose wheel or not.

Yealy cranked the big engine through sixteen blades, flipped on the mags and the Wright fired, sending clouds of oil smoke swirling about the canopy. The 13½ ft. prop blurred and Yealy ran down his checklist as the Wright settled into a sonorous throbbing mutter.

We taxied a mile in the Florida heat to the armament pad, where an ordnance team pulled the arming

The OV-10 could carry half a dozen fully-equipped troops in the fuselage cargo pod if they were properly motivated, and that was done occasionally while supporting the Special Forces and recon people in the clandestine war in Laos and Cambodia. Normally, the airplane carried a full complement of smoke rockets, anti-personnel bombs and a brace of 7.62 mm miniguns instead.

pins from our load. We carried two 750 lb. bombs, four 500 lb. bombs, simulated napalm and CBUs.

We held just off the active while a U-10 floated in and touched down at 30 mph, Yealy grumbling slightly and rechecking his watch. Our arrival over the tactical range was timed to the minute, and the delay was not welcome.

On the runway, the four A-1s lined up in a staggered four-ship formation and the pilots checked in. Yealy fed throttle to the Wright and we accelerated slowly, the A-1 at first demanding full right rudder, gradually lessening as airspeed increased.

The Spad broke ground at about 105 knots, some 3,000 ft. down the runway, and climbed like a very old man. The gear came up, unheard amid the bull-throated roar of the engine.

Yealy reduced power from 56 in. and 2800 rpm to 45 in. x 2600 rpm, and we climbed at 140 KIAS. Rate of climb, at this weight, moved slowly from 300 to 700 fpm. We climbed straight ahead, carefully, out over the Sound and the rendezvous point over the open ocean, the other three planes falling into a loose finger-four tactical formation to left and right, trailing slightly.

The power came back to 30x2200 as we flew westward up the coast and turned inland beyond Holley Field, heading for the tactical range.

Range 77 came equipped with a variety of targets, including hootches, a short truck convoy, a truck park, a bunker and some gun positions. The student FAC already was orbiting the area in his O-2. His call sign was Erade 22.

"Baffy Red Leader, this is Erade 22," he announced in our earphones. "I have you in sight. Target: truck convoy, five north of your position—" He continued, giving target location, terrain, weather, recapped the type and location of the expected ground fire, the route from which he wanted the target attacked, the A-1s' egress route and the area where he would orbit to watch the results. He would mark the target with a Willie Pete, a white phosphorous rocket, just before we made our run.

The weather was hot and muggy, but visibility was good; perhaps ten miles. The truck convoy was plainly visible from 5,200 MSL—5,000 ft. above ground—on a dirt track through the scrub pines. We were to make our runs from south to north and break to the west. The FAC would hold north.

"Baffy Red Flight, set 'em up, push 'em up," said Yealy to his brood—meaning, arm the 750 lb. bombs and increase the rpm.

Smoothly, the A-1 tipped up on its left wingtip and streaked earthward in a forty-degree dive, the airspeed reading 280 knots. Carrying this kind of load, you do not rack these birds around ham-fistedly, lest you stall and perhaps spin. At maximum load, you have some 30 knots' margin between cruise and stall, wings level. A heavily loaded A-1 gives little or no stall warning, and recovery can require 5,000 ft., even if you can jettison the external stores.

Yealy pickled his bomb at 2,700 MSL—2,500 above ground—and pulled out at 1,000 ft. to avoid damage from his own bomb burst, though these, of course, were inert training bombs. The pull-out was at a steady 3 G rate, less than half that pulled regularly by the OV-10s and due to a temporary restriction until the wing spars on all A-1s were beefed up to cope with occasional fatigue problems due to old age. Normally, the pull-off was at 5 Gs.

Yealy racked the A-1 steeply in its climbing turn, looking back to score his own strike. No. 2 was coming down the chute, leveling his wings, and I knew Capt. O'Dean "Stretch" Ballmes was holding his breath, peering through his gunsight. Ballmes was good. They were all good—the trucks would have been thoroughly demolished by eight solid hits in the kill zone—but Ballmes put his bombs side by side less than three yards from a truck, in two passes.

Around and around we went, in a racetrack pattern from 5,200 ft. We attacked the bunker with the simulated napalm, purposely aiming a few yards short so the flaming jellied petroleum would fan out and spray across the position.

We bombed the hootches with the smaller bombs, sprinkled CBU among the gun positions and wound up by strafing an ill-concealed truck. Yealy came in lower, flatter, perhaps fifteen degrees nose down. The sudden hammer of the 20 mm cannon was startlingly loud, and though only two of the four guns were loaded, the one-second burst slowed the airplane appreciably.

Thin ribbons of powder smoke trailed from the wing, and there was the quick sparkle of brass as the empties cascaded out the underside.

Yealy pressed the target, pulling out at 50 ft. above ground, and our wingtips etched broad contrails in the moist sea air. "You press as necessary to accomplish the mission," he explained later. "Otherwise, you'd normally stay high."

The strafing was in a random pattern, with the A-1s making their firing passes each from a different quadrant, each at a different angle, and never along the same track twice. It is a valuable tactic, designed to spoil the aim of enemy ground gunners, but one that demands timing precise as a dancer's.

I thought back to Yealy's long and individualistic pre-strike briefing, when he warned, "Get in there and get your target and roll out of there before those slope-heads get a bead on you." He explained, "This guy's been livin' with this gun now five or ten years, and he's had people drop ordnance on him every day. He's pretty smart. If you're gonna underrate him, then you're in trouble. He's damn' smart, and he's gonna have you."

I thought, too, of the remark in a training manual that said "Hair raising maneuvers near the ground will serve to stop the enemy gunners from shooting at you so they can watch you bust your ass. . . ."

For nearly an hour, we worked over the targets on Range 77 and, watching, I was very glad I would never be attacked by a Super Spad.

No bomb struck more than twenty yards from its target, and you could sit in the cockpit and watch the big 20 mm shells punch holes in the steel of the truck cabs and imagine the results inside.

Finally we were all Winchester—out of ordnance—except for No. 3, who had a hung bomb. He departed alone for the base, and the other three A-1s slid into tight formation for the trip back to Hurlburt.

The formation was too tight, too sharp for photography. I looked out, and our right wing overlapped our No. 2's left wing by 3 ft., sometimes twice that. He was 3 ft. below us. And I could not see No. 4's helmet, for he was hidden by No. 2.

I touched the mike button and asked them to open it up a little, so all the airplanes would show. I particularly wanted No. 4, for he was flying a single-seat A-1H, a slightly better combat plane—slightly faster, trickier, with a marginally better ordnance load, a different aft fuselage and less fin and rudder area.

We swung wide around Hurlburt and came over the active runway in our tight show formation, then broke sharply left in the much-loved 360 degree overhead approach. No. 1 . . . No. 2 . . . No. 4. By the time 4 broke, we were halfway to the ground.

Then back on the power, and gear and flaps came down. Final approach at 100-110 KIAS, back on the stick, ease off on the power, Yealy touched the rudder gently to counteract the changing torque effects, and the airplane touched softly, three-point.

Walking in, carrying our harness, sweat-drenched and loose, I grinned at this cheerful, deadly little gentleman at my side, my newfound friend, and I said, "Hey, I like your airplane! It's a comfortable old bird."

His eyebrows shot up. "Comfortable?" he asked, a smile tugging his lips. "It's not often we have anybody say that about it." But it is. It may be hot, crowded and slick with oil, but slipping into the Skyraider is like slipping into an old shoe.

"If I had to go back, I think that's what I'd like to go back in," said Dick Skeels of the old warhorse. And I

Standard operating practice called for slamming the OV-10 down hard on landing, in order to activate the squat switch in the main gear and allow the pilot to pull the power levers back into the reverse range for quick stops. Author had trouble getting his reflexes to allow him to do that. The odd bird really was an excellent design.

understood exactly what he meant. There was a feeling that the airplane would take care of you in unfriendly skies.

I went away from there with a small, round silver pin. It is a simple little thing, with a propeller and the legend, MACH Nix. It probably cost less than a nickel to make, at the time. I put it on my fly-in hat years ago. It's tarnished now, but it's still front and center on the hat. I'm proud of that pin!

And as I flew away from Hurlburt Field in the rainy morning light twelve hours later, I peered through the haze at the ranks of OV-10s and A-1s, T-28s, A-37s and scattered C-123s and U-10s. As an airman, an American and a taxpayer, I was very proud, too, of the Air Commandos.

They did good work.

Just how good, I learned two months later—when they raided Son Tay prison in North Vietnam! Many of my Hurlburt friends were involved in that mission.

First printed in *Air Classics*, October 1986.

The Super Spad carried a bigger load and more varied ordnance into combat on a mission than did the World War II B-17: iron bombs, napalm, cluster bombs, four 20 mm cannon, a dozen rockets, and pilots all agreed that in 1970 what the USAF needed in Southeast Asia was another thousand A-1s and maybe that many Douglas A-26s. They didn't have them. Both types slowly disappeared due to combat losses and lack of spares.

Chapter 19

Helio AU–24

The unknown warhorse

Over the last twenty-five years or so, it's been my good fortune to make the acquaintance of a double handful of highly memorable airplanes.

It's also been my good fortune to fly the Helio Courier, Super Courier and Stallion plus their military permutations. In part, this is because my original home was only twelve miles from the factory where they were built. Some of the people I grew up with worked in the factory. I knew both the factory test pilot and the ace tech rep very well. There's not much about Helios I haven't seen at one time or another. There are very few things about them I dislike—and I am not alone in that opinion.

I believe my wife would swap me for a Helio! And while I wouldn't go quite that far, I'd certainly be tempted to rent her.

Would I do it for an AU–24?

Maybe.

But if I did, I'd taxi around behind a convenient hangar at the first fuel stop and disconnect that Houdaille damper the FAA required!

The first time I saw N9991F, it was still clearly an AU–24. The bullet holes in its OD hide were covered with raw patches; the shipping label from Bangkok, Thailand, was still taped to the massive flank. There were rough, unpainted fiberglass tip tanks on the wings and a hastily daubed black registration on the aft fuselage. But it was still as military as an old combat boot.

The last time I saw 91F, it was decked out in a gleaming new orange and white finish. Leatherette and carpet covered the interior. It looked no more

military than a Cessna 150; instead, it was just another civilian airplane looking for work. A rare and singularly capable one.

To me, it still looked ugly. Most turboprop airplanes are ugly, but the AU–24, little-known military version of the Helio Stallion, and the even uglier Fairchild (née Pilatus) AU–23 Porter are somewhere toward the front of that particular parade. Both have a wing like a discarded door; both look like the result of a mad moment between an anteater and a pelican.

Turboprops are also noisy. They snarl and whine and squeal and growl in a quite astonishing range of discordance. And they stink. They reek of kerosene instead of the clean, tangy odor of honest high-test gasoline.

But beauty is in the eye of the beholder, and to Paul Davis, the Stallion is lovely. Davis, of course, doesn't know any better. He learned the mechanic's trade on jets and turboprops.

And he learned to fly in this airplane—in Cambodia. In combat. Worked on the Mekong River at night with a 20 mike-mike Vulcan cannon thrusting its deadly multi-barreled snout out the side of the airplane—a highly unofficial way for a civilian tech rep to go to war. The fact that this airplane and its two sister ships survived at all is largely due to him and a handful of dedicated Khmer airmen.

The thirty-two-year-old Davis was a contract technical representative for Helio Aircraft in Southeast Asia from 1970 until June 1972, while the airplanes were working in Vietnam and Laos. In October 1973, he was called back to perform the same function in Cambodia, since fourteen of the sixteen

AU-24s originally purchased by the USAF had been reassigned—minus spares or support equipment—to the Lon Nol government.

"I was one of the last people out," said Davis, running a hand through his sandy hair. "I was senior person in the country at that time attached to the Embassy," which was then limited to 200 names, total. He left Phnom Penh in April 1975, and three months later left Helio as well.

"I learned to fly in Cambodia to protect my own skin," Davis explained. "I knew the Stallion would get me out. Also, we didn't have anyone else to do functional test flights." With approval from the Embassy, Davis began going aloft, though "I didn't actually do any takeoffs and landings for almost a year." Pilot in command was a Cambodian maintenance officer. "We flew out wrecked airplanes and so on, and I got a little bit of time in a U-10 (Helio Courier) that belonged to the Embassy."

Though he had no license, Davis had 383.6 hours in an AU-24 by the time he came home, including over 100 hours of night combat missions and considerable instrument time. Davis recalls flying a repaired AU-24 to Phnom Penh, 2½ hours' IFR on the same day a T-28 and a C-123 were lost due to weather.

"I decided I'd better get my private license, so I got that in a Cherokee 140" at Tulsa after returning to the States, finding, in the process, that "everything was totally opposite from the Stallion I'd learned to fly in Cambodia. I find myself gettin' in trouble sometimes in another airplane," added Davis, who now has logged more than 700 hours.

Shortly after he earned his private license, Davis got a call from some Alcor representatives in San Antonio who were interested in buying three surviving AU-24s which had ended up in Bangkok, flown out of embattled Phnom Penh in USAF cargo planes. The Helios were now up for sealed bid, and the callers wanted to know what the aircraft should be worth.

Of the three, the Alcor bidders got one. The other two went to Anchorage investors Mike Schachel, Jack Turinsky and Gene Reed, who bought them sight unseen after looking up a description in Jane's *All the World's Aircraft*. Since they already had two of the three, they also succeeded in buying the third from Alcor.

Davis called the Alaskans and offered to get the planes out of Bangkok. "I told them I guaranteed nobody else was gonna get 'em out of the country for them. I knew where the records were." Thus, Davis went to Bangkok late in May 1976.

The three planes arrived in the States sixty days later, to the surprise of the Thai government, which had planned to block their removal, and, perhaps, the US government as well. They were the first US military export cargo to return home since the early 1960s.

Originally intended for CIA/Air America use and various "sneaky Pete" missions, the AU-24s are among the least-known military aircraft of all time. Both they and the AU-23s were used for flights into Laos and

Hardly anyone has heard of the AU-24, militarized version of the Helio 550A Stallion turboprop. There were only 16 of them, and they spent most of their time doing things folks weren't talking about in the early 1970s—but the fact is, the airplane was one of the great unsung success stories of the long, bitter air war in Southeast Asia. Fifteen went to Cambodia to support Lon Nol, and a dozen were in action on the last day of the war. Only three had been shot down! Three of them escaped the final collapse in Phnom Penh and were spirited out of Thailand and back to the United States. This is one of them: 9991F.

northeastern Cambodia from Vietnam. Later, they were turned over to the VNAF and, when the United States began direct support of the Lon Nol regime in its war against the expanding Khmer Rouge, they were transferred to Phnom Penh.

Davis, an unabashed partisan, calls the Fairchild/Pilatus "the box the Stallion came in," explaining there's no difference in cost, the Porter is less forgiving, the fuel consumption is higher, the speed lower and the useful load 300 lbs. less. He also says the airplane had to be beefed up to carry 5,100 lbs., and it lost the tail when powered by the geared Garrett engine.

In contrast, Davis notes, "we'd normally fly three or four missions a day, an average of 2.9 hours per mission," in the AU-24s. "We had the highest utilization rate in Southeast Asia.

"Three days before the close of the war, in 1975, every AU-24 in Southeast Asia except for one already shipped out in a box on a C-123 was available and flyable. That's twelve airplanes—at the end of the war. It's phenomenal. And it was all done by the Cambodians," despite a total lack of spares. "When we closed the war down, they didn't quit like the Vietnamese did. They just kept flyin' 'til they ran out of gas."

Of sixteen Helios built, one crashed in March 1973 with munitions and six personnel on board—over gross, out of CG and with inexperienced personnel. This was the incident that first sent Davis to Cambodia. One was lost at sea in the Tonkin Gulf on the last day of the war, out of fuel. Three were shot down and not repaired. The balance were at two

117

AU-24 was derived from this airplane, the one-off Helio Stallion. Powered by a Pratt & Whitney PT-6A-27 of 680 shp driving a 101 in., constant-speed prop, the H550A was certificated to a gross weight of 5,100 lbs. The military birds were certified to 6,300 lbs. at a 3 G load. There are over 300 minor changes between the H550A and the AU-24, but few are significant. Major points are: airplane will take off and land in two plane lengths (80 ft.), climb at a maximum deck angle of 34 degrees and cruise at 160 to 206 mph—not bad for a single-engine, eight-place airplane with a 2,800 lb. useful load.

Cambodian bases, and only the three that made it to Bangkok were salvaged.

The Military Equipment Delivery Team-Cambodia (MEDTC) had T-28s, AU-24s, C-123s, AC-47s with quad fifties, regular C-47s and UH-1H gunships and slicks. They had a team of six to nine joint-service personnel. "We flew night missions, with rockets and 20 mm and so on, for almost a year before the (military) mission recognized it," pioneering attack methods in the AU-24. On the other hand, the T-28s didn't fly at night under any conditions until very late in 1975, when they joined the Stallions on interdiction patrols up and down the Mekong.

Several times, Davis recalls receiving accurate ground fire and coming home to find holes in the wings and fuselage, but "nothing earth-shaking. Normally I never even knew I had a problem."

Back at base, there were other troubles. "We were getting an average of 75 rounds a day, incoming, on the airport" from Red artillery around the embattled Cambodian capital. Davis recalled walking out of his office at the field one day and going to his car. "I came back and my office was gone."

But the aircraft suffered worse than the personnel. No Americans were killed. "It just seemed we were lucky. We were in the right place at the right time."

On the other hand, the first of the restored survivors, now a veteran of civil flying in both Alaska and

the Andes, had over 800 bullet holes in it. Others were as riddled. Even so, the fleet racked up an estimated 19,000 hours' total time, much of it combat use. "We had one with 2,400 hours' total time. It was no problem. It flew great."

Helio, of course, is no longer producing aircraft and is virtually defunct, but Davis predicts "somebody will probably pick the Stallion up and put it into production someplace. There are a lot of inquiries. The Department of the Interior wanted me to demonstrate it in Boise. There's a possibility that some of the military agencies are interested for overseas operations. There's some Canadian interest. I could put three of them to work in Canada right now."

He estimates an initial market for fifty a year for the first two years and ten annually thereafter, but says, "The people I'm working with, there's no way they can produce the airplane." He adds, "I'd like to see the Stallion returned to production, and I'd like to go to work for 'em. That would be my goal."

Powered by a Pratt & Whitney PT-6A-27 680 shp turbine, the AU-24s cost the government $292,000 each in 1972. Since then, the cost of engines has jumped by $50,000. Unlike the one-off civilian-certificated Stallion, which had a certificated gross weight of 5,100 lbs., the AU-24s were flown by the military at 6,300 lbs. gross at a 3 G load. There are over 300 minor changes to the military bird, mostly to fit it for a spotter/ground attack role. That's why it took Davis over a year to get the airplanes recertificated in the standard category.

During that time, I flew the AU-24 twice, once from the right, once from the left seat, and found much that was familiar. The business office is almost identical with the civilian H-550A, a gray panel with a torquemeter, tachometer and flowmeter prominently displayed. There is the same machined aluminum T-handle on the power lever, a bangalore torpedo-shaped affair hefty enough to chin yourself on. The stick was purely military, a great curved club with a shaped grip, festooned with buttons to control radios, guns and bomb and rocket releases.

Starting involves fuel transfer pump off, fuel shut-off valve (red knob) on, starting control lever off, power lever at idle, prop control on full increase, generator switch off, battery on, boost pump on and at least five pounds per square inch (psi) on the fuel pressure gauge. At that point, you flip on the combination starter/ignition switch, watch the tach wind and the battery drain and when the PT-6A has stabilized for five seconds on at least twelve percent, move the starting control to low idle.

The ignition switch must be held "on" afer lightoff until the tach stabilizes at low idle, roughly thirty-five percent. Maximum allowable starting ITT is 1090 degrees C., and should decrease promptly as the engine begins to idle. Finally, cut in the generator at sixty-five percent rpm to recharge the battery, because starting takes a lot of juice. And you're in business.

Actually, starting is simple, it just sounds complicated. Davis contends it's easier to start than a piston engine, and if you boil it down to switch-flipping and button-pushing, it is. But the Helio ancillary systems get more frequent use than normal airplanes, and there are more gauges to watch. Different ones, anyway. There's some retraining required.

The big three-bladed paddle prop out front moves lazily around, slowly picking up speed as the turbine lights off, and by the time the engine has stabilized, the prop blades have come out of feather and gone to work. Fortunately, cabin soundproofing is excellent, because outside, close up, the pervasive whine of the machine is almost unbearable.

The droop snoot slopes away ahead of you, the massive windshield wraps around and over you and, since your eye level is nearly 9 ft. in the air, the effect during taxi is like riding in a space-age elephant howdah.

At the far end of the runway, the before-takeoff checklist consists mainly of scanning the forest of instrument faces. Basically, the AU-24 is a very simple airplane. The beauty of a turboprop is, you set the prop governor for the desired rpm (generally 2000-2100) and forget it. From then on, you do all your flying by advancing or retarding the power lever.

To me, there has always been a curious lack of feel to the Stallion, both on the ground and in the air, and the military version is no different. I remarked that, although just about any pilot could check out and fly the airplane in an hour or two, it would probably take fifty hours before he could wring the last ounce of performance out of the machine. Davis quickly agreed, but he added a couple of caveats: "Any competent tail-dragger pilot," he said. And he put the learning period at about 100 hours.

Davis should know. At this moment, he probably knows more about the AU-24 than any single man in the world. Not only did he engineer the design changes needed to make them suitable for civilian use (including the tip tanks and a 700 lb. increase in allowable gross weight), he also flew the test program, which was extensive, exhaustive, sometimes a bit hairy and involved one forced landing. "Once is enough," he declared three weeks after finally obtaining the standard airworthiness certificate. "I wouldn't care to go through it again. It was an awful long project."

We pulled onto the active, locked the tailwheel, set twenty degrees of flap and advanced the power lever. The percent power needle, which had been hovering at eighty, leaped frantically up the scale, reach-

N9950A shares airframe with later AU-24, along with control system. The AU-24, however, had tip tanks and reinforced structure to accommodate 20 mm side-firing Vulcan. The Stallion and AU-24 use a combination of short, broad-chord ailerons and spoilers for super-fast, ultra-positive roll control. The FAA insisted upon a stick force augmentation system (STFAS) that provides 55 to 100 lbs. of stick push force under certain conditions, making Stallion/AU-24 an iron-jawed brute. The airplane already had a Houdaille damper on the elevator, which should have rendered the SFAS unnecessary. The Stallion won't really stall, but it will become elevator limited at about 38 knots, or 45 mph.

A no-nonsense gray instrument panel and Bangalore torpedo-like throttles distinguish turboprop Helios. The AU-24 also has hard points beneath the wings and fuselage for smoke bombs, containers of anti-personnel bomblets or rockets. A good, honest, high-performance airplane, the Stallion lacks control feel because of the SFAS and damper required by the FAA for certification. It's like taking a shower with a raincoat on.

ing for 100 percent. The engine whine reached a hellish crescendo, and you could feel the airplane fighting to move. The Stallion has excellent, powerful brakes—but even with them locked, you can almost skid the wheels on dry paving. On wet paving, it's a cinch.

I released the brakes and the airplane lunged forward. We rolled about 100 ft. and jumped off the ground like a frog off a hot rock. Unlike the frog, we kept going. We weren't trying to set any records—climb angle was only about fifteen degrees, and the Stallion is cleared for a maximum continuous deck angle of thirty-four degrees—but, with only two aboard and 1,000 lbs. of fuel, we registered a sustained 2,800 fpm climb rate at 90 knots.

I flew the original 550A half a decade ago, and as the AU-24 pulsed in my hands, it all came flooding back to me.

N9991F was just like N9950A with a few new instruments and tip tanks. There was the same peculiar lateral response to control inputs: wiggle the stick rapidly to and fro, a foot each way, and the big bird barely quivers in the air. But slam the stick over and hold it there, and the AU-24 will roll so fast it'll leave your eyeballs hanging in space. That's because the Stallion, like all Helios, uses a combination of conventional ailerons and retractable spoilers, and the latter, deploying after the ailerons, are what really do the number.

There was the same iron-jawed brute feel to the elevator, a result of the Houdaille viscous damper (which resists rapid control movements and any reach toward the travel limits) and of the stick force augmentation system. The SFAS provides up to 55 lbs. of forward push at 42 knots IAS; sometimes up to 100 under certain conditions—and leaves a newcomer to the Stallion feeling he's been suckered into an arm-wrestling match with King Kong.

There was the same need to keep the controls coordinated. The Stallions are rudder airplanes. The wing spans 41 ft. and the bird is 39 ft., 7 in. long. The fin and rudder are 8 ft. high. That's a lot of mass moving in the sky, and, at low speeds and with the PT-6A pumping torque into the 101 in. prop, you can get yourself into an awful mess unless you fly the rudder just right.

In fact, if you fly a Stallion really in the STOL mode—right on the bottom fringes of the performance parameters—you are going to be very busy. It will require every bit of your concentration. And you will get an awful lot of healthful exercise. It's significant that the Stallion pilot notes, as written by Helio, say, "It should be emphasized here that the Stallion, during takeoffs and landings, must be masterfully controlled by the pilot," and goes on to say that any incipient swing demands "immediate corrective action."

However, it's amazing that the airplane is not much harder to handle than it is. A Stallion pilot can expect to go from 680 hp to zero hp to minus something on any trip—which should do weird things to directional control in all three axes. In fact, to me, there's a surprising lack of torque effect in any axis or flight mode. Not everyone has felt this way.

Helio claims its airplanes won't stall. And they won't; not really. But you can get some hellacious sink rates. And you can just about run the Stallion out of rudder in the air, holding the nose up under power until it finally swings determinedly leftward despite full right rudder.

In 91F you can work the airplane down to 38 KIAS at sixty percent power (450 hp), but at that point it becomes extremely unstable in the roll axis. Hold it there and work the nose just a tad higher and it will finally fall off on a wing.

The FAA defines the stall in these types as the point where they become elevator limited. In both the AU-24 and the original 550A, this is about 38 knots, or 45 mph, clean; 36/42 with the flaps down.

We didn't do it, since this was a private-venture airplane and not a factory demonstrator, but I knew what Davis was talking about when he said at the break he was almost at the top of a hammerhead. I recalled a similar experience in the 550A. Davis also said with more throttle, you can end up in what amounts to a vertical torque roll, with the airplane tailsliding corkscrew fashion back down its own flight path. The Stallion is tough, but it's not designed to do aerobatics.

We also tried a maximum performance ground attack, involving a wingover into a fifty-degree dive with the prop in deep beta once, but we dropped that

because it made Davis nervous about the prop and because he said in practice it wasn't used much in combat due to lateral snaking. We were indicating 80 knots and descending 3,500 fpm.

That's the beauty of a turboprop. Back off the power lever to thirty percent at 100 mph and the prop blades actually begin holding you back. It's like throwing out the anchor.

You don't have to fly the Stallion down at the hairy end of the performance envelope, of course. If you fly it like a normal airplane, that's what you've got, and one with a satisfyingly high degree of performance. This is the way the military flew it, using the STOL ability simply to fly heavy loads safely out of high, hot areas.

On the other hand, fly it light and you get impressive speeds. Davis recalled in his flight test program "I've hit 225 knots (260 mph) easy on the deck on a cool day. It'll accelerate to that." He cited a series of five runs at 50 ft. AGL (approximately 1,000 MSL) on a 50 degree F. day. The plane was timed at 205 to 210 knots (236-242 mph) on every run, and, he added, "Yesterday (July 9, 1978) at 12,500 MSL I was truing 214 mph on a very hot day during a cross-country over Arkansas. And we've had it to 378 mph TAS, coming out of 24,000 MSL indicated 235 knots in about a thirty-degree dive, full throttle" during the test program.

Normal cruise is considered to be 206 mph (seventy-five percent power) to 160 mph (sixty percent). That's not bad for a single-engine eight-place airplane with a 2,800 lb. useful load. And, among other changes, Davis got the official service ceiling upped from 20,000 to 24,000 ft. and suspects it will go to 30,000. He notes it was still getting 800 fpm rate of climb at 5,800 lbs. and 20,000 ft.

It's really pretty cheap to fly, too. Fuel costs $35 per hour, and Davis figures a sinking fund of $10 per hour on the engine. "You have less maintenance per hour on this airplane than you do on anything else."

Ugly or not, AU-24 or civilian 550A, the Helio Stallion is a thoroughbred performer. And it's a shame that production has stopped. But, if you just can't live without one, well—91F is for sale. And the price? Only $287,500, a bargain! The first AU-24 restored sold for over $300,000!

First printed in *Air Progress*, May 1979.

Chapter 20

DeHavilland Vampire

Thirst of the Vampire

I saw my first Vampire sitting on the ramp of my home airport probably twenty years ago, the property of a local contractor. It sat there for a long time. I think I saw him move it once. I have no idea how often he actually flew it, if ever.

At the time, I had no idea why it got so little use, for I never got the chance to talk to the owner about it.

Now, looking at the airplane from the vantage point of my own limited experience, I consider it a pussycat to fly but with somewhat demanding systems (gear, flaps).

On the other hand, if I owned it—and I wish I did—it probably wouldn't fly much either. In my case at least, that's because I couldn't afford to buy either the fuel required or pay for the asphalt repairs around the airport resulting from normal operation. Nevertheless, it is a historically significant airplane and an absolute ball to boot around the sky.

The single-seat Vampire is an attractive airplane, but grafting the Mosquito nose onto the little jet did nothing for its lines. On the other hand, two-seat airplanes are more fun than single-seaters because you can share the fun.

One nice thing about a jet: There's no need for a run-up at the end of the runway. You just taxi that rascal right out onto the runway, lay the nose wheel on the white line and go to full power.

It was probably noisy outside, as the 3,500 lb. static thrust Goblin went to 10,750 rpm and sent the Vampire Mk 35 hurtling down the 4,200 ft. Runway 17 at Tulsa, Oklahoma's Jones airport. Comfortable inside

the sealed, mildly pressurized (3 lbs. per sq. ft.) cockpit and my own earphones, I never noticed.

I was much more worried about incinerating some more of their runway. That, and the fact that the only way to control this unguided missile on the ground is by quick little alternate stabs of the brakes.

The British apparently knew nothing of nose-wheel steering in 1945.

My next problem was getting the gear up. Evidently concerned that someone would cycle the gear inadvertently, they fixed things so the chance of that happening is as remote as a Soyuz trip. They use the standard wheel-shaped gear handle, all right, but they flank it with a couple of extra pull handles.

The idea is to palm the gear handle, squeeze the pull handles into your palm, push outboard, pull the whole thing back and then up—and to do it all between your 100 knot unstick speed and the 115 knot gear retraction limit speed with external tanks.

For a raw colonial boy, this is fairly challenging the first time or two.

The next trick is to get the flaps up. This is much simpler but likewise requires an outboard push to get the wing-shaped lever out of its notch.

From then on, I was home free. Following Larry New's instructions from the right seat, I reduced the power to 10,250 rpm (500 below the fifteen-minute allowable maximum climb setting) and trimmed for a 240 knot climb (up from my initial 170 knots immediately after leaving the pattern), making coordinated turns en route.

I got so busy I forgot to look to see what the initial rate of climb was. I asked New later and he said probably 3,500 fpm, but a specification sheet I got later on the airplane shows 4,000 fpm initial, and a time of 3.5 minutes from brake release to 10,000 ft. at an average flying weight of 10,075 lbs. (two pilots, full internal fuel). I'd guess that's about right. It certainly didn't seem to take long.

New was busy, too, trying to get some cool air inside the cockpit. Four or five times, he reached down between the seats and fiddled with something, and every time I got a blast of air on my throttle hand hot enough to cook knuckles. He finally just gave up on the thing.

Leveling out below the continental control zone, I left the power where it was and allowed the airspeed to stabilize. Within approximately two minutes, it settled at close to 300 knots which, at our density altitude, equated to 350 true and about 403 mph.

Backing off to an economy power setting of 9500 rpm dropped the airspeed to 260 knots indicated for 302 knots true or about 346 mph. Clearly, the Vampire is no slouch in the speed department, but on the other hand I swear I could actually *see* the fuel needle creeping around counterclockwise.

The spec. sheet shows that eighty-eight percent rpm at 15,000 ft. produces 311 knots true and best range, while Vmax, SL, is 450 knots indicated. High-altitude cruise is 400 knots true, and normal high-altitude cruise 350 knots.

Fuel consumption "varies greatly with power settings," from a minimum of 160 gph at 35,000 ft. to a rule-of-thumb 300 gph down low. A setting of 250 knots below 5,000 ft. will yield approximately 250 gph or less. Basically, it's a gallon per nautical mile. The airplane carries 393 US gallons internally, 240 gallons more in the external drop tanks.

A few turns and some deliberate control displacements proved the airplane was very sensitive in pitch, neutral in roll, stable in yaw but easy to trim to fly hands off, using the big metal trim wheel under my left hand.

I looked over at New. "Mind if I do a few rolls?" I asked. "No," he replied. "Do whatever you want." So I proceeded to do one to the right, one to the left and another to the right.

My first slow rolls in a strange airplane are usually pretty sloppy, and these fit neatly into that category.

The Vampire's nose is much heavier than I had anticipated and the roll rate slower, and since I didn't pull it up high enough or push enough, the first one ended up pretty much on point but about ten degrees nose low. The second was a little better, maybe five degrees low, and I determined to nail it on the third. Full-aileron roll rate is probably sixty to seventy-five degrees per second at 260 KIAS, with the drop tanks attached. I understand it rolls at least ninety degrees per second and maybe a little faster, clean.

I pulled the nose up probably twenty degrees above the horizon, leaned on the stick and started around, feeding in forward pressure to hold the point

as we rolled inverted. Everything was going great until we went negative, when my seat let go somewhere down around floor level and I suddenly shot three inches toward the canopy. My feet came off the rudder pedals. It occurred to me I had not thought to pre-flight the seat. I didn't like it at all. My left hand joined my right in a death grip on the stick. I did a particularly lousy job of finishing the roll, ending up with the nose thirty-five degrees right of my intended point and ten degrees low again.

I mentioned that later to Denny Sherman, who used to own this airplane, and he said, "You know, the same thing happened to me. . . ." He explained that that means the vertical adjustment pin was not locked in place.

Having discouraged myself with inverted maneuvers, I proceeded to the stall series—and quickly found the Vampire is a real sweetheart here. At 6,500 ft., it stalled clean, power off, at 90 KIAS, and racked into a sixty-degree bank and pulling 3.5 Gs with probably 9500 rpm, at 160 KIAS. Somehow, I never did get into stalls with gear down and full eighty-degree flaps.

The next thing was to learn whether the airplane would have been easy to fight with. Fighter pilots talk about the buffet zone as pebbles, rocks and boulders to describe how deep in the stall regime you're operating. I got the Vampire into some pretty good-sized rocks and found I could roll the airplane rapidly from left to right and back again with perfect ease and full control. Turn radius seemed excellent. The sink rate went to 6,000 fpm, but she remained completely docile—a good fighting machine.

Sherman recalled as a teenager witnessing a formation of single-seat Vampires do a 360 degree turn inside of a mile at an air show, and said the airplane will do a positive-G loop in 3,000–4,000 ft., with an entry at about 320 KIAS.

Having gained a degree of confidence in this big blue bat, I aimed the bulbous nose at the old Muskogee AFB, forty miles away in the afternoon heat haze, to shoot my first landing.

We were there in no time! The only problem was, Davis Field's 7,200x150 ft. concrete runway is aligned 13-31, and the wind was 180 degrees at 30 knots with gusts to 40 or slightly better. I was certainly going to get to see how the Vampire handled in a crosswind!

I flew down Runway 13 at 1,000 ft. AGL (only way to get a jet fighter on the ground is out of a 360 degree overhead, right?) and 220 knots, chopped the power right back, pitched out to the left at about 2 Gs, threw out the speed brakes (little green lever at one o'clock on the throttle quadrant), followed with the gear at 145 knots, dropped thirty-degree flaps followed by full (there's a neutral detent on the flaps that you have to watch for, going either way) and brought the power back up a bit. These early jet engines have a slow spool-up time, and unless you lead them, you can develop a real problem for yourself.

I flew the downwind at 150 knots, base at 130 and carried 110–115 down to the runway—which is a bit

Entering service in 1946, the de Havilland Vampire never saw combat, but it did have a distinguished multi-national peacetime career extending nearly two generations. Indeed, Switzerland got rid of its last Vampires in 1990. The first-generation jet fighter was built initially as a single seater, but de Havilland soon adapted the Mosquito nose to their new jet and produced a two-seat night fighter/trainer configuration. An excellent airplane to fly, the Vampire's big drawback as a civil sport plane is its terrible thirst—roughly a gallon per nautical mile or six gallons per minute at low altitude. Author is in left seat, preparing to lift off the Goblin engine.

much, but I wrote it off to crosswind insurance. The right wing was down maybe ten or twelve degrees, on the average, with left rudder to match, and I proved the Vampire flies very well cross-controlled.

I also proved it will float very well. I went sizzling along like a Mooney just off the runway, the deHavilland bucking in the gale as I tried to feel my way down to the paving without sliding sideways or chopping quite all the power until the upwind main touched. Then, of course, I had to remember to tap the brakes with my toes to steer the thing.

It was an interesting few moments. New thought so, too. He woke right up and waved his hands some—but, to his credit, didn't try to interfere.

Neither one of us liked that experience much, so we taxied back to the departure end of the runway and took off for Jones/Riverside again. We agreed we'd rather shoot touch-and-goes on a short runway into a 30-40 knot wind than a long one with a fifty-degree crosswind.

I surely do love fast airplanes! Especially fast airplanes with plenty of power and a wing loading high enough to dampen out most of the low-level bumps.

I came steaming downhill in a wide circle to a right pattern to Jones' Runway 18R, broke to the right over the hangars, chopped the throttle, threw out the boards, threw out the gear, threw out the flaps, brought up the power a shade down final, chopped it again when it was certain I had the field made and crossed the fence at about 105 knots.

The moment I flared out and touched down, I had the speed brakes up and was bringing up the flaps, even as I steered my high-speed scooter down the runway. With the flaps started up, I advanced the power, and as the throttle hit the stop I dropped my hand to the nearby flap handle to set it at thirty degrees for takeoff. Just as I got the flap set, it was time to lift the nose and fly off, reaching for the gear.

A fellow can get busy in a hurry doing that.

This time, I simply bent it around to a right downwind, reduced power, dropped the gear, dropped the flaps and put it on the numbers at 100 KIAS.

The Vampire has a concave (double-tread) nose wheel tire and anti-skid brakes—and needs them.

I am not used to such devices, and had to keep reminding myself that I was not about to burn out the brakes, as I trod heavily on them to halt the airplane by the time we arrived at the far end of the runway. This thing wants to roll forever!

I turned off the active, and as New popped the hatch, I thought back on what I had just learned.

I would agree with Denny Sherman's spec sheet, which says the airplane requires a sea level takeoff distance of 2,000 ft., average, and 3,000 ft. to clear a 50 ft. obstacle at 20 degrees C. (68° F.) Furthermore, it takes at least that far to get it stopped again—so you can see 4,200 ft. was none too much runway to be shooting touch-and-goes, no matter how strong the wind.

Still, that's not bad for a 10,000 lb. load carried by 262 sq. ft. of wing pushed by the 3,500 lb.s.t. Goblin 35. That's a wing loading of 38.45 lbs. per sq. ft. and a power loading of 2.88 lbs. per lb.s.t. Empty weight of this aircraft is 7,082 lbs.

The twin-boom deHavilland DH 100 Vampire first flew Sept. 20, 1943, and the first production model, the Vampire F Mk 1, flew Apr. 20, 1945, in single-seat interceptor form. Intended as an answer to the Luftwaffe's Me 262s, the Vampire did not see combat, entering service with the RAF in 1946. Two hundred forty four were built, including four for Switzerland

and seventy for Sweden. Interestingly, the Dominican Republic bought twenty-five Swedish Vampires in 1955, operating them alongside later fighter-bomber models. Later fighter marks went to Mexico and to the the US civil market (twenty-five F.3s from Canada).

Vampires and the derivative Venoms with revised wings and slightly more powerful Ghost engines (4,850–5,150 lb. s. t.) quickly became the RAF's chief day fighters, and navalized versions served aboard aircraft carriers. The two-seat night fighter was developed by deHavilland in response to a 1949 order from Egypt, but in the event were taken over by the RAF. Ninety five were built. The company then produced a trainer version as a private venture, the first flying in November 1950. The Vampire attracted widespread foreign interest from the outset, and became Britain's all-time best-selling jet aircraft, serving in some countries into the 1960s. Zimbabwe had some still in military service in the 1980s.

Seventy-five were exported to Switzerland and another 100 were license-built there. Two hundred eighteen more were built in Australia by a subsidiary, half of them two-seat trainers. A further 433 were produced by SNCASE in France, and Jacqueline Auriol set a new women's world speed record of 515 mph over a 100 km. closed course in one of these on May 12, 1951. Even India built a few, at Bangalore. Total worldwide production finally reached 4,206 aircraft.

NX11924, serial number 4140, is a Mk 35, the final evolution of the Vampire series. It differs from the DH 115 T.11 trainer by the addition of hydraulic brakes and an anti-skid system. This aircraft was built in 1953 and served with the British Royal Air Force as a navigator trainer before it was seconded to the Australian Air Force in 1961.

Entirely rebuilt and certified as a new aircraft, NX11924 came to the US civil registry in late 1969, one

Built by de Havilland in 1953, NX11924 is a Mk. 35 (hydraulic brakes and an anti-skid system) used by the RAF as a navigator trainer and seconded to the Australians in 1961. One of 14 imported to the United States in 1969, it passed through a series of civilian owners, but total *airframe time was only 2,670 hours when this flight evaluation was made in the summer of 1989. Author is flying lead for a pair of DH Venoms, an improved Vampire with faster, thinner wing and uprated engine.*

of fourteen imported from Melbourne by Jim Cullen of Westair International, Broomfield, Colorado. It was civilianized and used by four different owners—but not much, due to the profligate fuel consumption of the simple axial-flow turbojet. Total airframe time currently is approximately 2,670 hours.

It is now one of six flying Vampires in the United States, although thirteen remain on the register. Another flies in England and an eighth in Australia, plus perhaps several examples still held by the Swiss Air Force and those in Zimbabwe.

The Vampire spans 38 ft., and the double-tapered low-aspect ratio (6.2) wing, twin tail booms and fuselage pod lend a bat-like appearance, hence the name. It is 34 ft. 6 in. long and 6 ft. 6 in. high.

A cantilever mid-wing monoplane with an EC 1240 series airfoil section, the Vampire has an all-metal, flush-riveted aluminum structure—except for the nacelle, which sports a monocoque nose piece of plywood and balsa sandwich construction forward of the bulletproof windshield. The rearward-tilting blown canopy is hydraulically operated, and one of the first items on the pre-start checklist is to remove the lock pin from the yellow-painted, L-shaped actuator centered behind the twin seats.

The cockpit is snug, and stiff, angled projecting "ears" for the lap belt digging into my hams on both sides made it clear the airplane was not designed for overweight middle-aged gentlemen. The Vampire was the first aircraft equipped with the popular Martin-Baker ejection seat, and Sherman said with those original seats, it was much worse since they were angled forward at the top.

The stick moves fore and aft normally, but the uppermost 12 in. or so is hinged and pivots left or right for aileron control—another strange British invention. Rudder pedals and the seat backrest are adjustable.

The 20.8 sq. ft. split flaps and 2.96 sq. ft. rotating air brakes are mounted in the wings and are hydraulic, as is the tricycle landing gear, which has both a track and wheel base of 11 ft. 3 in. Brakes in earlier models were pneumatic. Curiously, ailerons and rudders have internal mass balances, but the elevator carries external mass balance weights. The air brakes deploy equally above and below the wings, but still produce a mild pitch-up above 200 knots.

Of the Goblin, Sherman said importer Jim Cullen reported the Australians set TBO at 1,200 hours. "I've heard it's as low as 900 hours; that it's on condition.... So it's a mystery. I believe every air force had a different TBO. They inspect the cans, and if you've got cracks in 'em, you're allowed to weld the cracks."

Except for the critical tailpipe temperature and its inordinate thirst for fuel, the Goblin seems pretty bulletproof, anyway. Sherman said stock Vampires have no oil pressure or temperature gauges, just the tailpipe temperature and a tachometer.

"The engine idles at 3000 rpm, and you can't make the airplane move off the chocks until you've got 5500 rpm," he said. "If you noticed, the temperature comes up with your arm to 650 degrees, but once at 5500 rpm or so, the temperature rise stops."

Light-off actually is quite simple: with the throttle closed, hit the master, hit the fuel pump, hit the red "start" button and hold for not more than two seconds, and, as the automatic sequence takes hold and the engine begins to wind, advance the red fuel petcock lever from "closed" forward to "open" above 700 rpm.

Because the tailpipe rides low to the ground, you're likely to scorch the asphalt as you move away, and new owner Red Stevenson said the first time he, Larry New and Bill Harrison tried a formation takeoff in the Vampire and a pair of just-acquired former Swiss Air Force Venoms, they left three burned spots on the end of the runway.

Summing up, then, the Vampire is a historically significant aircraft, a straightforward and uncomplicated fighter plane that offers comfort, excellent performance, a reasonable degree of challenge for the pilot and probably low maintenance. Its only drawback is the fact that it burns approximately three gallons a minute.

As Sherman said, "If you have the engine running for 30 minutes, you'll spend eight or 10 on the ground. Then you take off, climb to 12,000 ft., do a stall, a loop and a roll and come back and you've just used 180 gallons. But a T-bird, at full throttle, burns 855 gph at 1,000 ft. and holds 813 gallons...."

Last year, Red Stevenson was flying one of the Spanish Hispano Ha-200 Saetas. This year, it's the Vampire and one of the gloss-black Venoms, having sold the other to warbird aficionado, sometime business partner and longtime good buddy Bill Harrison.

I asked him why, and he—predictably— replied: "We buy and sell everything from 18 horse to 10,000 horse. And people call us because they know we'll give a legitimate bid on anything that'll fly. The guys called me and wanted to know what would I give, and we always give a price that is very, very close to the actual true market value. I bought one in Florida, one in Houston and one in Dallas, but I happened to do it all about the same time.

"I think they're a delight to fly. I think they're safer than the T-33. The Venom has the same performance parameters as an F-86, but the accident rate was less than 2% of the F-86. It's nine minutes to 50,000 ft. Above 35,000 ft., the Venom will outperform the F-86!"

Like all Stevenson's airplanes, both the Venom and Vampire are for sale—cheap. And the Vampire comes with full King solid-state IFR avionics, dual glideslopes, RNAV and dual high-pressure oxygen consoles. If I had a spare hundred grand, I'd buy it in a minute!

Meanwhile, he's promised me I can fly it some more.

First printed in *Warbirds* September-October, 1989.

Chapter 21

Republic F–105 Thunderchief

Thud!

Ground attack in a modern tactical jet is one of the most exciting contact sports ever devised.

One contact with the ground, and it's all over. Permanently.

Nowhere have I ever had a better introduction to that than in the now-retired F-105 Thunderchief! You sit there, strapped in six ways from Sunday, swaddled in heavy flying clothes, and watch the earth mushrooming toward you with nightmare speed.

Obviously, the closer you can "press," the more accurately you can deliver your iron bomb. Obviously, the faster and steeper your approach, the harder it is for the defenders to hit you.

Equally obviously, if you misjudge your pull-out by a heartbeat, someone else will be writing your family.

I recommend it to everyone at least once.

As for the airplane, what can I say? It was a great flying machine, especially on a windy, gusty day in Kansas. The Thud was totally unaffected by turbulence. It was as stable as your office chair. And it had the instantaneous response every fighter pilot loves. In short, it was a hell of an airplane. I'm sure those who took it into combat remember it fondly.

From 3,000 ft. overhead, the dull brown tones of late winter flatten the flinty contours of the Smoky Hill Weapons Range southwest of Salina, Kansas.

The sun is fiercely bright, the thick, double perspex of the canopy scrupulously clean. A windy March day ensures 100 mile visibility. But there is little to see below as we whip past from south to north at nearly eight miles a minute.

This range property is roughly triangular in shape, 8½ miles wide by 10½ miles long; 8,100 acres of the 33,877 acre total actually comprising the range itself. Not really very big, at our speed and altitude. There are a few dirt roads, a conspicuous building with maintenance equipment huddled close alongside, a couple of spotting towers for range officers, three white aiming circles, two rectangular white gunnery areas and a clutch of "tactical targets" scattered around—truck convoys, armor, aircraft, surface-to-air missile sites and anti-aircraft gun emplacements.

In the front cockpit, Lt. Col. Edward L. Cummins is setting up his weapons selector panel for bombing. "See that lighted 'C' on the button about midway in the panel?" he asks through the intercom. "That means we can drop a bomb."

In the headphones, the range officer reports surface winds are 18 to 24 knots, with gusts up to 36 knots at altitude. Cummins acknowledges. We are established now, well south of our intended target and at right angles to it, eastbound.

"Four-two, on final," says Cummins, as the big fighter-bomber dips an ocher-and-green wing and rolls lazily left like a feeding shark, its needle nose dropping below the horizon to steady on the 300 ft. white bulls-eye of the bombing target and the tiny orange triangle that marks its precise center.

Ahead, housefly-size in the armor-glass windscreen, *Husky 41* is pulling off the right-hand target, banking gracefully away to the left. A puff of white smoke, perhaps 500 ft. high, is drifting rapidly downwind.

With a mammoth J75 jet engine producing 26,500 lbs. of thrust in burner and a wing loading that reached 127 lbs. per sq. ft., the Republic F-105 is so big a man can walk under the wing without stooping. The bird had a difficult service introduction but later proved to be the outstanding attack airplane of the Vietnam War. Launching at combat weights above 26 tons, the Thud could outrun everything else down in the weeds.

Cummins doesn't touch the throttle, but the airspeed indicator zips up from 450 to 480 knots. The Republic F-105F is a clean airplane, and twenty-two tons of metal and fuel, even going downhill at only a ten-degree angle, picks up speed in a hurry. The orange triangle swells dizzily in the pipper of his reflector gunsight as he zeroes in for a visual bombing pass, dropping his 25 lb. practice bomb the hard way.

Passing through the 1,000 ft. level, he depresses a red button on the control stick and releases the bomb, then, at 900 ft., pulls smartly back on the stick to begin the round-out.

The Thunderchief squats on its haunches, fighting to change its direction from "down" to "up" in a hurry, and the G meter, which measures the result of force applied against moving mass in terms of gravity units, goes to 4½. The airplane begins to vibrate, a rapid *tramp, tramp, tramp,* like the granddaddy of all centipedes at the quick march—as the wingtips stall, trying to keep an applied force of 100 tons from falling out of the sky.

Once the pull-out begins, F-105 pilots don't dawdle. If they did, they'd find themselves excavating their own mine shaft. "You shoot and pull," says Cummins. "That's the name of the game."

The Kansas Air National Guard's 184th Tactical Fighter Training Group and its flying squadron, the 127th TFTS, has never had anyone fly into the ground, and Cummins remarks, "We don't even like to talk about it. We try to impress that on 'em greatly."

The Kansas Air Guard runs three distinct training programs for would-be F-105 drivers at Wichita's McConnell Air Force Base, and the most common, for pilots who have not been combat-ready in a fighter for the last five years, is six months long. The chief reason for the length, says Cummins, is that "it takes that long to teach 'em to hurl their pink body at the ground."

On the right, the 80 ft. range tower flashes past, on a level with the cockpit. The nose pitches up to ten degrees above the horizon, the left wing snaps down, pointing vertically at the flint rocks and sere prairie grass. And the G load goes on and on as Cummins bends the big bird around in a near-maximum combat turn.

"By golly, that's clever," I gasp in the earphones as the G suits sense the relentless pressure and go to work, inflating with air, clamping the frail human bodies in a tight embrace to force the blood back up into the brain and upper body despite its efforts to pool in legs and feet.

Cummins chuckles. "Smart little rascal, isn't it?" he says. And it is. It keeps fighter pilots and weapons systems operators from blacking out due to lack of blood. But still, lungs are laboring under four times their accustomed load, hearts are slugging painfully in the chest cavities. The heavy plastic helmet, the padded "bone dome" designed to protect against head injury, forces the neck down into the shoulders. Arms weigh more than 50 lbs. each, and even the spine is compressed. It is no wonder old fighter pilots often suffer lower back problems.

Despite this, the unit's instructor pilots—all full-time Air Guard technicians—average over eleven years of military flying and over 1,700 hours in the F-105. One has 3,000 flight hours in the Thud.

Cummins is fifty; flies the F-105 a minimum of five hours a month; says "I like to go at least two or three times a week, if possible;" says the sustained high G loads don't bother him. Col. Ted Coukoulis, group commander, is about the same age and also flies regularly; he holds the range gunnery record.

But it must be a lot like George Blanda playing football. The recuperation periods have to get longer and longer.

That they continue is a measure of the fascination their job holds for them. In truth, it is so enjoyable it is almost sinful. The state adjutant general, Maj. Gen. Edward R. Fry, jokes it is "one of the best-kept secrets in the Air Guard. If the taxpayers knew how much fun it was, they'd complain."

It's fatiguing, of course. Pilots returning from an F-105 mission are pale and drawn, rumpled and sweat-stained—and tired. This kind of flying is hard work. At times, it's like pulling a plow. And it's very demanding, perhaps in particular the ground attack work.

The Republic F-105, known colloquially as the Thud-Five, or Thud for short, is the biggest, heaviest single-engine fighter ever put into service anywhere by anyone. Half an hour earlier, at takeoff from Wichita's McConnell AFB, this airplane weighed in at 49,000 lbs.—24½ tons—including 14,500 lbs. (2,154 gallons) of fuel. In combat, a decade ago, it launched regularly at weights of more than twenty-six tons. That's within a couple of tons of the loaded weight of the four-engine Boeing B-17 heavy bomber of World War II.

The single-seat D model is 64 ft. 3 in. long; the two-seat F is 69 ft. 7 in. Capt. Russ Axtell, up ahead in *Husky 41*, is flying a D. Cummins' *Husky 42* is an F, the type used for Wild Weasel SAM suppression missions over North Vietnam.

As they stand waiting on the ramp, a tall man can walk under the wing of either without striking his head on the weapon pylons. In their cockpits, pilots sit 12 ft. above the ground, and the great tail fins rise 20 ft. in the air. Both have a wingspan of 34 ft. 11 in. and a normal wing loading of 127 lbs. per sq. ft. at takeoff.

A product of the mid 1950s, the F-105 is a complicated machine that initially suffered from a definite predilection for burning off its own tail feathers, leading to a series of derogatory nicknames like Ultra Hog and Super Sled (derived from Lead Sled, the tag hung on the earlier F-100) and, finally, Thud, with its obvious connotations.

There is no doubt that the Thud is an earth-lover of the first magnitude. Even its mighty Pratt & Whitney J75 turbojet, rated at 16,100 lbs. of thrust, would be hard pressed to hurl it off the 2½ mile long McConnell runway without afterburning, which provides a boost to 26,500 lbs. by injecting extra fuel directly into the tailpipe. Pilots joke wryly that "if someone built a runway around the world, Republic would build an airplane that couldn't take off from it."

But the thing will fly at 855 mph (745 knots) at sea level and 1,390 mph (1,210 knots; Mach 2.1, or slightly more than twice the speed of sound) at altitude, and it will haul 9,000 lbs. of bombs, and rockets, and extra fuel tanks and other add-on garbage to a maximum of 12,000 lbs., plus its internal five-barrel 20 mm Vulcan rotary cannon and 1,029 shells. And in combat over North Vietnam it proved that it could brave the hell of radar-guided flak and missiles and strike Hanoi day in, day out, with better success and fewer losses than anything else we had.

Cummins and Axtell and others in the Kansas Air Guard's 184th TFTG are proud of their airplane, which they have operated with perfect safety for more than a decade now, at a rate of more than 6,000 flying hours annually; and they're proud of their current mission, which is training all Thud drivers for the active USAF. Since the fall of 1971, they've trained more than 300 flying students plus another fifty in ground school only.

"It's an outstanding racer at low altitudes," explains Cummins. "It will go so fast, carry such a big bomb load. That and its survivability. Because of the great speed, your chances of surviving are greater."

Unfortunately, the supply of spare parts is drying up, and the remaining 200 odd flyable Thuds (of 833 built) are being phased out of the active military inventory. The 184th will be operational in 1980 on the newer McDonnell F-4 Phantom, which is still in production.

The Phantom is conceded to be a better mount for air-to-air combat and at high altitude (what the F-105 least likes to do is climb), but is not so efficient below 15,000 ft. or in ground attack. "We do hate to get rid of it," says Cummins, the group's operations director, in discussing the impending loss of the Thud.

There are few things more impressive than a low-level mission in an F-105.

It starts in the briefing room of the Air Guard complex on McConnell's west side, where Axtell, the flight leader, runs down the details of the mission.

Start-engine time will be 12:35 p.m., radio check-in at 12:45, takeoff at 1 p.m. Time en route to the target will be thirty-five minutes, along a zigzag course totaling more than 250 miles and into headwinds ranging up to 25 knots. Altitude will be 500 ft. above ground.

We will spend just over thirty minutes on the range, and will be back on the ground at McConnell by 2:30 p.m. Timing is critical and precisely planned to ensure adequate fuel for the return. Jet engines do not run on air alone, and an F-105, power off, has a gliding angle only slightly better than a falling safe. Bingo fuel—the quantity needed to fly the 100 odd miles from the range to base and land—is 4,000 lbs., or about 615 gallons.

The big J75 has a flow rate like a small creek, consuming the high-grade kerosene at a normal cruise power rate of 1,000 gph. At full military power for takeoff, the rate goes to 1,500 gallons, which is increased fourfold by the use of afterburner—6,000 gph.

"You stay in burner, it makes for a short flight," observes Axtell succinctly. Considering the high power settings needed for the range attacks, we will have a total endurance of approximately ninety minutes.

Zipped into one-piece coveralls and the trouser-like G suits, carrying 40 lbs. of parachute and survival gear plus a 5 lb. helmet, the pilots scale ladders and clamber into the cockpits. Inside, they pass heavy elastic cords through steel rings attached to the inside of the "knee garters" to position the legs in case of ejection, don helmets and plug in the radio and oxygen connections, lock the survival cushion to the seat and fasten shoulder and lap straps, tightening them down carefully.

In tail number 628294, Cummins signals the crew chief, M/Sgt. Jerry Tomlinson, and the ground power unit revs up, providing the electrical energy needed to start the big engine. The turbine begins to whine and, at about twelve percent, the engine lights off with a blowtorch "whoosh" from the tail.

Across the way, in 610145, Axtell is going through the same procedure. As engine instruments stabilize, both pilots check in on the squadron comm net and toggle the switch to close the clamshell canopies. The crew chiefs unplug their telephone jacks, pull the chocks and signal to see the removed safety pins from the ejection seats.

Slowly, the birds begin to roll as the pilots advance the throttles and go to ground control frequency. Fifty feet from the parking area, Cummins taps the brakes briefly as a ground crewman checks to see if the horizontal tail moves, trying to dampen out the nose dip—an indication the stability augmentation system is working.

On the taxiway at the departure end of the runway, both aircraft stop again for final checks and undergo inspection by a small ground crew stationed there.

Axtell rolls into position on the runway, the hollow roar of the engine swells to a crescendo, he releases the brakes and begins to accelerate. Ten seconds later, Cummins follows as a heavy boom announces Axtell has gone to afterburner to lever *Husky 41* off the ground.

The runway flows beneath *Husky 42*, faster and faster, and as the 2,000 ft. marker flashes past, the vertical-tape airspeed indicator reads 125 knots (143 mph). At 176 knots (203 mph), Cummins eases the stick back to lift the racing nosewheel off the ground, and cuts in the afterburner with a brisk outboard push on the heavy throttle quadrant. It is like a hard boot in the rear.

Wrapped in thunder and passing through 191 knots (220 mph), the Thud hurls itself off the runway 1¼ miles from its starting point as Cummins' hand flashes to raise the landing gear. If gear retraction is not accomplished within the next 35 knots of acceleration, air pressure will prevent the nosewheel from folding forward.

Climbing at a twenty-degree angle under the relentless push of the afterburner, the F-105 hurtles north-northeast across southern Wichita, rattling windows in countless buildings as the airspeed tape winds rapidly to 450 knots (520 mph) indicated.

Cummins comes out of AB, and lurches forward against his shoulder straps as the acceleration drops off suddenly. It seems very quiet in the cockpit as Axtell's aircraft swims into view, in a shallow right bank a mile ahead. *Husky 42* cuts inside *41*'s turn and slides up fast from below and to the right, Cummins playing the speed brakes to cut back to 420 knots (485 mph) and keep from overshooting.

Once clear of the city, the two Thuds ease back down until they are within 500 ft. of the ground, knifing eastward to pass south of El Dorado.

The heavy fighter-bombers are rock steady in the bumpy, gusty air as the tiny wings punch through the Kansas turbulence. They look purposeful, relentless, like a pair of greyhounds after a rabbit.

A slight left turn, and the flight is headed generally toward Eureka. The ground flees away below at 425 knots as Cummins murmurs, "She's just loafin', now." The Thuds are forbidden to exceed the speed of sound over Kansas, but Cummins notes, "It'll come so close to goin' supersonic right now, carryin' a bomb load, it's unreal," indicating Mach .97, or more than 600 mph.

The course runs from near Eureka to southwest of Council Grove to northeast of Herington, slices between Woodbine and White City, angles southwest, then turns sharply back to the north to enter the range. It's a route that cuts across the historic Santa Fe Trail, and is chosen to avoid, as far as possible, any disturbance to people, livestock or property below.

Dozens of high-performance military jets fly this route every day, and cattle, long since inured to the racket, graze peacefully beneath the rocketing wings.

In the pressurized cockpit, swaddled in protective gear and bathed in sunlight, the flight is oddly restful. There is no vibration, no stress of any sort; merely a warm, comfortable, utterly stable platform with a world unreeling below.

At the range, all that changes within seconds.

There are six bombs to drop, the last two at a forty-five-degree angle. And there are five gunnery passes. That's a total of eleven high-G pull-outs, flirting with the 5-G limitation established for F-105s with drop tanks. Plus, of course, the 3- and 4-G combat turns.

It is a long, exhausting half hour. And for Cummins, a frustrating one.

The cannon is loaded with 100 rounds of ammunition, plus a few spares. Since it fires at a rate of 6,000 rounds per minute, that means he has one second of firepower—although, because it takes a fraction of a second to bring the electrically operated weapon up to full speed, it's actually slightly longer.

The idea is to fire twenty rounds on each of five passes—a single "burp" from somewhere underfoot—at a range of roughly half a mile, out of a ten-degree dive and within 1,000 ft. of the ground, centered on a circular white fabric target.

Hits are scored acoustically, by individual rounds, and the read-out is displayed immediately in the scoring cab. Coukoulis' range record is 118 hits. This day, Axtell—an accomplished strafer—scores 79. Cummins' total, for the five passes, is seven hits, despite the utmost care and the saving of half his total ammo until the last (and hopefully most accurate) pass.

Later, ground crewmen discover the airplane's gunsight is malfunctioning. Also, it is not aligned with the gun. Today, it is small consolation. "I never claimed to be the best in the world," mutters Cummins, "but I know I'm not that bad!"

Bomb scores are somewhat better, averaging under fifty yards from the orange center triangle for both men. Dropping visually, that's pretty good bomb tossing. But a later flight of four Vought A-7 Corsair IIs averages less than half that over the same course by using their onboard computers.

Delivery angles vary, with the last pair of bombs dropped out of a thirty-degree dive. Pull-outs are well

Kansas National Guard ended up training USAF pilots to fly the big attack airplane. The program commonly took six months—chiefly because "it takes that long to teach 'em to hurl their pink body at the ground." The idea was to dive at the target at around 450 to 480 knots, shoot and pull. Recovery often was below the level of the 60 ft. scoring tower, despite a 4½ to 5 G pullout. Sadly, the Thud now is gone from the skies—permanently.

below the level of the scoring cab and the G meter is flirting with five before Cummins racks it over into a more comfortable 4 G turn.

Rocks and grass stream past off the left wing and Cummins chuckles softly, merrily into his oxygen mask at the scores, like Jack the Ripper on a Saturday night.

In my own, I can taste rubber and, somewhere at the back of my tongue, the sour threat of vomit from a stomach that tolerates much higher G loads with equanimity—but never over such a long, sustained period.

Ordnance expended and less than thirty minutes' fuel remaining, Cummins eases the stick fractionally back and vaults two miles high, into the afternoon sky. I shoot a few pictures of Axtell's plane, and then Cummins turns the beast over to me.

Tentatively, I play with the effortless, power-boosted controls. "It rolls nice," murmurs Cummins. "Go ahead, try one." "My cameras," I demur, weakly, thinking of my stomach. "Just do an aileron roll," he suggests. Against my better judgment, I proceed. And Cummins is right. It rolls nice. It is beeauutifulll! Control response is instant, precise. It will roll as fast as you can twitch your hand, or as slooowly as you wish. I slam through a left roll, a right; try one from knife edge to knife edge. . . .

And my stomach goes on strike—violently.

I have just enough internal control left to announce formally, "You have the airplane"—and to fumble for the barf bag thoughtfully tucked into a knee pocket of my flight suit by my outfitter. I have embarrassed myself for the first time in years, but I refuse to mess up the interior of the ground crew's airplane.

Stomach and I come to terms just as Cummins begins a businesslike approach to McConnell. Over the runway at 1,600 ft. AGL and 350 knots (405 mph), the sharp pitch-out so well loved by fighter pilots, ending with gear extended, headed downwind and curving around for landing.

Across the runway threshold at 198 knots (228 mph), 20 mph above the speed where the airplane quits flying, and there is the sudden rumble of high-pressure tires on smooth concrete as the aircraft touches down at 170 knots (196 mph).

Cummins deploys the ribbon parachute stored in the tail, and the Thud decelerates, rolls easily into the Air Guard area and shuts down.

Flight time: seventy-eight minutes.

It's been a long afternoon.

First printed in *Air Progress*, Winter 1980.

Chapter 22

McDonnell F–4 Phantom II

Smoke and thunder hog

How would you like to fly an airplane that burns 2,000 gallons of fuel per hour and takes, on average, over forty hours of maintenance per flight hour?

US taxpayers have been footing such bills for more than thirty years in the case of the McDonnell F–4 Phantom II, the airplane that proves the exception to the old claim that if it looks good, it'll fly good. The big two-seat twin-engine F–4 looks so bad it's often called "Big Ugly," but even in 1990 it's acknowledged to be one of the world's best multi-role fighters.

Many airplanes will do some things better than the Phantom. A few more recent designs do everything as well or better than the Phantom, but this big, heavy airplane with the droop snoot and the funny wings and tail remains as dangerous today as in 1958. More dangerous, since the type has been retrofitted with more effective avionics and engines.

Still in first-line use by more than a dozen nations in the 1990s, it's obvious that the Phantom will soldier on well into the twenty-first century. It should. It flies good!

The Phantom rolled hard to the left, stacking up the Gs, as Col. Rowland F. Smith tipped the airplane over and poured it downhill, partially inverted.

"Tally-ho!" he called into the mike, reversing his turn and hauling the nose back up through the horizon as he maneuvered to cut off his adversary. A mile off to the left, a lizard-painted jet fighter rocketed out of the depths below, going straight up.

Smith angled to close the gap, throttles right to the wall as full afterburner hurled seventeen tons of

F–4D into the hot blue Kansas sky with maximum thrust. A moment before, the racing airspeed indicator touched 600 knots—about Mach .95 (ninety-five percent of the speed of sound) at our altitude. Now the numbers were hustling back down the other direction and the altimeter was going wild, the thousands hand whirling madly around the dial.

He eased the stick gently back, climbing now about ten degrees inverted, as the airspeed slid down through 140 knots and the altimeter whizzed through 24,000. In the cockpit, headsets suddenly filled with a series of aural warnings.

The first was the warble of the pitch indicator, the second the rattlesnake buzz of the heat-seeking missile lock-on, the third a warning tone registering an alien radar sweep.

The target Phantom, slowing even more, was at eleven o'clock and perhaps 500 yards, climbing at the same angle, and it seemed obvious Smith was only seconds from a kill. Suddenly from the depths somewhere down below, Lt. Col. Virgil "Woody" Johnson, locked in combat with *Zorro 1*, called, "Knock it off! Knock it off!" and Smith abandoned the pursuit, easing out to the right and heading for the "safe" area to prepare for the next engagement.

Briefly, the altimeter touched 26,000 ft. and the airspeed dropped to 120 knots. At its present weight, the Phantom quit flying 40 knots higher than that—but in its ballistic trajectory, that mattered not at all. The accelerometer, which a minute ago had been reading 4.5 Gs, or 4½ times the force of gravity, now quivered near zero. The automatically inflating G suits relaxed their iron grip around our lower bodies.

Far below, the blue waters of Fall River Reservoir glinted in the clear Kansas sun. It was a long way from the steamy verdant hills of North Vietnam, where Smith earned the Air Force Cross a decade and a half ago for dueling with communist guided missile sites in an F-105 Wild Weasel. But the mission, basically, was the same. Smith is a fighter pilot. His job is to fly and fight and win against whomever he encounters, whether a radar trailer controlling half a dozen SAMs near Hanoi or a flight of MiGs four miles up. And to train others to do the same.

He is a snub-nosed, fair-complected man with short, thinning white hair and the build of an oak stump who's been in the fighter business for twenty years and 4,000 hours. He earned his nation's second highest award for bravery by remaining over an enemy target to protect his downed wingman even though his own plane was hit and crippled, then nursing the burning machine south to a safe landing on a friendly airstrip. The airplane never flew again.

Technically, he is on leave from Trans-World Airlines, where he was a flight engineer in a jetliner—but, somehow, he never went back.

Smith is vice commander of the 184th Tactical Fighter Training Group, Kansas Air National Guard, now upgraded to a complex of more than fifty of the hulking McDonnell-Douglas Phantom fighters and 1,200 personnel whose job it is not only to train other Air Guard and USAF pilots to fly and fight in Big Ugly, (the Phantom's nickname) but to conduct advanced training as well.

And, occasionally, to do other things. . . .

Not too long ago, ten F-4s and 326 men slipped away in the middle of a Kansas thunderstorm and deployed nearly halfway around the world for more than two weeks of hush-hush training in the deserts of the Middle East. That mission originally had been slated for a regular USAF fighter squadron, but when Col. John McMerty, 184th commander and a veteran of twenty-two years' Guard service, heard of it, he "made sure they knew of the fact that we were ready and eager to do that."

For political reasons, neither McMerty nor others involved in the deployment are free to comment publicly on where they went or what they did, but informed sources indicate their destination was a desert airstrip and "tent city" in Oman, on the Arabian Peninsula, where for eight days they fought aerial war games against Hawker Hunters and Panavia Tornados flown by pilots under contract to the Omani government.

Much of the flying was at ground level and supersonic speeds, with few restrictions.

Sentry Tornado, as it was called, was the Wichita Guardsmen's first overseas deployment in sixteen years, and McMerty noted, "We're the first Guard unit to go east of Suez." The selection of the 184th to make the deployment is an indication of its increased importance in the nation's total force structure. Within the last few years, with the replacement of the

The McDonnell F-4 Phantom II is an exception to the ungrammatical old aviation axiom that if an airplane looks good, it will fly good. The fact is, Big Ugly wouldn't win a beauty prize if it were the sole contestant. It looks like something put together by a bored sixth grader in a history class. That did not prevent it from being the most versatile combat airplane in the world for nearly 20 years. Able to climb 28,000 fpm or better, accelerate from Mach 0.92 to Mach 2.05 in three minutes, reach better than Mach 2.5 (more than 1,600 mph) and carry eight tons of underwing ordnance, more than 5,000 Phantoms were built. Many still serve with US allies around the world.

Republic F-105 Thunderchief with the F-4, the Guard complex at Wichita's McConnell Air Force Base has expanded from roughly 600 personnel and one squadron to twice that, seventy percent of them full-time Air Guard technicians.

That's because the nuclear-capable, Mach 2+ F-105, despite its abilities and its outstanding ground attack record in Southeast Asia, always was a limited-production item. Fewer than 1,000 examples were built, none was used outside the USAF and spares were becoming a serious problem. On the other hand, well over 5,000 F-4s were built, and despite its ongoing replacement with later-generation machines, the F-4 will continue to soldier on with active-duty USAF,

The F-4's J79 jet engines always produced a telltale smoky trail, leading pilots to refer to it wryly as the "smoke and thunder hog." The smoke gave away the airplane's position in the skies over Vietnam—a serious handicap in combat. Despite this, and the demands of constant ground attack missions, the F-4 posted an air-to-air victory record of 2.48:1. The airplane weighs 14 tons empty (it has the density of a concrete floor) and will hit 29 tons fully loaded for combat.

Navy and Marine units for many years to come, as well as with the British, West Germans, Israelis and other US allies. That means new pilots have to be trained, experienced ones upgraded.

The new 177th Tactical Fighter Squadron runs what was once called gunnery school, teaching pilots and weapons systems operators just out of flight training how to fly and fight in the F-4 and turning out combat-ready crews. Most are Guardsmen, but some are USAF active-duty personnel. Each trainee gets twenty-eight air-to-air and twenty-seven air-to-ground sorties, a total of around fifty-five flying hours, plus 110 hours of classroom instruction plus various other briefings, delivered in two- to four-week modules to accommodate the trainees' civilian schedules.

The 177th is running three concurrent classes totaling an average of twenty aircrew each, and class size may be expanded in the future to keep up with demand. The 127th TFS, the 184th's original flying unit, now continues the function of the USAF's F-4 fighter weapons school at Nellis AFB, Nevada, teaching experienced pilots what they need to know to serve as tactical advisers to unit commanders. The squadron also trains F-4 instructors. "It's essentially the graduate school for fighter pilots," explained Smith.

The first course takes a total of about six months, the second twelve weeks. It all adds up to a lot of flying—and a demand for a lot of airplanes. If the F-4 is not the wildest, farthest-out, fire-breathingest monster in the whole wide world, it certainly was just a few short years ago—and it hasn't lost any of its zip and exhilaration since. Several of the Phantoms on the McConnell ramp have neat red stars painted beneath the cockpit, denoting MiG kills over Vietnam, where the USAF Phantom drivers' success ratio was 2.48:1 against the MiG jockeys.

Originally designed for catapult launching off the Navy's big first-line carriers, the F-4 weighs fourteen tons empty and has a maximum takeoff weight of twenty-nine tons. It can carry up to eight tons of underwing stores, and in clean condition can climb 28,000 fpm and accelerate from Mach .92 to Mach 2.05 in three minutes. For an air combat maneuvering flight at subsonic speeds, like the one in which Smith was engaged, its 2,000 gallons of internal fuel gives it an endurance of just about one hour—precise time depending on the amount of afterburner required.

Afterburner increases an engine's power by injecting extra fuel into the flow of incandescent gases expelled from the "hot section." It boosts the thrust of each of the F-4's twin engines from 10,900 to 17,000 lbs., but fuel consumption jumps from 1,300-1,500 gallons per hour to four times that. Without power, the F-4 glides like a Buick driven at high speed off the Royal Gorge. That's one good reason for the fancy ejection seat.

"You don't use afterburner unless you really have to," said Smith later. "That's why we ended up with a lot more gas. If you can run the other guy out of gas, it certainly helps. A kill's a kill, no matter how you get it. You can't just call 'bingo' (low fuel) and go home; you've gotta escape. You've gotta get to a safe area before you run out of gas."

Afterburner is required for takeoff, providing breathtaking acceleration and hurling a clean fifteen-ton Phantom off the runway at 210 mph in less than 2,000 ft., even in the Kansas heat. And the airplane can carry 1,270 gallons in drop tanks, providing an unrefueled range of 2,300 miles. For anything beyond that, in-flight refueling is needed.

It weighs so much because it has the density of a concrete sidewalk. And that, of course, is why rotation speed is 175 knots, allowing the airplane to fly off at 180 or 190 knots! Big Ugly is just that kind of airplane. The wonder is that it can maneuver like it does.... It's hard to believe, but the first Phantom flew May 27, 1958, and the Navy took delivery of its first airplane Dec. 29, 1960. The F-4A set a 100 kilometer closed-circuit record of 1,390 mph on Sept. 25, 1960, involving a continuously sustained centrifugal load of more than 3 Gs through the tight Mach 2 turn, and demonstrated initial climb rates up to 35,000 fpm. The F-4B, with more powerful J79-GE-8s, set a world absolute speed record of 1,606.342 mph on Nov. 22, 1961, and went on to set a further fourteen world records, including reaching 30,000 meters (98,425 ft.) in 6:11.43.

The first USAF Phantom was the F-4C, 583 of which were purchased at $1.931 million each. Intended for air superiority, interdiction and close support, the first machine was delivered May 27, 1963, and by June 1965 they were deployed to Vietnam. They quickly established the best safety record in the inventory—many accumulating well over 100 flying hours per month (one had 139.8)—and the lowest combat attrition rate. In just under two years' service, they accounted for forty-one MiG-17s and 21s in Southeast Asia. Many of these MiG killers are still in service.

The C is armed with Sparrow III AIM-7 semi-active radar homing air-to-air missiles (AAM) and AIM-9 Sidewinder infrared heat seekers. It carries a 600 gallon centerline tank and two 370 gallon wing tanks. It can accelerate from Mach .92 to 2.05 in 3.5 minutes.

The F-4D was the same airplane with improved air-to-ground weapons delivery systems, inertial navigation systems and radar. The E model had a Vulcan 20 mm cannon firing 6000 rpm, solid-state fire control radar, -17 engines delivering an extra 900 lbs. of static thrust each in afterburner, a seventh fuel cell in the rear fuselage, a slotted tailplane and fixed inboard wing leading edges.

The D first flew Dec. 8, 1965, and more than 800 were built by the time the final aircraft was delivered in February 1968. The same airplane was sold to Iran. Es went to Israel and Japan.

Specs on the D are a length of 58 ft. 3⅛ in., a span of 38 ft. 4 ⅞ in., a wing area of 530 sq. ft., and a height of 16 ft. 3 in. Service ceiling is 79,000 ft., and maximum speed at 48,000 ft. is Mach 2.4 (1,584 mph). Combat radius is 900 miles. Low-level tactical radius with 6,000 lbs. of ordnance is 400 miles at 420 mph, and the thing will hit 950 mph (Mach 1.2) at 1,000 ft.

It can outrun and out-accelerate the Soviet MiG-21, though not out-turn it, and has better armament and weapons systems. The airplane can pull well over 9 Gs without airframe damage. It is no Tinker Toy.

The F-4 is a sophisticated airplane crammed full of complex systems, and demands a lot of maintenance. There are 256 circuit breakers in the aircraft, seven of them in the front cockpit.

McMerty says the ratio of maintenance man-hours to flight hours was 34:1 a couple of months earlier, "but that was unusually good. Normally we run 44:1. Our serviceability rate right now is 60% fully mission capable, 75% flyable. Those are really good numbers! To have 50% FMC in any environment's really good." Smith said much of the electronic gear in the F-4D is "pretty primitive by today's standards," and suffers as well from unreliability. "What we need," he said, "are a better radar, better smokeless engines and a new heat-seeking missile that can shoot from any angle." If that were done, he continued, "the old F-4 would still be a pretty good airplane."

He grinned and added, "But even with the equipment we've got, against the average pogue in the squadrons, we can fight pretty even with the F-15s and -16s." Translated, that means the experience and professionalism of the Air Guard Phantom jockeys tells when pitted against the kids in the USAF's newest-generation super fighters. . . .

McMerty agreed with Smith's summary, tacked a better inertial navigation system on the wish list (the current equipment requires servicing an average of every third flight) and said with those additions, "we could do the job without any degradation in capability. We're competitive with the threat. The quality of the training will have a bigger effect than the quality of the weaponry. Given the fact that our training is better and we have a more experienced force, we'll do very nicely."

That attitude showed up throughout the training mission.

The flight started on the ground, well before takeoff time, with a short but detail-packed briefing by Johnson: it would be an air combat maneuvering (ACM) mission in the airspace between 25,000 and 6,000 ft. within a forty-mile-wide fan between seventy-five and 105 degrees from McConnell, in the Eureka High military operations area (MOA). We would be "Woody 1" and "Woody 2." Maj. P. T. Duke and Maj. Jim Ray would be "Zorro 1" and "Zorro 2." Capt. Bob Appleton would be our ground-controlled intercept (GCI) officer, guiding us from a radar trailer back at the McConnell flight line. Initial altitude would be 18,000 ft. Maximum G limit would be 6½. Bingo (break-off) fuel would be 3,500 lbs. There would be no

Loaded, the Phantom requires 210 mph to fly, off the runway and lands, stores expended, at around 190 mph—which makes the use of braking chutes an excellent idea. An F-4's arrival aboard an aircraft carrier is more of a controlled crash than anything else, but the airplane was designed for the Navy and is super-tough. Well, not too tough. It typically demands 34 to 50 maintenance hours per flight hour to keep it in the air.

supersonic flight, and all planes would maintain at least 200 knots. Takeoff for "Zorro" aircraft would be 1415, "Woody" aircraft five minutes later. Return also would be by elements.

"We'll be ready to fight when we cross 45 DME," said Ray, "Zorro 2" pilot. Afterward, each element huddled briefly to set up its own plans. "We'll set up a drag; pull and turn 135 degrees. Five seconds and 135 back. They'll be at our 1 o'clock," and very high, but we'll be off their scope at 10 o'clock," Smith explained.

First flown May 27, 1958, the Phantom set nearly a dozen and a half world records for performance and saw service in most air arms allied to the United States. Typically, the Kansas Air Guard's 184th Tactical Fighter Training Group was assigned to train not only Guard and Reserve pilots but regular USAF pilots how to fly and fight in the hulking fighter.

Taxiing out, it was hot in the cockpit, even with the canopy raised, and we were wrapped in the stink of high-grade kerosene as we paused at the end of the runway for a final systems check by the ground crew.

With the canopy down and locked and the bone dome pressing against our temples, the noises of the outside world were almost sealed out.

There was little of the thunder of the twin hellfires kicking us in the rear as Smith accelerated hard down the runway, throttle right to the gate, then moved it inboard and forward into full AB. Runway lights flashed past like teeth in a comb. Suddenly the nose pitched upward at an impossible angle, the bird ran briefly on the mains and hurled itself skyward like a green-and-brown javelin.

We climbed steeply, McConnell falling away behind the tail, and lurched forward in the tight constricting harness as Smith eased the engines out of afterburner. We headed southeast. Within minutes, we were within the MOA. We made a wide, lazy turn and headed north at 18,000, cruising easily at 480 knots. Smith was having trouble with the black boxes. He gave me directions in the back; switches to flip, knobs to turn, a radarscope to scan. Nothing happened. One of those days.

On the first pass, we played target while the "Zorro" aircraft ran an intercept on us. There was nothing to see; merely an endless expanse of blue until an F-4 flashed past a mile below us, headed south. Smith racked the stick over and piled on the Gs, hauling the Phantom around. The G suit went to work, squeezing hard. We were just beginning to maneuver against an "enemy" airplane when Johnson's "Knock it off" sounded in our ears. Later, Smith remarked, "If I'd have done a hard 135 after I blew through, we probably could've got back into it."

The second encounter was even less conclusive, but the third was much more active. Initiated at much shorter range (less than twenty miles) due to the low fuel state, the four Phantoms engaged too early and the clash quickly disintegrated into what fighter pilots call "a big fur ball." It ended up with one plane out front and everyone else behind.

"When we entered the fight," said Smith later, "I saw two aircraft, and it was difficult to tell whether Johnson was being attacked or doing the attacking. At that moment, I had to make a decision as to what I was gonna do." In the process, "the other aircraft saw us and started maneuvering on us, so all of us ended up engaged simultaneously in that little bit of airspace."

Later, in debriefing, Johnson remarked, "We pulled a lotta Gs and fought for our life most of the afternoon out there." Johnson is a nineteen-year USAF veteran with 213 missions in the F-4E in Southeast Asia, more than 5,000 hours total time and 3,000 as an instructor pilot. He is the USAF adviser at McConnell now.

The radarscope in Smith's plane was on strike, and Capt. Steve Filo, Johnson's "wizo," was providing tactical information for both "Woody 1" and "2." He picked up the incoming "Zorro" flight at fifteen miles, called "Bandits" and gave the range and general location information.

Smith, leading, was spotted visually by the incoming "Zorro 1" and "2," who were spread laterally about three miles. They immediately began a short pincers movement, calling a kill on Smith just about the time "Woody 1" joined the fight, and all four airplanes locked briefly in a swirling battle of maneuver.

It all ended when P. T. Duke, the youngest pilot in the group (and the only part-timer) called "bingo," indicating he had only 625 gallons of fuel remaining—a "no foolin' bingo" which gave him just enough endurance to cruise the seventy-odd miles back to McConnell, fly the pattern, land and taxi back to the ramp without sweating blood about his fuel state.

Not more than twenty minutes had elapsed since entering the maneuver area.

Already, it had been a long day.

Fighter pilots try to avoid pulling any more Gs than absolutely necessary because to do so scrubs off speed. Getting it back costs fuel, and high fuel consumption shortens engagement time. Energy management thus dictates a vertical scissors, because by getting over on his back, the Phantom pilot can make a sharper turn. Johnson spent "quite a bit" of time in burner because he was largely on the defensive. He and the other airplanes logged 0.9. Smith never pulled more than 4.5 Gs, and we were airborne 1.1 hours by the time we finally landed.

"The important thing is to have a plan and execute that plan," said Johnson. "Theirs was better than ours, 'cause they wound up more offensive than we did. I shot 'Zorro 1' on one pass, and I guess you all got killed in the last one."

The flight formed up for a little photo work en route back to McConnell, and Smith led the formation down the runway in the 360-degree overhead "break" so beloved by fighter pilots. He rolled the big fighter up on a wingtip, hauled back on the stick and popped the gear, eased back on the power, rolled out on downwind and said, "You got it."

Hot damn! I acknowledged; cautiously felt out the Phantom's response to stick and rudder as we proceeded downwind. The nice thing about little airplanes, aerobatic airplanes and fighter planes is that most don't take long to communicate with you. They're light, tight and responsive, with controls as taut as a high E string.

Civilized airplanes are all right, and I like them, too—but I just flat *love* these razor-balanced machines with lightning responses and rattlesnake tempers! The Phantom is definitely one of them. The F-4's fast-acting controls are hydraulically boosted, of course, and what little stick feel there is is totally artificial. Who cares? The airplane is so responsive, so easy to fly, it's like being freed from gravity.

I shot a couple of landing approaches in the pattern, getting used to the airplane, then pulled off to the east twenty miles or so, grabbed a few thousand feet of altitude with a quick shot of power and did a few fast rolls—so neat, so precise, so easy to do it gladdened my heart for months, just thinking about it. Regretfully, then, I turned back to McConnell and our final pattern.

Over the runway, I banged the stick over and sucked it back as Smith worked the gear from the front seat (the rear cockpit has emergency extension only), rolled out on downwind, curved around base and lined up on final, on down to 160 knots and perhaps 200 ft. when Smith's nerves won out and he called, "I've got it."

We touched down, nose high, runway flashing past beneath us. As the nose dropped, Smith popped the braking chute and we rolled to an easy stop, dropped the chute on the concrete and taxied in, canopy open, engines whining. The end of a perfect day.

Imagine getting paid to do this!

First printed in *Air Combat*, May 1986.

Chapter 23

McDonnell Douglas F–15 Eagle

Pick of the pack

If I were king of the world, I believe my personal airplane would be a McDonnell Douglas F–15 Eagle!

Here is a flying machine that will operate in about the same runway length as a heavy-laden Cessna P210, pull straight up and accelerate just about as far as you want to go. Around St. Louis's Lambert Field, they do that all the time to get out of the elephant herd of airliners in a hurry. They call it the Viking departure, and it cannot be described. It must be experienced.

But that's not all. The Eagle has a controllability range that runs from zero to 1,700 mph, will fly so high the sky deepens from horizon to navy blue, will do a 180–degree turn in half a mile while riding the edge of the Mach.

In other words, this is a hell of a flying machine. It's also a hell of a fighting machine, but that's another story.

The problem, of course, is that it's a damn-the-expense airplane, and the USAF unit that maintains a serviceability rate of sixty percent for any extended period of time is certain to earn a medal for its CO.

Who cares?

This is another airplane I'd pay to fly!

"I think you'll find we'll be airborne in about 1,200 feet," said Maj. Bob Caster as Jazz 11 Lead rolled easily onto Runway 04 at New Orleans' Alvin Calender Naval Air Station.

Jazz 11 was a flight of four McDonnell F-15 Eagles of the 122nd Tactical Fighter Squadron, 159th TFG, Louisiana Air National Guard, and Lead was a two-seat TF-15B. Its back seat supplied me with most of

the requisite goodies for sampling the performance envelope of the airplane widely considered to be currently the world's best air combat machine.

We assumed our position at the right front as 1st Lt. Joe "Ninefingers" Tumminillo rolled up and stopped at our eight o'clock, 40 ft. away. Behind him, the second element, composed of Maj. Dave "Dusty" Rhodes and Capt. Aubry "Junior" Landry, slid into place for our formation departure.

Caster didn't bother with the afterburner. He just slammed the nested throttles of the twin Pratt & Whitney F100-100 augmented turbofans to full military power.

The Eagle squatted slightly on its haunches, and twenty tons of gull-gray airplane shoved me in the back. Hard! The runway lights began to blur.

Caster was right. It didn't take a dime's worth over 1,200 ft. of runway.

He lifted the nose at about 130 knots and we flew off 20 knots later, accelerating rapidly to 350 knots and making a formation climb-out at an easy fifteen degrees nose up and 5,000 or 6,000 fpm for the convenience of ATC.

An afterburner Eagle departure is a sixty-degree climb at the same airspeed and 30,000+ fpm.

We punched up through 2,000 ft. of stratus and broke out into a brilliant sunlit world at 14,500 ft., still in formation, headed for our air combat maneuver area, Eagle Golf, forty miles to the southeast.

Two was off to our left about a quarter mile, but three and four were no longer tucked in within close visual range. Well, they'd be back. They were the opposing element for today's hassle!

This was the second time Caster and I had tried to go flying. We'd been saddled up and strapped into the bird the preceding afternoon—only to break it right on the ramp! When Caster hit the starter for No. 2 engine, the shaft sheared. The other two-seater already was redlined with control problems, so that left us with nothing to do but retire to the squadron lounge to drink beer and eat popcorn.

The aborted mission had been a two-plane flight, pitting us against 1st Lt. Mike Canatella one-on-one, so in a way, today's four-plane mission offered more possibilities. And the time wasn't wasted. It gave me a chance to get to know some of the Coon-Ass Militia pilots, and get a feel for what they think about their new mount.

The 159th TFG is the first National Guard unit to receive the F-15, and they're proud of it. Justifiably. But their selection was not altogether unexpected.

The New-Orleans-based Guardsmen have been known as air combat specialists since they were flying F-100s, and when they transitioned into F-4s, they became the only air superiority fighter Guard unit in Tactical Air Command.

They received their first F-15 in July 1985, started flight training in August and were declared combat-ready in May 1986. Today, a pair of 122nd TFS F-15s crouches armed and ready in the alert shelters, their pilots lounging nearby. These are the airplanes scrambled to intercept unidentified aircraft in the Air Defense Identification Zone off the Louisiana coast.

"Used to be, that was a good place to catch up on your sleep, but not anymore," Caster remarked casually. "They've had five scrambles this week."

The routine assignment of a Guard unit—even so proficient a unit as the Coon-Ass Militia, speaks volumes about the role of the "part-timers" in the national defense structure. And it's another reason the 159th is operating F-15s!

Lt. Col. Dohrm Crawford, the squadron commander, remarked, "I can do *anything* in this airplane. In this airplane, you *are* the 900-pound gorilla!"

But there's a down side to that, too. For one thing, "We've always flown old worn-out airplanes," observed Crawford. "But now that we've got this airplane, it's like [we're] Notre Dame. There's no mistakes allowed. If it ain't perfect, it sucks."

For another, he continued, "You lose proficiency [at this type of flying] very quickly unless you do it a lot." Crawford wiggled his fingers; noted they sometimes betray him. "The little devils are always doin' somethin' wrong" under the pressure of a dogfight—much like a touch typist making a typographical error.

The F-15 is a HOTAS airplane; the pilot never has to release his grip on throttles and stick, because everything he needs—weapon selectors, radar modes, communication, the works—all are controlled by the buttons that cover the knobs in his hands like clusters of warts.

But at near Mach 1 speeds and God knows what kinds of G loadings, errors are a lot more likely. And in a jet fighter, you can practice only an hour at a time. Then it's home for some more juice. Or a date with a tanker.

For that reason, the average squadron pilot gets 120 hours and 130 sorties a year. They launch twenty sorties a day! When Caster told me that I shook my head and exclaimed, "And you guys get *paid* for this!"

Said Crawford: "We've got some killer lieutenants! They're really good. I don't think I've seen a better bunch." He flashed a grin. "It's very hard to be a lieutenant and be an F-15 pilot," he added. "Lieutenants are supposed to be humble."

Maj. Tom "Snake" Donaldson, the group's operations officer, declared: "The biggest thing in the F-15 I think is not to get greedy. If you can't kill somebody within a minute, you better leave. And when you want to leave, you can usually leave."

That's one of the up sides to the F-15, but only one among many. For one thing, its acceleration is awesome. As Rhodes remarked, "It's almost as if the airplane is out of control and you're just hangin' on."

Indeed. I came down final, flying the Eagle from the back seat, and bled the speed back to 160 knots across the threshold, 300 ft. in the air.

Then Caster sucked up the gear and flaps from the front seat, we stroked the burner and went to 350 knots in less than a mile! And woke up everybody on the base in the process.

It was one of those high points in life.

The F-15 is the latest in a long line of airplanes that fighter pilots have predicted gloomily would be "the last of the sports cars." Pilots said that about the P-51. They said it about the F-100 Super Sabre. They said it about the F-5. Now it's the Eagle.

Note, first of all, that winged sports cars are getting more expensive. Back in 1945, North American was selling Mustangs to Uncle Sam for $47,000 apiece. An F-15 costs $30 million—and inflation hasn't been *that* bad.

On the other hand, you get a lot more for your minidollars. Someone—Robin Olds, I believe—remarked a while back that the ejection seat alone on the F-4 was more complicated than the whole P-51. I'm not sure I believe that, but it sounds good and is certain to be quoted for many years.

At any rate, it makes the point that today's fighter is *much* more complicated than yesterday's fighter. And that's true. In spades!

But from the cockpit, the F-15 is about as close to a simple airplane as fighter jocks can get these days. That's one reason its pilots love it. They'll tell you the Eagle has a generous "hard" wing, whereas the F/A-18 Hornet and the F-16/AFTI live-wing experimental version of the Electric Jet do not.

And they'll add that the F-16 (nobody calls it the Fighting Falcon except some jerk in the Pentagon) and the F/A-18 both are computer-controlled, fly-by-wire airplanes. The F-15 is not.

Of the various jet fighters the author has sampled so far, the big, twin-tailed McDonnell F-15 Eagle is his hands-down favorite. A supersophisticated piece of machinery, demanding at least as much maintenance as the F-4, the Eagle nevertheless is a simple airplane from the pilot's standpoint. There are no start carts, braking chutes or problems. The airplane will fly off loaded (nearly 21 tons in the intercept role) at 150 knots in 1,200 ft. of ground roll, depart the field at a 60-degree pitch angle and 50,000 fpm, fly at better than Mach 2.5 (1,653 mph)—and yet come down final at 130 knots, touching down at 70 knots with the nose up 12 degrees. Visibility is superb. Maneuverability is incredible. It even makes a good glider!

For the pilot, that means he can do whatever it takes to win!

He can run the F-15 down to flat *zero* airspeed, and it won't bite. The predecessor F-4 Phantom, from the same maker, will auger a very deep hole if you try that!

If he's man enough, the Eagle driver can pull enough Gs to bend the airframe, and the airplane will obey. Try that in an F-16, and the computer will intercede, moderating the pilot input to save the airplane. The Hornet tries to do the same thing—but it at least can be overruled with enough effort.

We didn't go that far. We only pulled 7.6 Gs, eighty-six percent of allowable, hassling with the other Eagle drivers. Just enough to leave me permanently 3 in. shorter. It didn't bother the airplane!

In short, the F-15 is one of those airplanes that works *with* a pilot, instead of arguing with him. Flying against later types like the F-16 and the F/A-18, it finally comes down to the old question of who's the better fighter pilot. And the Coon-Ass Militia has the gun camera film to prove that.

"In dealing with the Vietnam-era MiG-17s, -19s and -21s, it's strictly no problem in the -15," said Tom Donaldson. "The same with the MiG-23s and -27s." And the MiG-29? He shrugged. "There, we may have a problem. We don't know enough about the capabilities of the airplane yet, but they seem very similar to the Eagle."

"In dogfighting with the F-16, it becomes pilot experience," Donaldson continued. "Down around 250 knots, we *are* the superior airplane. The F-18 is the only airplane I've ever seen that has the capability to fight us like that." And as for the F-5s used to simulate MiG-21s for Red Flag training, "it does not take very long to beat an F-5!"

Crawford concurred. The F-16 is "tough, properly flown," he said. But, he pointed out, the average pilot experience in the 122nd probably is 2,200 hours in fighters, "which is a lot!"

Crawford continued: "The bottom line is, an excellent pilot in a mediocre airplane will beat a hamburger in the best airplane in the world, every time. A hamburger wrapped in gold is still a hamburger."

The F-15 is a *big* airplane, fourteen tons empty, nearly twenty-one tons takeoff weight as an interceptor, twenty-eight tons maximum gross. It spans 42 ft. 9¾ in., has a wing area of 608 sq. ft. (providing a wing loading of 68.26 lbs. per sq. ft. for the intercept mission and a maximum loading of 92.923 lbs. per sq. ft.), is 63 ft. 9 in. long and 18 ft. 7½ in. to the tips of its slightly canted twin fin/rudder assemblies.

Advertised maximum speed is 1,653 mph (Mach 2.5+) above 36,000 ft., clean, carrying AIM-7s, though Caster says their tired birds, USAF hand-me-downs which have been in service since 1974, won't do Mach 2 clean. Listed Vmax on the deck is "over 921 mph" (Mach 1.22), and initial climb is in excess of 50,000 fpm as an interceptor, 29,000 fpm at maximum gross weight.

Service ceiling is said to be "70,000 feet plus." At any rate, it's good enough for the airplane to serve as the launch vehicle for the successful 18 ft. long, 2,600 lb. direct-ascent US anti-satellite missile.

The 159th's A models can carry 11,635 lbs. (1,940 gallons) of internal fuel and a six-ton external load, and have a ferry range of 2,878 miles with three external tanks. Clean, they have a normal combat mission endurance of about ninety minutes, depending on altitude and the need for what the British call "reheat."

In burner at low altitude, the airplane uses 2,500 lbs. of fuel (417 gallons) a minute, but Donaldson said at 43,000 ft. and 430 knots, fuel burn drops to a ton per engine per hour.

He told of flying from Macon, Georgia, 520 nm to Michigan, loitering on station for an hour, engaging two flights of four A-7s each and landing with 2,500 lbs. of fuel remaining. "Even in the maneuverin' phase, I never had to go to afterburner," he reported.

Maximum flight duration to date, with refueling, is fifteen hours; unrefueled, with conformal fuel tanks, 5.25 hours. The new F-15E Strike Eagle, which first flew in December 1986, routinely carries a pair of low-drag conformal fuel tanks that fit the fuselage like a fat man's avoirdupois and hold another 9,000 lbs.

Intended eventually to replace the swing-wing F-111 as a long-range tactical strike fighter, the E has a WSO in the back and a maximum gross takeoff weight of 81,000 lbs. It can pull nine Gs with 6,000 lbs. of external bombs attached!

Personally, said Caster, he'd rather do it all himself. He much prefers the single-seat A model, 739 of which were delivered to the USAF. Forty more went to Israel, sixty-two to Saudi Arabia and a dozen to Japan. Mitsubishi is building eighty-four more.

The F-15 first flew July 27, 1972, and the first two production airplanes were delivered to Tactical Air Command Nov. 14, 1974, at Luke Air Force Base, Arizona. Considered the best fighter in the world due to its extreme maneuverability, it can outfly almost any other US machine *using only military power.*

Its gimbal-mounted Huges APG-63/70 X-band pulse doppler radar has eight to ten times the search volume of earlier fighters, look-up/down capabilities and "excellent" ECCM capability. It can detect helicopters and low-flying cruise missiles against a terrain backdrop and maintains lock to gross angles even during rapid roll-and-pull maneuvers, enabling the Eagle driver to fire accurately longer than other aircraft.

It is equipped with an IBM onboard central computer, a Head-Up Display, an internal navigation system, internal countermeasures equipment and the usual IFF and TACAN.

Some 26.5 percent of the airplane's structure weight is titanium, including most of the rear fuselage, while non-metallic composites are used in the tail-feathers and the dorsal speed brake.

Initial claimed unit cost was $7.5 million, but a more realistic figure is $30 million a copy. The E's price tag is $32 million.

In November 1982, F-15s captured five of the top six places in the William Tell weapons meet at Tyndall

Hero picture. Author told Coon-Ass Militia (122nd Tactical Fighter Squadron, 159th Tactical Fighter Group, Louisiana Air Guard) to draw up a purchase contract for the airplane after an ACM (air combat maneuvering) session and he'd sign it, no matter how much it was. However, he said he'd insist they maintain it. The F-15 is one super-flying airplane; it handles like a baby carriage—a very fast, very adroit baby carriage. As one squadron stick put it, "In the F-15, you are the 900 pound gorilla!"

The latest version of the Eagle is this F-15E dual-role aircraft, configured also for ground attack. Able to carry a dozen Mark 82 bombs on stub pylons attached to the conformal fuel tanks, LANTIRN (Low Altitude and Targeting Infrared for Night) pods and four Sidewinders, the F-15E is a formidable foe. The Eagle's acceleration is awesome. So is the maneuvering ability. McDonnell Douglas.

AFB, Florida, against F-4s, F-101s and F-106s from the United States and Canada.

The F-15 was the first US fighter to complete initial flight testing without a loss. It now has amassed more than 900,000 operational flight hours, and has a loss rate of 4.2 aircraft per 100,000 hours—lowest rate ever. It has a claimed kill ratio of 58.5:0, including destruction of three Mach 2.9 MiG-25 Foxbats.

Sitting on the ramp, an Eagle driver's eye level is roughly 10 ft. off the ground. The automatically variable intake duct for each of the turbofans is big enough to house a porpoise—or to make meat puree of the unwary in a heartbeat. And to provide 23,930 lbs. of static thrust with afterburning, for a total thrust to weight ratio comfortably in excess of unity (1:1).

The airplane's dash and maneuver capabilities go far to outweigh the handicaps of its size and cost. "The reason this airplane is so big is, it's got a powerful radar," explained Donaldson. The radar will "paint" a target at fifty miles, and enable the Eagle driver to shoot at twice the enemy's range, one-on-one.

The F-15 is armed with four AIM-7F/M Sparrow radar-guided missiles, four AIM-9L/M Sidewinder infrared-guided missiles on lateral rails under the wing, an M-61-A1 20 mm rotary cannon with 940 rounds, an alternate eight AMRAAMs and the full range of air-to-ground ordnance to a total weapons

Part of the penalty for the Eagle's awesome acceleration is a prodigious thirst for fuel. This Coon-Ass Militia F-15 slakes its thirst at the boom of an aerial tanker. McDonnell Douglas

load of eight tons, excluding the gun. Normal external load is six tons.

One of the things that endears this big bird to pilots and ground crew alike is that a boarding ladder is the only external item needed to get under way. There are no start carts, as there are no braking chutes. There aren't even any thrust reversers!

Engine start is by hydraulic accumulators, each of which gives the pilot two shots at starting an engine before somebody has to get out and get under to hand pump it back up—a matter of some 300 strokes.

No. 2 first, Caster mashed the start buttons and the big engines moaned into life, their intake lips snapping down at a thirty-degree angle as they lit off. The canopy came down, and we eased out of our parking place and down the taxiway, leading the pack.

Visibility was marvelous. I could rest my forearms comfortably on the sides of the cockpit, and see through a total arc of perhaps 310 degrees without shifting position. By neck turning and mild twisting against the shoulder straps, I could see directly aft, right through the twin fins.

The idea of this mission was to provide practice in element defense against beam attacks. Weaponry was limited to Sidewinders and guns. There was no GCI. We were strictly on our own. We owned an airspace block running from 8,000 to 50,000 ft., roughly forty miles in either direction.

Blasting off the runway, we made a thirty-degree right turn and climbed through the cloud deck, leveling at 25,000 ft. in brilliant sunshine, cruising at 420 knots. Joey Tumminillo's airplane sat off our left wingtip at half-mile range, nose up perhaps five degrees, keeping pace.

Caster turned the airplane over to me, and I tried a few mild maneuvers to get the feel of it. I progressed quickly from alternating Dutch rolls to seventy-five-

Four F-15s from the Coon-Ass Militia over St. Louis, Missouri. McDonnell Douglas

143

degree banks pulling up to about 3 Gs at 160 knots indicated, deep in the buffet; a half roll and split-S and an eighty-degree climb back to altitude.

Pulling off the power, I slowed the Eagle to 70 knots, pulled the nose to a thirty-five-degree pitch attitude—and found the big fighter a good deal better behaved than the average general aviation machine. It just wouldn't bite! And control response remained excellent, though naturally I had to add hefty amounts of power to keep from rapidly sinking tail first into the cloud deck.

"Hey, I like your airplane," I called to Caster over the intercom. He chuckled. I spent a few moments maneuvering after Tumminillo in a few "follow the leader" twists and turns, and then Rhodes and Landry reported their element was in place.

"Fight's on," called Caster—and the fun began!

Within the next half hour we were up, down and round and round, sometimes hanging poised in the sky, sometimes pulling so many Gs the oxygen mask did its best to wipe off my face and deposit it somewhere down around my belly button.

Presumably Caster's radar set told him just where everyone was all the time. Ninety percent of the time, I never was sure. Occasionally I'd spot a streaking gray airplane, and once we made a head-on pass on an F-15 that whipped over the canopy at about ten o'clock and very close with a closure rate of nearly a thousand miles an hour as Caster jinked abruptly to the right.

The most impressive thing I saw in the whole fight was the 180 degree level turn we made at 450 knots within a radius of well under a mile! Caster and Tumminillo were bounced twice and twice bounced the other element. Everybody had a great time, despite a certain amount of confusion.

Sometimes it's pretty hard to tell who's who in a big fur ball of identical airplanes—or what's happening to whom. Caster, for example, assumed from the kill call on one pass that he was dead, and therefore disengaged. In debriefing, it turned out the kill had been on Tumminillo.

Because he was trying to save gas for me to play with, Caster never went to burner during the whole series of engagements. He didn't seem noticeably handicapped.

About all I had to do in the back seat was grunt and tense my stomach muscles against the insistent pressure of the G suit, try to keep my head upright and roll my eyeballs until they clicked against the stops, tracking the other airplanes. It was cool in the cockpit, but within twenty minutes sweat was beading my forehead inside the heavy bone dome.

A fellow passenger on the airliner en route home asked me what it was like. I first compared it to a date with an absolutely stunning lady, then paused and added, "But it helps if you're a masochist. There's a lot of discomfort involved."

Aerobatics is always physically punishing, but you can get used to it through regular sessions. Also,

the guy doing the flying can always tolerate more Gs than a passenger, simply because he knows what's coming—and when. That's one of the reasons WSOs lead a hard life. Aerobatically, I was out of shape. It showed.

I made it through the air combat sequence okay, but when Caster quickly handed the controls back to me and I essayed a fast aileron roll immediately afterward, my abused stomach let me know in no uncertain terms it was on the thin edge of rebellion.

I gave the stick back to Caster, freed the oxygen mask and spent the next three or four minutes arguing my stomach back into submission. It turned out I didn't need the barf bag, but about one more half roll and I would have!

We were down to 15,000 ft. by the time I recovered. I left the oxygen mask off and spent a few minutes sloppily trying to fly formation on Tumminillo. I never did get the throttles adjusted quite right, but I was impressed by the fast power response and the freedom from worry about compressor stall.

Caster took over to enter the pattern and fly a circuit to familiarize me with the speeds and airplane attitudes, then called, "You've got it."

It's interesting to fly a pattern at 2,500 ft., with a 220 knot downwind leg, 200 across base and 175 on final, bleeding off to 160 knots across the fence!

I made three circuits, including the one with the afterburner sprint, and was pleased with all of them. Caster—an airline copilot on Boeing 757s and 767s in civilian life—had to coach me a bit on pitch attitudes the first time, but never said a word the last couple of circuits.

The F-15 was impressively stable yet responsive with the gear and flaps down, and it was easy to set up the proper pitch attitude and control the sink rate with minute power adjustments.

There are airplanes that feel honest, and others that do not. The Eagle is one of those that does.

We swept across the threshold and touched down at about 120 knots indicated, and Caster held the nose up for aerodynamic braking. "This airplane is aerodynamically balanced at 70 knots and 12 degrees nose up," he remarked as the nose wheel finally thumped to the asphalt.

Turning off the runway, Caster popped the canopy and hung an arm down the rounded flank of his big gray steed.

"It's the world's greatest air-to-air machine," he declared with great conviction.

"I'm sold," I replied. "Write out the purchase contract and I'll sign it right now and fly it home today. But you have to maintain it!"

Let's see, now. Surely the 159th TFG needs a centrally based PAO pilot person. And of course he'd need an assigned airplane for proficiency.

Wouldn't *that* be fun!

First printed in *Air Progress*, May 1987.